Love So Amazing

Love So Amazing

Expositions of Colossians 1

D. Martyn Lloyd-Jones

Baker Books

A Division of Baker Book House Co
Grand Rapids, Michigan 49516

First published 1995 by Kingsway Publications, Eastbourne

First North American cloth edition
published 1995 by Baker Books
a division of Baker Book House Company
P.O. Box 6287, Grand Rapids, MI 49516-6287

Printed in the United States of America

ISBN: 0-8010-1011-X

Contents

Chapter 1

An All-Inclusive Message

Whom we preach, warning every man, and teaching every man in all wisdom; that we may present every man perfect in Christ Jesus (Col 1:28).

In Colossians 1:28 the apostle Paul sums up his ministry, his work as a minister and as a preacher of the gospel. He has already reminded the people at Colosse that God had called him to this, had made him a minister, and had given him what he calls 'the dispensation of the gospel' (v. 25), and here he sums up his work. He looks at himself, as it were, and asks himself a question that he might answer it not only for himself but for them: What is this preaching? What am I doing? What do I preach? What is my message and why do I preach it?

Now it is important, if we are to understand the full significance of what Paul says here, that we should realize what led him to do this. And the answer, unfortunately, is all too simple. He is writing to these members of the church at Colosse, whom he had never actually seen – he reminds them, in the second chapter, that many, perhaps most of them, had never seen him, they had heard of him but they had been converted under somebody else's ministry – however, all that does not matter, he is writing to them because of a certain confusion, or danger of confusion, which had arisen among them. There were certain clever people at the very beginning of the first century, who went round these early Christian churches and muddled the believers. They claimed to be very able,

very learned men, and they called themselves philosophers;
so Paul says in the eighth verse of the second chapter, 'Be-
ware lest any man spoil you through philosophy and vain
deceit, after the tradition of men, after the rudiments of the
world, and not after Christ.'

Now this is a comfort to those of us who are Christians
at a time like this, when there is so much confusion in the
church and when so many ideas are being passed off under
the name of Christian. You see them in the newspapers and
in the correspondence columns: people claiming to be
Christian but denying the Old Testament or this, that and
the other Christian truth. So people are utterly confused as
to what it really means to be a Christian, as to what
Christianity is and why they should believe it. It is, therefore, a comfort to know that there is nothing new in all
this. Even in the early church there were false teachers,
people who had insinuated themselves into the life of the
church and were claiming for themselves an unusual degree
of knowledge, learning and insight.

The false teachers had a most complicated system – these
systems are always very complicated when you put them
by the side of the gospel. They were teaching that between
man and God there was a whole series of angelic beings
who acted as intermediaries, and if men and women wanted
to have communion with God, they had to go from one of
these to the next. And at the top of this list was this 'Jesus'
who was but the highest intermediary between man and
God. That was their teaching in its essence, and they were
confusing the people at Colosse, and various other places
where they went with their newfangled ideas and their false
gospels.

The Apostle's sole object in writing this letter was to
check once and for ever this devilish teaching, this denial of
the gospel that masqueraded under the name of gospel. He

wanted to expose this philosophy which was just a mixture
of human ideas, a sort of mysticism, some vague human
experience. Its proponents claimed that it was wonderful
and they liked to contrast it with the simple preaching of
Paul. They said, 'That man Paul is always talking about the
cross, about the death of Christ, it is always the same old
thing; but this is the real thing!' They sounded so marvellous, so intellectual, so modern and up to date.

It was in order to expose all that for what it really was
that the Apostle wrote this letter and explained what the
gospel is and how he preached it. And I feel that I can do
nothing better than to repeat what the great Apostle did
here, for today also there is appalling confusion as to what
Christianity really is. That is almost incredible but it is
true. All sorts of notions are current. Some think that
people make themselves Christians; others that Christianity is a wonderful philosophy, and we are confronted again
by the same confusion. So the masses of the people, I sometimes think, are outside the Christian church because they
say, 'Well, what is Christianity? These Christians themselves do not seem to agree! Here are some people getting
up and utterly denying what others are saying.' The man in
the street is tempted to say, 'I am not going to bother with
it until these people decide among themselves what it really
is!'

How, then, can we know what it is? Surely there is only
one answer. The Christian faith is not what *I* think or what
anybody else thinks; it is what is plainly taught in the
Scriptures. The Christian church is established upon the
foundation of the apostles and prophets. I know nothing
apart from what I have in the Bible, and my business is
simply to expound it and to allow it to speak for itself. The
moment people begin to stand in judgment upon it and say,
'This is not true, I accept that but I do not accept this,' then

they have substituted their authority, and what they think, for the teaching of the Bible.

But that is not our position. We know nothing apart from what we have in these records. And indeed in this very chapter the apostle Paul himself is careful to tell us, as he does everywhere else, that his preaching was not his own idea, it was not the result of his own meditation and cogitation. He says, 'Who now rejoice in my sufferings for you . . . whereof I am made a minister, according to the dispensation of God which is given to me for you, *to fulfil the word of God.'* And 'to fulfil the word of God' means to give it full scope, to let it show itself. 'That is all I am here for,' he says in effect. 'I am simply here to open out the word to you, to fill it full in that way.' He knew nothing apart from that which was given to him by the risen Lord who commissioned him on the road to Damascus; and for Paul there was no other authority.

So then, let us take this opportunity of reminding ourselves of certain fundamental and primary truths. It is all clear in verse 28. Let me divide it for you in this way. Let us notice first of all what the Apostle tells us about *the nature of this message.* 'Whom we preach' – a better word there would be, 'Whom we proclaim.' The Apostle says: I am a man who is proclaiming something; I am making an announcement; I am making a declaration.

And that at once tells us a great thing about this gospel, does it not? You see, Paul is a proclaimer of the great good news. He is proud of it. He says, 'Whom we proclaim'! He is like a man who has been commissioned to sound a trumpet call. He calls everybody to listen. He has the most marvellous good news to give his readers, the most thrilling good news that this world has ever heard. This message that we are considering together is the greatest thing in the world at this moment. There is nothing to compare with it.

It is the most glorious, the most wonderful thing.

Charles Wesley wrote a hymn which says:

> O for a thousand tongues to sing
> My great Redeemer's praise!

Could you sing that honestly? Would you really mean it? Do you wish that you had a thousand tongues to proclaim what you know about the gospel and what you feel concerning the Lord Jesus Christ? Do you feel that? Charles Wesley did; Paul did. So, you see, the way we test whether we believe the gospel or not, at the very beginning, is to ask ourselves: Is this the most glorious and wonderful thing we have ever heard of or ever can hear of? If it is not, then it is not the gospel. Take the idea that you make yourself a Christian by living a good life – there is no good news about that, is there? There is nothing thrilling. You do not need a thousand tongues to proclaim that. But this, says Paul, is good news, it is a proclamation!

Then the second thing which Paul says about it is that *it is a very clear message.* You see, when you are making a proclamation, it must of necessity be clear. You do not proclaim a speculation; no, you talk quietly about that. But when you come to the gospel, you proclaim it. The evangelical prophet Isaiah has already revealed this: 'Lift up your voice,' he says (Is 40:9). The town crier! The man is making a proclamation. Yes, he is going to shout the message, and that means that it is simple and clear. That is why you can shout it out and proclaim it; it is a clear and mighty declaration.

This is no uncertain speculation. Have you ever heard a man making a proclamation, and saying, 'Well now, friends, on the whole I think this may be going to be true.' Is that a proclamation? Have you ever heard a man making a proclamation like that when something important happens? Does he deal with ifs and possibilities and perhapses and suppositions? Of course not! I proclaim! I announce! That is the gospel. So these words of Paul tell us at once that the gospel is not something uncertain or speculative.

Christians are not, therefore, in a 'quest'; we are not searching after truth. We are not like some philosophical society trying to come to some understanding. That is not it at all. 'Whom we *proclaim*,' says Paul. I have a message. It is a clear one and I know exactly what it is.

And here Paul gives us a summary of it. So let us get rid of this notion that you cannot tell what Christianity is – that it is just some vague feeling, some wonderful experience you cannot describe. Let us get rid of the idea that you cannot define it. If it is a proclamation, it has to be absolutely clear and, by the grace of God, it is clear.

But that leads me to say this third thing about it. Notice how Paul keeps on emphasizing the words *every man*. 'Whom we preach, warning every man, and teaching every man in all wisdom; that we may present every man perfect in Christ Jesus.' Now why does he repeat those words three times? Is he just one of these people who goes on adding unnecessary words? Is this tautology? Is it just the carelessness of a writer or bad literary style? No, Paul does it very deliberately because he wants to drive his point home, and this is very wonderful to me. You see, these false teachers said quite openly that their message was only for certain special people. They were teachers of what became known later as 'the mystery religions', and the whole point about these mystery religions was that there was something secret about them, you had to be initiated into the mystery.

Now there are societies like that today: they have secrets which we outsiders do not know. They have some marvell-

ous secret in there, but you have to be 'initiated'. This
secret is not for the common people, but only for those
who are allowed in. And that was what those false teachers
in the early church were teaching; that was the heresy, as I
am reminding you, that the Apostle is countering; that is
his reason for writing his letter. So you see he answers it by
repeating *every man*, three times! This is not simply for
some special initiates, it is for all, it is a proclamation to the
whole world. 'But now God commandeth all men
everywhere to repent' (Acts 17:30) – and this is still true.

So I draw a second deduction from this 'every man' –
and again I thank God for this as I stand in a pulpit and try
to preach – since the message is for 'every man' *it is obviously not dependent upon our ability or understanding.*
Have you ever tried reading a book on philosophy? Well,
take my advice: do not, unless you happen to be specializ-
ing in that sort of thing! It will be a sheer waste of time;
you simply will not be able to follow it! Philosophers have
their terms and their arguments and their subtleties, and
unless you are gifted with unusual ability and have had special training, it will mean nothing to you. Philosophy is
only for certain special people. You must have the knowledge, and the capacity to understand it. But thank God
that does not apply to the gospel! Here is a message that
does not depend upon our abilities but is 'the power of
God unto salvation to every one that believeth' (Rom
1:16). Yes, 'every one', 'every man' again!

In other words, it is an all-inclusive gospel and I rejoice
in this. Paul says, 'I warn every man, I teach every man,
that I may present every man perfect in Christ Jesus.' He is
challenging the whole world. This is a point he often
makes. Listen to him saying it to the Romans: 'I am a
debtor both to the Greeks, and to the Barbarians; both to
the wise, and to the unwise' (Rom 1:11). 'Every man'!

What a gospel! Nobody can write as Paul does in Romans 1:11 but the preacher of the gospel! Oh, your philosophers can say, 'I am a debtor to the Greeks.' Yes, the Greeks were natural philosophers; Greece was the home of philosophy. But confront a great philosopher with a congregation of barbarians, people who have never studied philosophy, and he will say, 'What are you insulting me for? I cannot speak to people like that, they do not understand my terminology; my categories mean absolutely nothing to them. Give me a man who can understand and I can address him. I cannot speak to common people, ignoramuses like this.' He is a debtor to the Greeks but not to the barbarians; he is a debtor to the wise, but not to the unwise. But that is not my position, says Paul.

In other words, this is Paul's challenge: I have a message for the greatest philosopher in the world, and I have a message which he cannot understand, which is beyond him, which leaves him baffled and completely without understanding. I have a message that is so great and glorious and infinite and eternal that the mightiest intellect cannot comprehend it. I am a debtor to the mighty, to the Greeks, to the philosophers, to the wise.

But Paul is able to say at the same time that he is also a debtor to the barbarians, to the unwise, to the ignorant. And this little man, of course, exemplifies all this in his own personal life and story. There he is standing on Mars Hill in Athens, of all places, addressing a company of Stoics and Epicureans, and he can meet them on their own level; he has a message for them – 'every man'! But thank God he can visit the Galatians – excitable, emotional, ignorant people – and he can address them also, and he has quite as much to give them. That is the glory of this gospel: the greatest mind in the world cannot understand it, but it can save a little child; the mightiest intellect cannot comprehend it, but the most ignorant fool can be saved by it. It is for everyone, it is universal, because it does not depend upon our intellectual capacity but upon the power of God in the person of his only begotten Son. That, then, is the nature of the message.

Secondly, what is *the content of the message*? The Apostle is anxious that we should be as clear about the content of the message as we are about its nature – and here there is no difficulty. His first word tells us everything we need to know. What is the message of Christianity? What is the Christian preacher commissioned to preach? Is he sent in order to give his own views about various subjects, about politics and international affairs? Is that Christianity? Is it having a Christian view of this, that or the other?

No! Primarily the preaching of this message is '*whom* we preach': this blessed person! 'To whom God would make known what is the riches of the glory of this mystery among the Gentiles; which is Christ in you, the hope of glory: whom we preach . . .' (vv. 27–28).

> O for a thousand tongues to sing
> My great Redeemer's praise!
> *Charles Wesley*

It is he! He is the beginning and the end, he is the alpha and the omega. Christianity is Christ. And if he is not at the centre of all your thinking and experience you are not a Christian. What matters, is not your views on a thousand and one questions, but your attitude to this person, your relationship to him. The vital question is, 'What think ye of Christ?'

This is what I am preaching, says Paul; this is my proclamation – not endless intermediaries between man and God, not a hierarchy of angelic beings to bring you into the presence of God. There is only one whom we preach! And God forbid that I or anybody else should ever preach anything but this blessed person! 'We preach not ourselves,' says Paul to the Corinthians, 'but Christ Jesus the Lord' (2 Cor 4:5). I am not here to talk about myself or to tell you stories about myself or anybody else. I am here to sing,

> My great Redeemer's praise,
> The glories of my God and King,
> The triumphs of his grace!
> *Charles Wesley*

'Whom we preach'!

What, then, is the message? Well, you start with his person. Christianity consists of the amazing proclamation that God 'hath visited and redeemed his people' (Lk 1:68). 'God so loved the world, that he gave his only begotten Son' (Jn 3:16) – that is it! It is all about him, this person, and the facts concerning him. Who is he? That is where you must begin. We have not started with Christianity until we have confronted this Jesus, this baby who was born in Bethlehem and brought up in Nazareth; the man who worked as a carpenter for all those years; the young man who began to preach at the age of thirty; who worked those miracles; who died upon a cross; who was buried in a grave; and who rose again. That is Christianity – this person!

Now this is the good news. Here we are in a world of trouble and pain, a world of uncertainty and unhappiness. We see the great statesmen and others grappling with the problems and failing. What is Christianity about? What is the church here for? Is it to tell those people what to do? No, it is to say that God has done something; he has sent his Son into the world. Let us look at this person. How the apostle Paul rejoiced in doing this very thing! Read again these great verses from the first chapter of Colossians and if you are not thrilled by them I do not see how you have any right to claim that you are a Christian.

Jesus of Nazareth is:

> . . . the image of the invisible God, the firstborn of every creature [or, 'of all creation']: For by him were all things created, that are in heaven, and that are in earth, visible and invisible, whether they be thrones, or dominions, or principalities, or powers: all things were created by him, and for him: and he is before all things, and by him all things consist. [They all hold together. If he disappeared they would all vanish and disintegrate.] And he is the head of the body . . . who is the beginning, the firstborn from the dead; that in all things he might have the pre-eminence. For it pleased the Father that in him should all fulness dwell (Col 1:15–19).

That is the person we are speaking of!

Then see what Paul says about Christ in Colossians 2:3: 'In whom are hid all the treasures of wisdom and knowledge.'

Verse 9: 'For in him' – this is Jesus of Nazareth – 'dwelleth all the fulness of the Godhead bodily.' That is who he is! That is Paul's answer to those teachers who talked about intermediaries, with Jesus being but one of them! That is the answer to people today who say, 'I believe Jesus was a good man, I believe he was the greatest religious teacher the world has ever known, I like his life, I like this and that . . .' but who do not go any further. The answer is, 'In him dwelleth all the fulness of the Godhead bodily'!

In other words, this is our message: that the eternal Son of God has entered into this world; that the baby of Bethlehem was the second person in the blessed holy Trinity, everlasting God; that all the fulness of the Godhead dwelt in that infant bodily!

That, then, is why I say it is a proclamation, it is thrilling good news. The King of heaven has come down! That is what the Christian church means. It is because of this thing that happened nearly two thousand years ago. God has done it; the Son of God has been in this world! Is that the most thrilling thing you have ever heard? That is what Christianity is about – this person! The incarnation: God becoming man, the Word being made flesh and dwelling among us, taking human nature, living and teaching, with all the miracles and manifestations of his power. And then the cross, the death, the burial! And the amazing fact of the resurrection, his appearances unto his people, his ascension into heaven. *Whom* we preach.

That is the Apostle's message. That is what he went around proclaiming – that the Son of God has been in this world! Yes, but the important thing to understand is this: What is the significance of it all? Someone may say to me, 'All right, I have always known that. I was taught, when I was a child, that Jesus of Nazareth was the Son of God, but I do not see that it has any relevance to me. I do not see what application it has to my life and to my way of living and to my whole course in this world. What is its relevance?'

Well, here is the Apostle's answer: 'Whom we preach, warning every man.' *Warning!* What is he warning them about? That is how Paul preached this gospel. It always started with a warning. Indeed, all gospel preaching starts like that. The first preacher in the New Testament was John the Baptist and he was a man who had a warning. He looked at certain people who came to listen to him, and said, 'Who hath warned you to flee from the wrath to come?' (Lk 3:7). Our Lord Jesus Christ preached in exactly the same way: 'Repent,' he said, 'and believe the gospel' (Mk 1:15).

The apostle Peter, the first preacher under the auspices of the Christian church as we know her, preached on the day of Pentecost at Jerusalem, and this is what he thundered forth: 'Save yourselves from this untoward generation' (Acts 2:40). Then, what is the meaning of the last book in the Bible, the book of Revelation? Oh, it is a great warning of something that is going to happen. And the greatest need of every man and woman in the world today is to pay attention to this warning.

What do we need to be warned of? The judgment of God! This is what the Apostle preached. He said: I have a message for every man and woman in the whole world, and the message is this: God has made you and your world – you did not do it. You are proud of yourselves, of your knowledge and your achievements, but it is God's world and God has made you. Whether you know it or not, whether you believe it or not, he has made you, and you are responsible to him. He has given you certain powers and abilities, not that you may consume them on yourselves, not that you may yield to them and enjoy yourselves.

God made men and women in his own image and for his own glory, and the object of their creation was that God might be glorified. They are set in this world to glorify God and to enjoy him for ever. God has made this quite clear in his commandments: 'Thou shalt love the Lord thy God with all thy heart, and with all thy soul, and with all thy mind, and with all thy strength' (Mk 12:30). We are all under God and we are responsible to him, and we, every one of us, will have to give an account of ourselves to God. 'Warning every man. . . .' The great philosopher has to stand before God like everybody else; and the utter ignoramus has to stand in the same place. That is the message of the Bible from the very beginning to the very end.

'But,' you say, 'where does Jesus Christ come in? How does Jesus Christ and the truth about him come to me as a warning?'

Let me answer that quite simply. Why did Jesus Christ come into this world? Why did the incarnation – that most amazing thing that has ever happened, that babe of Bethlehem who contains the whole fullness of the Godhead – why did it ever take place? What does it mean? There is only one answer and our Lord gave it himself. He said, 'The Son of man has come to seek and to save that which is lost' (Lk 19:10). Consider John 3:16: 'God so loved the world, that he gave his only begotten Son' – Wonderful! But why did he do it? Oh – 'that whosoever believeth in him should not perish.' *Perish!* The danger is that of perishing!

We men and women are not merely animals, we are not merely bodies with minds and a certain amount of reason. We are more than that. We have a soul, we are related to God. And when we go out of this life we will stand before God who made us, the Judge of all the earth, and we will give an account of what we have done with the gifts that he has given us. That is what makes life such a tremendous thing, and that is the tragedy of this present time. Nobody is thinking about that. It is more, 'How are we going to get on? How can we get more money and do less work at the same time? How can we get more pleasure?' These are the things that everybody is thinking about.

But the thing to be concerned about is the fact that every one of us is only here on a very temporary lease. 'Brief life is here our portion.' Let me tell you about a young widow and her infant child. The husband, the father, a young doctor, died recently. I believe I am right in saying that he was not yet thirty years of age, with life before him, and prospects. But now there is to be a funeral service for him. What does it all mean? In the midst of life we are in death! Suddenly taken ill without any warning, dead in a few weeks! 'Warning every man'!

This warning is not only for those who are tottering on the brink of the grave! I am not only referring to octogenarians or nonagenarians; I am preaching to the child and to the young man or woman. I warn you. You have got to die, and so have I, and then what happens? Well, you stand before God in the judgment! And you will be judged as to what you have done with the gift of the soul which God gave you. You will be judged as to whether you have lived your life to his glory or to your own glory; whether you have lived to please him or to please yourself. 'Warning every man'!

There is a final judgment, and we shall be judged according to God's standard. He has given it to us in the Ten Commandments, the moral law. Here God has depicted the kind of life he wants men and women to live, and we have all got to face it. A verdict will be delivered in that judgment. It will be one of two, and there are only two. As a result of that judgment, all of us will either go on to spend eternity in the presence of God, in the glory and with the holy angels, or to spend it in eternal misery and wretchedness and unhappiness.

That is the teaching. 'Warning every man'! It is not Paul's idea. Christ said it. He talked about the place where 'their worm dieth not, and the fire is not quenched' (Mk 9:48). There is a hell, whatever the modern man may say. He is only speculating, he does not know. The Son of God said there is a hell, so the Apostle 'warns' every man. Every one of us has got to die and face God, and then there will be one of those two things – heaven or hell! Joy and bliss indescribable, or misery and wretchedness that are too awful to contemplate. It does not matter who or what you are, nor what you know, nor how much money you have, nor what your prospects are – we have all got to come to this, every one of us.

Thank God our message does not stop at a warning. But it does start with it. People say, 'Nobody comes to Christ these days!' I will tell you why that is: they see no need of him. They say that they have got all they want. They think that sloppy, sentimental people listen to the appeal 'Come to Christ', and such people will listen to any appeal!

'But,' say these others, '*I* do not need it, I am all right.'

Are you? When you realize that you have to face that eternal God in the judgment, then you will begin to see your need of Christ and then you will listen to the teaching. 'Warning every man, and teaching every man in all wisdom.'

What is this wisdom? It is the wisdom of God. It is this teaching about the Son of God, our Lord and Saviour Jesus Christ. Why did he come into the world? He came to save us. He came into the world for this reason – because face to face with God and his judgment we are all lost, we are all undone, we are all condemned. The most moral people are utter, miserable failures. They may not have done this, that and the other wrong action, no, but they have not lived to the glory of God, they do not know God, they have not thought of God. They are as damned as the greatest drunkards or prostitutes. 'All have sinned, and come short of the glory of God' (Rom 3:23). 'There is none righteous, no, not one' (Rom 3:10). 'Teaching every man'!

But oh, what a privilege it is to teach this old, old teaching! Here it is: Jesus of Nazareth, the Son of God, in whom dwells all the fullness of the Godhead, came into the world to save us. And, the teaching says, he did that by dying for us.

For it pleased the Father that in him should all fulness dwell; and, having made peace through the blood of his cross, by him to reconcile all things unto himself; by him, I say, whether they be things in earth, or things in heaven. And you, that were sometime alienated and enemies in your mind by wicked works, yet now hath he reconciled in the body of his flesh through death, to present you holy and unblameable and unreprovable in his sight (Col 1:19–22).

Here is more of the blessed teaching: 'God was in Christ, reconciling the world unto himself . . .' (2 Cor 5:19). The Son of God took on a human nature in order that he might be our representative. That was the only way to deliver us. He made himself one of us in order that he might deliver us. What did he do then? Well, he took our sins upon himself, he made himself responsible for our position. That is why this is thrilling good news. Here am I, lost and damned, dying, facing God and knowing that I am going to hell, and I can do nothing about it. It is no use my saying that I will live a better life – my best will be unworthy because God is perfect and I must live entirely to him. I can do nothing. I am completely helpless. But suddenly I am told that God's own Son has taken all my failure and guilt and shame upon him, has taken my punishment, has died my death, and thereby has satisfied the demands of God's Law, and God is ready to forgive me freely.

That is it! That is the teaching – God's way of saving us, God's way of reconciling men and women unto himself. There was no other way. If there had been, this would never have happened. Think of the Son of God leaving the everlasting glory, coming down into a world like this, a world of sin and shame and unhappiness, and sharing our life and dying that awful death. Why did he do it? It was because it is the only way whereby he could save us – and he did it.

And so the blessed teaching is just this: that the only way to be saved, to be forgiven, is to believe this message, to believe on the Son of God. Justification is by faith only, our works will never save us, all our good deeds are not enough.

Not the labours of my hands
Can fulfil Thy law's demands.
Could my zeal no respite know,
Could my tears for ever flow,
All for sin could not atone;
Thou must save, and Thou alone.

A. Toplady

The best people cannot save themselves; the most
learned will never understand. The message comes to us –
paupers, helpless, people in rags, hopeless failures as we are
– 'Believe on the Lord Jesus Christ, and thou shalt be
saved' (Acts 16:31). Whether you have touched the lowest
dregs that anyone can ever touch in this life, or whether
you are the most respectable person, it is all the same. I am
teaching 'every man'. I do not care what your antecedents
are. I am telling all that this is the only way, and it is a way
for all.

So all we are called upon to do is to repent, to realize our
state, to acknowledge and confess it to God, and, in our
utter helplessness, believe the message concerning the Son.

Just as I am, without one plea,
But that Thy blood was shed for me,
And that Thou bidd'st me come to Thee,
O Lamb of God, I come!

Charlotte Elliott

I do not understand; I am 'tossed about with many a
conflict, many a doubt'.

Come, he says, as you are. I am not asking you to understand, I am asking you to believe. 'Look unto me, and be ye
saved, all ye ends of the earth' (Is 45:22). That is all, he
says. I am asking you to come as you are in your need and
helplessness, and to believe that I have loved you and died

for you and that I reconcile you to the Father.
And what is the object of it all? It is, 'That we may present every man perfect in Christ Jesus'. What a wonderful
thing this is. You see, it does not merely mean forgiveness.
It does mean that; I am not depreciating that – God forbid
that I should. If we are not forgiven, then we are completely hopeless. Forgiveness is absolutely essential. But it
is not all, it is merely the beginning. To believe this message
does not mean you can believe that your sins are forgiven
and then go back into the world and go on living as you
were before, and go on sinning and then confessing and
being forgiven and back and forth. No!

'That we may present every man perfect in Christ Jesus.'
Present. When? At the last judgment. That is a part of this
great and glorious gospel. I do all this, says the Apostle, in
order that at the end I may present all who have believed
this message, and all have received the teaching, that I may
present them perfect, without spot or wrinkle or any such
thing, in the presence of God and his eternal glory.

Paul has already said this in verse 27: 'To whom God
would make known what is the riches of the glory of this
mystery among the Gentiles; which is Christ in you, the
hope of glory.' This is a very important and thrilling part of
the teaching. We are in this old, troubled, decaying world
– 'Change and decay in all around I see'; a world of war
and shame, sin and bloodshed. Throughout the running
centuries men and women have been trying to improve it
and make it a better place, but it gets worse and worse.

Is there no hope? Well, there is. Not from the human
standpoint, but from the standpoint of this teaching concerning Christ. Why did he come into the world? It is
because this is God's world. Our Lord did not merely
come to save us as individuals, but to reconcile all things
unto God, which are in heaven and on earth and under the

earth; there is to be 'new heavens and a new earth, wherein dwelleth righteousness' (2 Pet 3:13). The hope of glory! The glory which is to come! This is not the only world; it is a comparatively unimportant one. This is but a preparatory school, a stage of preparation. And Paul says: My object is to prepare the people who believe this message for heaven and for this glory which is coming.

We are not merely delivered from the guilt of sin, we are delivered from its power. We are to be made perfect. That is the Christian message according to the apostle Paul. It is for 'every man'. What about you? Have you heard the warning? Have you believed it? Have you realized that you have got to die and face God in the judgment? That is the warning. The judgment may come at any moment. Have you paid heed to it? Have you repented? Have you expressed your sorrow to God? Have you turned away from all that sin in your life and turned to God, giving yourself to him? Have you heard the warning?

Have you believed the teaching concerning the Lord of glory, who came down to earth and died for you? Have you completely ceased to rely upon yourself and your good works and your good ideas and all your good motives? Are you trusting entirely and only to what the Son of God has done for you? And believing that, are you preparing for the glory that is coming?

The apostle John says: 'Every man that hath this hope in him purifieth himself, even as he is pure' (1 Jn 3:3). Those who have heard and believed the warning, those who have accepted the teaching, those who believe that the Son of God so loved them that he left heaven and literally died that cruel death for them, are the people who say with Paul, '"I am not my own, I have been bought with a price." I must yield myself to him, body, soul and spirit.' They give themselves to preparation for the glory that is yet to come.

'. . . that we may present every man perfect in Christ Jesus.'

But what a glorious prospect! Are you rejoicing in it? Are you rejoicing in the thought that a day is coming when your old body even will be absolutely pure, free from sin and every stain, free from illness, free from weakness, a glorified body in a glorified spirit dwelling in a glorified universe? That is what is offered to all who believe on the Lord Jesus Christ, the Son of God.

Chapter 2

The True and Only Gospel

We give thanks to God and the Father of our Lord Jesus
Christ, praying always for you, since we heard of your faith
in Christ Jesus, and of the love which ye have to all the
saints, for the hope which is laid up for you in heaven,
whereof ye heard before in the word of truth of the gospel;
which is come unto you, as it is in all the world; and bringeth
forth fruit, as it doth also in you, since the day ye heard of it,
and knew the grace of God in truth: as ye also learned of
Epaphras our dear fellowservant, who is for you a faithful
minister of Christ (Col 1:3–7).

There is one thing about this letter to the Colossians that
makes it of particular interest. It is that the apostle Paul is
here writing to people who had not come into the Christian
faith as a result of his own ministry. As we have seen, many
of them had not even seen him. They had clearly become
members of the Christian church as a result of Epaphras.
Epaphras was a preacher, one who had been commissioned
to preach the gospel, but he was not an apostle, and I suppose that that is partly the reason why, when Paul comes to
write to the Colossians, to confirm them in the faith, he
reminds them of some of the first essentials and principles
of this our Christian faith.

He also does this, as we have seen, because of the false
teachers who were going around and confusing these early
Christians. The Apostle is anxious to rid his readers of this
false teaching and so to establish them in the faith that they
might enjoy it in all its fullness and receive all the great
blessings which it has to give.

So that is why Paul goes out of his way here to deal with the gospel in general and then in its particular propositions. And I call your attention to this because it seems to me that this teaching is more necessary today than perhaps it has ever been. We are confronted by the simple fact that in this country alone only ten per cent of the people claim to be Christians. The great majority are outside the faith, and that should be a matter of grave concern to everybody. Why is this Christian message rejected as it is, and not only rejected but ignored, dismissed, without any real consideration being given to it? We must address ourselves to this question.

There is great confusion, as we have seen, as to what Christianity really is. People have extraordinary ideas about it and that is why so many do not even come to listen and are not interested in it. They think they know what it is, but if you talk to them you will find that their whole idea concerning it is completely divorced from the truth. But there it is, there is this terrible confusion outside the church with respect to the real character of the Christian faith.

But, and I am sorry to have to say this, there is confusion, alas, inside the church as well. And I am not sure but that it is not this confusion inside the church that is mainly responsible for the confusion outside. The man in the street looks at us and says, 'When you Christians can begin to agree among yourselves as to what Christianity is, then I'll be prepared to listen to you. But,' he says, 'there you are, you call yourselves Christians and yet you all say things that are outright contradictions of what others say. What is it? What is your faith? What is your message?'

So we must face the facts. I am not here to defend the Christian church; that is not my calling. I am called, as I understand it, to speak in the name of God and the Lord

Jesus Christ, by the power of the Holy Spirit, to men and women in need and in trouble. I am not here to defend any institution as such, not even Christendom or the Christian church, but am here to try to make plain the message of this great and glorious gospel, in order that men and women may be saved by it. And here, in this introduction particularly, the great Apostle puts before us the very fundamentals and vitals of the Christian faith.

Let us look at it like this. Let us forget all about Christendom. Let us forget for the moment all we have habitually thought about the Christian church. Let us forget all about massive cathedrals or little chapels. Let us forget all about the great councils that are held in various parts of the world. Instead, let us try, as far as we can, to think about and to face this message as if we knew nothing about all those things; let us go back to the beginning. Let us do all this because we know very well, do we not, that any institution is always in danger of becoming something very different from what it once was.

That is true of everything human. We tend to change things and sometimes the change is so gradual and so subtle that people do not realize that it has occurred. And that is something, I suggest to you, which has happened to the Christian church. That is what I mean by saying that I am not here to defend Christendom but am here to preach the gospel. So let us forget all that we know and all that we have ever seen, and let us ask this simple question: What is this Christianity?

Now, there is no better way of discovering that than to ask the question: How did it begin? Go back to the origin of a thing – that is what we should always do. What was it at the beginning? And what we find is this. Here is the apostle Paul writing to a little group of people at a place called Colosse. He addresses them as 'the saints and faithfulbrethren in Christ which are at Colosse'. Now get rid immediately of any notion of a great cathedral or a chapel or anything like that; these people were meeting in a house. They were a group of people who came together regularly, and in their meetings they spent their time praying together, studying the Old Testament Scriptures as best they could, and talking to one another about the Christian life and their experience of it, endeavouring to help and strengthen one another so that they might go forward more and more in this life into which they had been introduced.

This was the primitive pattern, you see. You did not have an array of functionaries and dignitaries, and great pomp and ceremony. Nothing like that at all, just a house with a small company of people meeting together. One perhaps, who had a greater understanding of these things than the others, was a kind of leader, but they all took part, and they all spoke, and they all gave their experiences, and they all joined in praying together.

That is the picture, that is what is meant by 'the church at Colosse'. Now here is the question: What was it that brought this group together? How did the church at Colosse and similar churches come into being right through Asia Minor; indeed, right through the countries of the then civilized world? The Apostle puts it like this. He says, '. . . ye heard before in the word of the truth of the gospel; which is come unto you, as it is in all the world; and bringeth forth fruit, as it doth also in you, since the day ye heard . . .' And you notice that later on he goes on to say that this was preached 'to every creature which is under heaven'. That is a bit of hyperbole. What he means is that in all the countries of the Roman Empire these little groups had come into being and were called Christian churches. Now this is a remarkable thing; this is a great fact of history, a phenomenon, and I suggest that to ask why this happened is a very good way of approaching the whole question of what Christianity is.

What, then, was it that produced these little churches? The answer is that there, in pagan countries under the rule of the mighty Roman Empire, these little groups came into being as the result of preaching by certain people – by the apostles, by men like Epaphras, and others. These people went round and delivered a message. What was the message which produced this phenomenon? To ask that brings us directly to the question of what Christianity really is.

Now first of all, we must start with general principles. When I talk to people about these things I find so often that they focus on some particular question. But they cannot hope to understand the particular unless they are right about the general. You see, a man may come to me and say, 'I want to know about the Christian attitude towards war.' But I cannot discuss that with him unless he is a Christian, because if he does not know what Christianity is, how can he possibly know what the Christian attitude is? And as you get into these discussions you so often find that people are not arguing and disagreeing about war but about what Christianity is: that is the real difference between them. And people divide and go wrong in their views about war and other matters simply because they are not clear in their minds about that. So it is a part of this message to say that people cannot think in a Christian way until they have become Christians. They cannot hope to understand the Christian attitude until they have the Christian spirit within them.

Now I am not saying this; the apostle Paul says it. 'He that is spiritual judgeth all things, yet he himself is judged of no man' (1 Cor 2:15). The Christian, says Paul, is a man who in the light of this gospel which he has believed has an understanding of everything, but nobody understands him.

They say, 'What is the matter with that man? He is not what he used to be. He does not look at things in the same way.' Surely we have seen this. People look at such a man and say, 'Has he gone mad? Has he gone soft? Has he developed a religious complex?' They cannot understand him because something has happened to him. He has an entirely new outlook upon life and all problems. He has become an enigma. Why? He has become a Christian.

So, you see, before we come to the particular questions, we have got to understand the thing in general, the thing as a whole.

Here, then, is our question: What is this Christian message? And the answer is given us very plainly in verses 5–7:

> . . . whereof ye heard before in the word of the truth of the gospel; which is come unto you, as it is in all the world; and bringeth forth fruit, as it doth also in you, since the day ye heard of it, and knew the grace of God in truth: as ye also learned of Epaphras our dear fellowservant, who is for you a faithful minister of Christ.

Here, then, is the first thing: What is Christianity? And the answer is, *it is a gospel* – the word of the true gospel.

It is no use going any further unless we are agreed about this. Here is the broadest definition you can ever have of the Christian message, the Christian faith; this is its great central characteristic – a gospel. And what is a gospel? It means, *good news*; whatever else this message may be, it is good news.

Look here, says Paul, I am writing to you, you who are saints and faithful brethren at Colosse, you who are meeting together in your church. Why are you doing that? You are meeting because you believed. You heard, and you accepted, the word of the true gospel that was delivered to you – as it is being delivered everywhere else – in your case by Epaphras.

Gospel! The first thing, therefore, that we say about the Christian faith is that it is the announcement of some great and wonderful good news. So let me ask a question before I go any further, and let us be quite honest in our answer. As you have thought of Christianity has it always been in terms of good news? Is that your habitual way of thinking of it? If it is not, then you are already wrong. If you have thought of Christianity as just a very hard task; a moral life that we have got to live; an ethical programme to follow; something that demands great sacrifice from us and imposes a duty upon us: if that is your view of it, then, of course, there is no good news about it and you are already wrong.

Now I want to prove this because to me it is the greatest tragedy of all that people will persist in regarding the Christian faith as some terrible task that is put upon them. Indeed, I went through this phase myself years ago when I wished I had never heard of Christianity, this thing that stood between me and the pleasures I wanted to enjoy and the life I wanted to live. I wished I had not been brought up in that atmosphere. I wished I had not heard about it. What a terrible view to take of good news – the most thrilling and wonderful good news that has ever come into this old world of ours!

Look at the way in which the gospel is announced all along. Go back to the very beginning. One of the first men to speak about it was the father of John the Baptist. This man, Zacharias, was a priest and he was doing duty in the Temple on one occasion, when suddenly an angel gave him a message from God. But he could not accept it; he could not believe it. His faith staggered so he was struck dumb and he remained dumb for many months, until the time came for the circumcision and naming of the son who had been born, as the angel had said, to him and his wife Elizabeth. And then 'his mouth was opened immediately, and his tongue loosed, and he spake' – and what else did he do? – 'and praised God' (Lk 1:64). 'Zacharias was filled with the Holy Ghost, and prophesied, saying, Blessed be the Lord God of Israel . . .' (vv. 67–68).

This is how Christianity always starts. It is not a number of people deciding to draw up an ethical programme or resolving to protest against this or that. No, Christianity does not start like that. That is the belief of most opponents of Christianity. But this is Christianity:

> Blessed be the Lord God of Israel . . .

Why?

> . . . for he hath visited and redeemed his people, and hath raised up an horn of salvation for us in the house of his servant David; as he spake by the mouth of his holy prophets, which have been since the world began: that we should be saved from our enemies, and from the hand of all that hate us; to perform the mercy promised to our fathers, and to remember his holy covenant . . . (Lk 1:68–72).

That is Christianity.

But take another description of how it all began. Consider, for instance, what happened to the virgin Mary. She was visited suddenly, unexpectedly, one day by the archangel Gabriel. He began to speak to her and he addressed her in these terms:

> Hail, thou that art highly favoured, the Lord is with thee: blessed art thou among women . . .

Why? Well, he goes on:

Fear not, Mary: for thou hast found favour with God. And, behold, thou shalt conceive in thy womb, and bring forth a son, and shalt call his name JESUS. He shall be great, and shall be called the Son of the Highest: and the Lord God shall give unto him the throne of his father David: and he shall reign over the house of Jacob for ever; and of his kingdom there shall be no end (vv. 28, 30–33).

That is it – glory, rejoicing – 'Hail, thou that art highly favoured.' This is good news, something thrilling, something astounding!

Then Mary herself, when she addressed Elizabeth about this, spoke in exactly the same manner. 'My soul,' she said, 'doth magnify the Lord, and my spirit hath rejoiced in God my Saviour . . .' – read for yourselves her words in Luke 1:46–55.

And we find the same note of praise in the well-known passage about the shepherds. There they were, in the field at night, tending to their flocks as usual, when suddenly there appeared to them a host of heavenly beings singing. And what were they singing? 'Glory to God in the highest, and on earth peace, good will toward men' (Lk 2:14).

The heralds are shouting; everybody, archangels and angels, everybody is interested in this. Why? Because it is the most amazing and astounding good news that has ever come to this world. So is that your habitual way of thinking of Christianity? Or have you just thought of it as going to chapel or church on Sunday? Perhaps you have been made to go up till now – brought up like this, sent to the Sunday school, made to go to church with or without your parents? And you have hated the whole thing, and did not want to do it. And you say, 'Now at last I am free, I am going to do it no more!' Is that your attitude? But you do not know what Christianity is. You know nothing about it. You are not rejecting Christianity, you are rejecting something that you think is Christianity. This is Christianity –

> Hark! the herald-angels sing,
> Glory to the new-born King.
> *Charles Wesley*

'Glory to God in the highest, and on earth peace, good will toward men.' This amazing thing has happened.

This, then, is the first point we must always be clear about. If your thinking about Christianity is not in terms of glorious news; if you do not understand what the Scripture means when it says, 'The people that walked in darkness have seen a great light' (Is 9:2), you know nothing about it. Christianity is the fulfilment of that prophecy. The people who sat in darkness have suddenly seen a great light and they are filled with joy: the way out is being shown. That is Christianity.

Later on, when he began his ministry, John the Baptist said the same thing. He was preaching to the people and they said, 'We have never heard anybody like this before! This is marvellous! This man must be the Christ, the long-expected Messiah.' And when John heard that he turned on them and said, 'I am not the Christ . . . . He it is, who coming after me is preferred before me, whose shoe's latchet I am not worthy to unloose' (Jn 1:20, 27). I am the fore-runner, says John; I am merely the introducer; I am the prologue. It is *he* who is the Messiah.

Now this is Christianity, and all the writers who came later describe it in the same way. The apostle Paul, sum-ming it up in a phrase, calls it 'the glorious gospel of the blessed God', or 'the gospel of the glory of the blessed God' – whichever you like (1 Tim 1:11). Christianity is the great-est and most wonderful good news that has ever come into this world, that men and women can ever hear, thrilling in its immensity and in its glory. Is that our way of thinking of it? The Colossians, said Paul, received and believed 'the word of the truth of the gospel'. It is gospel. Then the second point is that it is the *true* gospel. This is a crucial point, and the Apostle emphasizes it, as we have already seen, because he is contrasting it with that other teaching which was trying to muddle the people at Colosse and everywhere else. He says: That is not true; *this* is the only true gospel.

Now what right has Paul to speak like that? And that is the question that many are asking at the present time. They say, 'What is your authority for preaching as you do?' I am often asked that. They say, 'I hear other people saying this, that and the other. I hear people denying the virgin birth and the unique deity of Christ but still calling themselves Christians. How do you know that you are right and they are wrong? You believe in miracles; these other people do not. You say that we are saved by Christ dying for us on the cross; those other people do not say that. They say his was the death of a pacifist. You say that he literally rose in the body from the grave; they say he did not. When they talk of resurrection they mean that his ideas went on influencing his followers. How do you know you are right? How do I know what to believe? Who is right? Is it not one man's word against another? Is one not as good as another?'

That is the position, is it not? You may even be thinking as you read this, 'That man is so dogmatic. He says that he alone is right, but that is arrogance.' Is it? Was the apostle Paul arrogant? Had he no right to say, 'You have heard the word of the true gospel, the other is a false gospel'? What right had he to speak like this? What right has anyone to repeat his message? What right had Epaphras to preach as he had done at Colosse? What is the test? What is the authority? How may we know what we are to believe amid the welter of theories and ideas that are, unfortunately, in the church as well as outside it? Well, let me try to answer the question in the very terms of the Apostle.

Here are some of the tests which we must always apply when we are concerned about this matter of authority, and when we would know for certain whether or not we have the true gospel. The first is that it is not human philosophy and speculation. Human beings speculate; they have considerable ability – some of them. Some are great philosophers and thinkers. But, for instance, one may say that he does not believe that anything happens to us after death. He does not believe in a future life, nor that we have souls. So what do we say? Well, my reply would be that that is nothing but that particular philosopher's opinion. It is what he thinks: he cannot prove it, he cannot demonstrate it. He has no authority whatsoever for his view except that it is what he thinks.

But I will even add something to that. He is not the only one who thinks like that. Many men and women who have never read a textbook on philosophy say exactly the same thing, and are equally entitled to say it because it is a matter of opinion with these people also. None of them know; none of them can prove it. And people, intelligent people, are ready to accept it simply because So and So says it. That, therefore, is your first test. What is such teaching based on? What right has a person to make such a statement? Is it merely a human philosophy, human speculation?

Then let me give you another negative test. You will find many people saying today, 'Well, of course, I cannot accept your gospel. You say that God hates sin, and that he punishes sinners, but I cannot believe in a God who is capable of that. I believe that God is love, and that he loves everybody. I believe, too, that everybody is going to God and to heaven. I do not believe in punishment and retribution. Therefore I do not believe in an "atonement".'

Now what about these people? Well the position there is that they, again, are basing their whole position upon what they think, upon what they can and what they cannot believe. 'I cannot believe that God . . . .' On what grounds? No grounds at all. Do they know God? Have they ever discussed it with him? Do they know the mind of God? Of course not! All they are doing is stating that they cannot possibly believe that. And because they assert it, we are expected to believe it! But, you see, that is nothing again but a human opinion.

Now there are people doing that with the Bible and at the same time calling themselves Christians. They cannot accept this, that and the other in the Old Testament and the New. But why is this? It is only that *they* cannot; it is their opinion and nothing else at all. They have no sanction, no authority, no basis whatsoever for their views. Indeed it does not tell me anything except that they cannot accept something. It tells me nothing about the truth itself.

So that is not the basis of authority, because if it is, then every man is his own authority and if I cannot believe a thing, it is not true. But then if another man can, it is! So anybody can believe anything at all and there is no authority whatsoever – chaos!

Then my last negative point is that we must be very careful about what is called 'tradition'. Someone once said that every institution tends to produce its opposite, and there is a great deal of truth in that. He meant this: Christianity starts, as we have said, as a group of people in houses; nothing institutional about it at all. But the church has become, what? A great world institution! You remember how Protestantism began? What is it today? Look at some of the things that are said in the name of Protestantism in

the Church of England at the present time. It has become
the exact opposite of what it was originally.

Look, too, at the beginning of non-conformity three
hundred years ago, then look at modern non-conformity
and, again, it is almost the exact opposite! Look at
Methodism two hundred years ago and look at Methodism
today. How much of it would John Wesley recognize?
Institutions tend to produce their opposites, because, over
the passage of the years, changes come in, tradition
develops and tradition becomes more important than truth.

As you read the Gospels you constantly find that the
Lord Jesus Christ was fighting about that. He said to the
Pharisees: 'You are worshipping the traditions of men; you
are putting aside the law of God and worshipping men's
teachings.' These so-called experts on the law of God were,
with their vain traditions, concealing the law of God from
the people.

So, if you are concerned about this question of authority,
I ask you to make quite sure that you are not just relying
on some tradition that has developed, something that you
have been brought up in. I stand for no denominations. I
am not interested in them. It is not my task to defend any
one of them, but to speak about the original thing; to ask:
What is the truth? What is the word of salvation? Institutions generally stand between people and the truth. So
authority must not be based on human tradition.

What then was it that gave the apostle Paul the right to
say that this is the true gospel and not that other? And here
is the answer – historical events!

Why did these apostles start preaching at all? Look at
this man Paul. Here was a Pharisee: trained as a Pharisee,
brought up as one, and a very able one, one of the greatest
of them all. Suddenly he left it all and became a preacher of
this gospel. What made him do it? What made Epaphras

ever go to Colosse and preach the gospel? What is the basis? What is the background? What is the authority? And what is the whole thing built upon? And the answer is – historical facts. Certain events have taken place.

Listen to the way the apostle Peter puts it at the end of his life, as an old man. Listen to what I am saying, he says in effect. I have not been weaving wonderful tales. I have not been getting round you and moving your hearts with stories, and a very clever philosophy and psychology that I have been working up to make you feel a little bit happier and better! Not at all! In his second letter, Peter writes: 'We have not followed cunningly devised fables, when we made known unto you the power and coming of our Lord Jesus, but were eyewitnesses of his majesty . . . when there came such a voice to him from the excellent glory [saying], "This is my beloved Son, in whom I am well pleased"' (2 Pet 1:16–18). That is it!

Now this is the argument; this is the whole basis for our faith; this is the authority for what I am trying to say – the fact of Jesus Christ! That is what has caused it all; that is where it all comes from: a baby born in Bethlehem. You remember the annunciation, and the shepherds, and the wise men? Who is this child? This is the explanation; this is how it all began. First there was the extraordinary birth, and then the boy at the age of twelve in the Temple at Jerusalem, arguing with the great doctors of the law, refuting them, turning their arguments back so that they could not answer him. And everybody said, 'Who is this boy? This is a phenomenon! What is he?' And after that for eighteen years you hear nothing about him – he went on working as a carpenter.

Then at the age of thirty he began to preach and to teach. He went back to his own town of Nazareth and entered into a synagogue on the Sabbath. They gave him the book of Isaiah to read; he opened it at the sixty-first chapter and expounded it and they were amazed at the gracious words which came from his lips! He attracted great crowds. Why? Well, because he could heal people. He could give sight to the blind. He could make the lame walk and jump. He could give the deaf hearing. He could raise the dead. He could calm a storm at sea. He was a phenomenon and the crowds went after him. What was this person?

And then listen to the claims he made for himself. He stood up and he said, 'Before Abraham was, I am' (Jn 8:58). He said, 'I and my Father are one' (Jn 10:30). He said, 'I am the way, the truth, and the life: no man cometh unto the Father, but by me' (Jn 14:6). 'All that ever came before me,' he said, 'are thieves and robbers' (Jn 10:8). 'I am come that they might have life, and that they might have it more abundantly' (Jn 10:10).

This is what gives rise to Christianity. It is not your opinions about war or peace, or a thousand and one other questions; it is not living a good life. No, forget all that and look at him. What is he? How do you explain him? He is a fact of history. He is a phenomenon.

And listen to him as he tells us why he ever came into this world. He says, 'The Son of man is come to seek and to save that which was lost' (Lk 19:10). Or again, 'The Son of man came not to be ministered unto, but to minister, and to give his life a ransom for many' (Mt 20:28). His friends say, 'Do not go up to Jerusalem. You know that Herod hates you. You know they are trying to catch you.' But he sets his face steadfastly to go to Jerusalem. They cannot keep him back. He says: I must. I have come to do this. The hour is about to strike; the hour is come.

Who is this? This is how you approach Christianity. That is what sent Epaphras down to Colosse: this man who said and did these things.

Not only that, those quotations, every one of them, point out all that is true of this person. And what happened in him and through him was a fulfilment of Old Testament prophecy. Here is a mighty argument. If you want to know my authority, here it is. Here is a great old book – the Old Testament – covering a number of centuries, and there, in each of its single books, there is a prophecy about someone who is going to come, some deliverer, someone who will set his people free. Zacharias quoted the Old Testament, so did Mary, and the angels, as we saw earlier. They all quoted it – the promise that was made to Abraham and to David.

The apostle Peter, again, employs the same argument. He says: I will tell you that I was on that mount of transfiguration with him. James and John were with me and we saw him transfigured. His face and his very clothing began to shine and the voice came from heaven saying, 'This is my beloved Son.' Believe me for that reason, says Peter. But I will give you a stronger reason, he adds: 'We have also a more sure word of prophecy' (2 Pet 2:19). Do not merely take it on my testimony, he says. Look at the life of this Jesus. Read your prophecies and you will see that he is the fulfilment.

These prophecies said the Messiah was to be born in Bethlehem, and he was. They said he was to ride into Jerusalem on the foal of an ass, and he did it. They said he was to be betrayed for thirty pieces of silver, and he was. Read your Old Testament, see what we are told about this coming Messiah, then look at Christ and you will find that his life tallies perfectly. 'All the promises of God,' says Paul, 'in him are yea, and in him, Amen . . .' (2 Cor 1:20).

That is our authority. It is not what I think; it is not what anybody else thinks. It is the extraordinary fact of history – the fulfilment of prophecy.

'But wait a minute,' says someone. 'This great person of

yours died on a cross in apparent weakness. Why did he not save himself? If he is, as you say, the Son of God, why did he die in such unutterable weakness?'

You are not the first to have thought of that! The people mingling round the foot of that cross, the crowd who saw him crucified between the two thieves, said, 'He saved others; himself he cannot save' (Mt 27:42). They hurled it in his teeth, we are told: You who said you are the Christ, give a demonstration of it. Who are you?

So he died upon a cross, and his body was taken down and buried in a grave; that is a fact of history. That is something that actually happened; but it is not the end of the story. If it had been, Epaphras would never have gone to Colosse; the apostle Paul would never have been a preacher; none of the apostles would ever have preached. What made them? Oh, he died, he was buried, he was laid in a grave, the stone was rolled in front, the seal was placed and the soldiers were on guard. But he burst asunder the bonds of death! He rose triumphant over the grave. He brought life and immortality to light.

Here is the most striking proof of all. Listen to the apostle Paul saying it to the Romans: 'Jesus Christ our Lord, which was made of the seed of David according to the flesh; and declared to be the Son of God with power, according to the spirit of holiness, by the resurrection from the dead' (Rom 1:3–4). He rose, he appeared to his followers – these disciples, these apostles and others.

And still more wonderful, in Jerusalem, on the Day of Pentecost, he sent down the Spirit upon them. He had promised he would. He had said: It is all right, I am not going to leave you alone. I will send you another Comforter (see John 14:18, 26). This is vital. Here is one apparently who is not just a man. He was about to die and he said: Do not let your hearts be troubled because I am leaving you.

That will be a good thing for you because when I go I will send the Holy Spirit to you. He will be in you, and he will bring me back to you in a more real sense and he will enlighten your minds and open your understanding.

Then after his resurrection he repeated that. He said: You men are going to be my witnesses in Jerusalem and in Samaria and to the utmost parts of the earth, but not yet; tarry in Jerusalem until you receive power from on high. You shall receive him, and when you do you will go out and be my witnesses (see Lk 24:48–49). And on the Day of Pentecost he fulfilled his promise and prediction. These are facts, these things have happened. There would never have been a church at Colosse, there would never have been a preacher, were it not for these facts. This is the basis, and the authority for our faith.

But then that brings me to the testimony of the apostles. These men had been with Christ during the three years. They had heard his preaching; they had seen his miracles; they had stood at the foot of that cross and had seen him dying; and they had seen him after his death and resurrection. They met together in an upstairs room, filled with fear, with all the doors locked because of the Jews, and suddenly he stood among them. He said: Do not be alarmed, I am not a ghost. A ghost has not got flesh and bones as you see me have (see Lk 24:38–39). And he sat down and ate a piece of broiled fish and honey, proving that he was the same person in his glorified body. These men were witnesses of these things.

You remember how crestfallen, disappointed and dejected they were when he died. And when he was buried they thought the end had come, in spite of his teaching. But once they had seen him, once they knew he was alive for evermore, and above all when he filled them and baptized them with his Spirit on the Day of Pentecost, they were

transformed men. They went out and testified. When the
authorities tried to stop them, they said: You cannot stop
us. 'For we cannot but speak' – of what? Not our theories,
not our philosophies, but 'the things which we have seen
and heard' (Acts 4:20). They were his witnesses. Christ
gave them power to work miracles. When Peter healed the
lame man, he said, 'Why look ye so earnestly on us, as
though by our own power or holiness we had made this
man to walk? . . . God hath raised [the Prince of life] from
the dead; whereof we are witnesses. And it is his name,
through faith in his name, hath made this man strong,
whom ye see and know' (Acts 3:12, 15–16). That is what
made these men preachers: the things they had seen and
heard, and the power that came upon them to declare it
through the Holy Spirit.

Then look at Paul. He was not one of the disciples. As we
have seen, he was a Pharisee and he hated Christ; he hated
these so-called apostles. He was not in their company, and
he did everything he could to destroy Christianity. He tried
to massacre Christian churches. And yet here he is as a
minister and a preacher of this gospel! How did it ever
happen to him? And Luke tells us in the book of Acts, in fact
he tells us more than once, quoting Paul's words when he
was on trial. It is a fact that Paul saw Christ on the road to
Damascus. He did not have a vision; he saw the risen Lord in
his glory. He saw him as certainly as the other apostles had
seen him in the upper room and on the seashore.

And what was that for? Well, he was to be a minister, a
witness and an apostle. He was a witness to the resurrection: he had seen Christ risen from the dead. It was this fact
that made him preach. He was not a Christian because of a
teaching or a theory but because he had seen, he bore witness to the fact of the resurrection. And he was given the
teaching by the Lord, the same teaching that was given to

these others. They all had the same message because they were all given it by the same person. And what the Apostle is saying here is that that was the message that was preached by Epaphras.

It is the true gospel, and, says Paul, it is the *only* gospel. 'For the hope which is laid up for you in heaven, whereof ye heard before in the word of the truth of the gospel; which is come unto you, as it is in all the world; and bringeth forth fruit, as it doth also in you . . .' – everywhere throughout the whole world. It is the only gospel because everything else is merely the product of human thinking, human imagination, and human ideas. Other religions originate from human leaders, and consequently are limited in their scope. But Christ is not just a man, he is the Son of God come down to be the Saviour of the world. That is why the herald angels were singing: they knew the Lord of glory had left heaven and had come on earth. That is why they all burst forth in acclamation. That is the good news: 'He hath visited and redeemed his people' (Lk 1:68). The Christian faith is the only, universal faith because it is of God, because the only Son of God has come. It is not man trying to rise; it is God coming down in his only Son to save us and to lift us up.

And that is why the apostle Peter did not hesitate to say to the authorities, 'There is none other name under heaven given among men, whereby we must be saved' (Acts 4:12). There is no second; there is no other Saviour. This is God's way in his own Son, and there is only one.

And it was for that selfsame reason that this apostle Paul in writing to the Galatians used the expression: 'Though we, or an angel from heaven, preach any other gospel unto you than that which we have preached unto you, let him be accursed' (Gal 1:8). Paul says: Such a person is a liar; he is a false teacher. Indeed Paul goes further: Even if I come to you one day, he says, and I contradict what I said before, then you can be sure of one of two things: I have either become an apostate, or else I have become a lunatic. Do not believe me. I shall be telling a lie. This is the one and only gospel.

Why does he say that? Is it because he is opinionated? No, it is because the gospel was given to him, not by the teaching of men, as he goes on to say in Galatians 1, but by Christ himself. If it had been his opinion he would not speak like that, it would have been sheer arrogance. He says, 'I certify you, brethren, that the gospel which was preached of me is not after man. For I neither received it of man, neither was I taught it, but by the revelation of Jesus Christ' (Gal 1:11–12).

No, says Paul, 'The word of the truth of the gospel which is come unto you, as it is in all the world' is Christ the Son of God, the Saviour of the world. This is why it is good news; this is why all these people are thrilled. Why, even the hymn-writers have joined in!

Hark the glad sound! the Saviour comes,
The Saviour promised long;
Let every heart prepare a throne,
And every voice a song.
Philip Doddridge

Have you got that song? Are you singing his praise? If you are not, it is because you do not know him; you do not know the truth. You do not know the message; you do not know the facts; you do not know your history; you have a false notion of Christianity and you are not a Christian. And not to be a Christian means that you are still in your sins, and under the wrath of God, and if you die like that you will go to an eternity of a similar nature, of misery and wretchedness and unhappiness.

But if you realize that God has so loved you, and so loved the world, that he gave his only begotten Son even to the death of that cross, that whosoever believes in him should not perish but have everlasting life; if you realize that that is true for you, you are bound to sing because it means that God is ready to forgive you, and the door of heaven is open to you. And you will start living a new life such as you cannot even imagine.

So stop for a moment and face the facts; face these events in history that led to Epaphras going to Colosse, and receive them as these people at Colosse did. And you will become a saint and one of the faithful brethren, and the gospel will begin to bring forth fruit in you as it did in them, and in everyone who has ever believed it.

Chapter 3

A Body of Doctrine

We give thanks to God and the Father of our Lord Jesus Christ, praying always for you, since we heard of your faith in Christ Jesus, and of the love which ye have to all the saints, for the hope which is laid up for you in heaven, whereof ye heard before in the word of truth of the gospel; which is come unto you, as it is in all the world; and bringeth forth fruit, as it doth also in you, since the day ye heard of it, and knew the grace of God in truth: as ye also learned of Epaphras our dear fellowservant, who is for you a faithful minister of Christ (Col 1:3–7).

I want now to deal particularly with the second half of verse 5 through to the end of verse 7. The Colossians, you remember, had become confused because of various false teachers who had come among them, and the Apostle is writing to encourage them and to establish them in their faith. In the last chapter we considered what it was that had brought that little group, the church in Colosse, into being. Putting behind us our tendency, in the twentieth century, to think of the church as an institution, we went right back to the beginning and saw how Christianity began. We saw that the Christian message was based upon the facts concerning Jesus Christ, witnessed to and preached by the apostles, and we emphasized that the Christian faith is the gospel – good news – the true gospel and the only gospel for all the world.

Those, then, are certain general points, and they are very important because it is no use going on to consider details unless we are clear about the whole character of the gospel.

53

There is so much today that passes as gospel which has not got an atom of good news in it! You get the impression from some people that Christianity is nothing but a negative protest. The newspapers give us that impression, do they not? Christians! What are they? They are people who are always protesting against something! And so the world thinks they are a negative, miserable lot of people and it is not interested, and I do not blame them because that is not Christianity; it is a travesty of it. True Christianity is the most positive thing in the world, the most thrilling, the most glorious – it is a gospel!

But, having seen all that, we must proceed to the next note which comes out equally prominently in these verses at the very beginning. I want to emphasize certain words here and the first is the word *word* itself. 'The word of the truth of the gospel; which is come unto you' – it is something that comes to people – 'since the day ye heard of it' – it is something you can hear – 'and knew' – you can know it – 'the grace of God in truth: as ye also learned of Epaphras.'

Paul's words here are of crucial importance, and that is why I am constrained to call your attention to them. As we have seen, there is much confusion at the present time as to what it is that constitutes the message of Christianity. And these words in the Apostle's statement here, bring us to the very heart of this question.

First, let me put it negatively, and let us be quite clear about this. Christianity does not primarily address itself, in the first instance, either to the heart, the emotions or to the will, but to the mind.

Now you see the importance of this? There are so many people today who think of Christianity and the Christian message in terms only of some vague general spirit – they talk about 'the Christian spirit'. Some of them even talk of

'catching it'. There was a popular slogan a few years back
that went, 'Christianity is caught, not taught'! We do not
hear it so much now but the theory, the idea behind it, is as
popular now as it ever was. And what it says is that the
Christian faith is not so much something that you understand and receive with your mind as a wonderful spirit that
you catch. It is a spirit of self-abnegation, a spirit of phil-
anthropy, a readiness to help others and to do good, and so
on. You cannot describe it, you just get it and you find that
it has got you and there it is! It is no use asking you to try
to analyze it because you cannot dissect some vague notion
or some subjective condition. Now we hear a great deal of
that. A spirit of brotherhood, mutual help, assistance, a
readiness to forgive, and so on: that is Christianity!

Others seem to think of it in terms of some general kind
of moral uplift, something that makes you a bit happier and
a little more comfortable. How you reach that point does
not matter, as long as you are made to feel better. So there
are many people who, in the name of Christianity, do not
preach from the Bible. They preach poetry, tell stories or
show films. It all becomes more and more vague, and more
and more general, but as long as we are moved and perhaps
shed a tear or two and feel happier, then that is Christianity
and we have come under its influence. 'Do not ask us what
it is,' they say. 'We cannot tell you. All we know is that we
did feel that we ought to be better; it gave us a nice comfortable feeling and we were moved by it.' And that passes
for Christianity!

Then there are others who think of it just in terms of an
appeal to live a better life. This version of Christianity is an
appeal solely to the will. Men and women decide to live a
more worthwhile life – they become moral crusaders; they
take up an ethic – it does not matter what it is, as long as
they make the world a better place and help others. And

they regard Christianity as an appeal for that. That, of
course, has been very popular for the last hundred years or
so and its great propagator was the famous Dr Thomas
Arnold of Rugby. That was his whole notion of Christianity; this kind of 'religion touched with emotion' as his son
Matthew Arnold afterwards put it. But it is nothing but a
kind of ethical campaign, just an appeal to us to be gentle-
men, as it were; to be upright men and women, to live a
good life and to help others to do so!

Then there are others who think of Christianity as just a
message which tells us that God loves us. You are having a
hard time, you are having difficulties, you are having trials
– but it is all right. God loves you and that is all you need to
know. So you are made to feel a bit better again and your
burden is lightened and your pain is eased somewhat. It is
an appeal to us to trust ourselves to the love of God. Well,
of course, that is in the gospel but I am going to show you
that that is not the gospel. The gospel is bigger and deeper
than that.

And finally, I would even say this: there are those who
seem to think that Christianity is just an appeal to people to
come to Jesus and all will be well. They do not tell them
how, they just say, 'Do you need a friend? Do you need
help? Do you need comfort? Are you in trouble? Then
come!'

I had to deal the other day with a very sad case which
seemed to me to be entirely the result of that position. There
was a man who had been going a bit astray in his profession
and things had also gone wrong between him and his wife.
So there was quite a tragedy in the family. I was given the
story and then I asked whether the man was a Christian.

'Well,' said the poor wife, 'I don't know exactly. He said
he was, he had thought he was, but now he says that he
isn't.'

'So what,' I asked, 'made him think that he was ever a Christian?'

Then she told me that he had been talking to a colleague of his one day who was a Christian. Her husband had told the man about the trouble he was in and his despair. He wondered what was to happen to him and what he could do. And the colleague had said, 'What you need is Christ. Believe in him and he can help you. He can put you right and deliver you out of this.'

Her husband had said, 'I am so desperate I will believe anything. If Christ will help me with this problem and get me out of this mess, I will believe in him.'

But, you see, he had only been offered Christ as someone who could help him out of his problems and it did not last very long. He is now saying that he is not a Christian at all. He is back living life as he was before. There was a temporary reformation but it did not last. And I am not surprised that it did not, because it was lacking the vital element that is before us in this passage.

This is a message – let me emphasize this again – which is not addressed primarily to our emotion nor to our will. It is a message that comes first to our mind, to our understanding, and I say that because of the words of our text: '. . . whereof ye heard before in *the word of the truth* of the gospel . . . . As ye also learned of Epaphras our dear fellow-servant . . . .' This is truth, this is a word. Or, to put it plainly, this is a body of teaching. It is not something vague, nebulous and indefinite. It is not something about which men and women remain uncertain because all they have is a wonderful feeling within them that all things are different with them. Now the cults can do all that, but that is not Christianity; it is not this message. Christianity is a word, a teaching; it is something which one has got to learn.

In other words, it is a body of doctrine, and I want to demonstrate this to you because at the present time there is a great objection to this very thing. We are living in an age which no longer believes in principles – that is why the Christian church is as she is; that is why the world is as it is. We are too busy to bother about fundamentals. We want what we want and we are not prepared to submit ourselves to God's way.

But the argument today is, 'What does it matter what people believe as long as they live a good life? Surely you are not still interested in doctrine and theology? The world is on fire,' they say. 'We want something practical. We want something that works, something that is going to make a difference! We do not want to be arguing with you about theology and doctrine.'

Now I do not propose to argue about this, but I propose to tell you what the doctrine and the theology are, because without them you will never know the power of the Christian gospel.

Sometimes the argument is put like this. 'The thing that matters,' people say, 'is your reaction to the person of Jesus Christ. Does he make you feel better? Does he make you feel that you would like to be like him? Does he create within you a desire to go out and follow him? Believe what you like about him but as long as he has that effect upon you, then you are a Christian.'

Now we have got to be clear about this. There are people in the world today, who are held up as the greatest Christians of this twentieth century, who deny that Jesus of Nazareth is the eternal Son of God. They deny his atoning sacrificial death and his physical resurrection. But the argument is, 'What does it matter? Look at their lives. Look at the sacrifices they make. Look at the good they are doing – they are generous, always ready to give, always ready to help – that is what makes people Christians.'

I am sure that you are familiar with that argument. What do doctrine and belief matter? What does anything matter as long as people are sincere and honest? And we are even told that they are like Christ, though they deny some of the elements of the faith.

So it is not surprising that so many are outside the Christian church, because if that is Christianity then you need not have a church. Your ethical societies, moral institutions and many other agencies are sufficient. You do not need to come to worship God and sing hymns. Just go out and do good and you have your happy feeling by reading poetry or looking at a sunset! What do you need a church for? It is unnecessary.

But that is not Christianity; that is not how the church at Colosse, or the church anywhere else in the New Testament, came into being. No, says Paul. You are what you are, you have come together, because you heard this word, you learned this truth, from my friend Epaphras.

So all these other ideas are wrong, because that is not what happened at the beginning. Now this is not a matter of my opinion. I know nothing except what I find in the writings of the apostles. As the apostle Paul puts it, the church 'is built upon the foundation of the apostles and prophets' (Eph 2:20). I must be certain that I am on that foundation. I have no right to assert my opinion. And when I look at the apostles, this is what I find: they say: A word has been preached. The Apostle also talks about a *deposit*. He says to Timothy: Keep the deposit that I have given you, that good thing that was given to you. Keep it and guard it and hold fast to the message (see 2 Tim 1:13–14).

What, then, is this truth, this faith? Now in 1 Corinthians we find the Apostle writing another letter to people who are in trouble and who are being confused by false teaching. And he puts it like this: 'Moreover, brethren, I declare unto you the gospel which I preached unto you, which also ye have received, and wherein ye stand; by which also are ye saved, if ye keep in memory what I preached unto you . . .' (1 Cor 15:1–2). He does not say, 'You are saved if you go on keeping that nice and wonderful feeling you have got or if you go on doing good.' No! You are saved, '. . . if ye keep in memory what I preached' – it is a body of doctrine – 'unless ye have believed in vain.' Then he goes on to say what it is: 'For I delivered unto you first of all that which I also received, how that Christ died . . . was buried . . . rose again . . .', and so on.

Now that surely ought to be enough for us. These men did not go round the ancient world just telling people to be nice, to be good, to be kind to one another, and to deliver a spirit of brotherhood and of friendship, because there was a wonderful person who had just been living in Palestine, who was always ready to deny himself and to give others a helping hand. The world was full of that sort of thing before Christ ever came. You need not go to Palestine for that. Greek philosophy taught it and many other teachings inculcated it.

But that was not it at all. Christianity was a body of truth, something that could be learned, a statement made and expounded. That is what you find in the New Testament, so what right have we to say anything else? What right have we to say that all this is immaterial and that being a Christian means having a nice feeling and doing a certain amount of good?

The New Testament tells me that all these preachers – the apostles and the others like Epaphras whom they delegated to go and do the work for them – they all had a body of doctrine. They all preached the same doctrine so that nobody could drive a wedge between what one said and what the other said. The Apostle makes this clear in chapter 2 of his letter to the Galatians. In verses 1–10 he tells how he went up to Jerusalem and when he was there he and the other apostles compared notes, and found that they were all preaching exactly the same thing. 'For,' says Paul, 'he that wrought effectually in Peter to the apostleship of the circumcision, the same was mighty in me toward the Gentiles' (Gal 2:8).

There was no difference between John and Peter, and Paul and James, and all the rest of them; they were all preaching the same message. They had conferences about this – you can read about them in the book of Acts. Take the one in chapter 15. Again they compared notes and found they were all preaching the same message. What right have we to say, therefore, that what you believe does not matter? Christianity was founded on a very definite body of doctrine. That, then, is how it began.

But it did not stop at that. The early ages of Christianity recognized the vital importance of this. So when difficulties arose in the churches and people began to say, 'That is wrong. This is what *I* say,' they would call a council. The great ecumenical councils really were ecumenical: they included all the churches of the world. And what did the delegates do in them? They drew up creeds, creeds like the Apostles' Creed, which is nothing but a body of doctrine. It is a series of statements, a series of definitions. And it came into being in order to correct these errors, these false teachings. The church leaders said, 'If that goes on there will be no Christianity left. It is a denial of the truth we began with; it is a denial of the foundation. So,' they said, 'we must define what we believe.' The Apostles' Creed, the Athanasian Creed, the Nicene Creed – that is how they came about.

Now the Christian church did that at the beginning because the apostles had done it before them. Christianity is not a vague feeling; it is something very definite. You can know whether you believe it or whether you do not. The creeds and confessions came into being because if you do not believe them you have nothing but chaos. If you do not believe in a body of doctrine, then what have you got? What is the message? What is Christianity? Who knows? Who can decide? One man says this, one man says that. One man's opinion is as good as another's, and you do not know where you are. And if people come to me in trouble, am I only to say to them, 'Try to feel better, my friend, God loves you. Come to Christ. He will take your problem from you,' and then leave them like that? Does that help them?

No! If you do not believe in a body of truth, you have no method of deciding when a man's teaching is false. You cannot define heresy. The New Testament is clear about the danger of heresy. The apostle John, in his second epistle, actually puts it like this: 'If there come any unto you, and bring not this doctrine, receive him not into your house, neither bid him God speed: For he that biddeth him God speed is partaker of his evil deeds' (2 Jn 10–11). Look here, says John in effect, this matter of what a man believes is as important as this. If one of these men comes in, who denies the true deity and the true humanity of Christ, do not ask him into your house; do not give him a meal. He is a danger, keep him out!

That was the view they took of this matter, so I press it upon you for this reason. We live in a world that is full of strange teachings and we can be easily deluded. There are cults and various other notions which come to us very plausibly and offer us help. They say, 'Follow me and you will feel better; your problems will vanish.' And people do, and often land in greater misery than before, because they are just relying on their feelings. They have no objective standard; they have no test that they can apply to find out whether the teaching is genuine or false.

So if you want to be saved from going astray, if you want to be saved from difficulty and confusion, and especially if you want to be saved at the end of your life, on your death-bed, from the realization that you have got nothing because you have been living on some sort of psychological self-suggestion or playing with your own emotions and feel-ings, then the only way is to come back and accept this word, this truth that Epaphras had taught to the people in Colosse.

And what is this? Well, Christianity and the message of Christianity are nothing but this apostolic doctrine. It is the teaching that is found in the Bible. You must not add to it and you must not subtract from it. There are churches that have added to it and have asked people to believe things that are not found in the New Testament. I deny that that is apostolic doctrine. All I know and the only message I understand is the message that I find here: the message of Paul, the message of Peter, John, James, Epaphras, Timothy, Titus; all of them, they were all preaching the same thing. So you must not add to it. But also you must not take anything out of the gospel and say that Jesus was not born of a virgin, or that he did not work miracles, or that he did not die an atoning sacrificial death. No, you take the teaching as it is.

'But wait a minute,' says somebody. 'Are you saying that the passage of the years makes no difference? Are you ask-ing me to believe that I have got to go back nearly two thousand years, and that the truth is what these men taught then? Am I to ignore entirely all the advances and the developments in knowledge and understanding? Am I to jettison all that has been guarded by the sages of the centuries? Are you asking me to commit intellectual suicide and go back to the first century as if that is the whole truth and there has been no addition since?'

Yes, I am, and this is why: there can be no development in this truth, and there has not been, because this is not truth that man works out for himself, but is truth which God reveals. Not one of the apostles was a discoverer of truth. The mighty apostle Paul never discovered the truth as it is in Christ Jesus. He had spent his time fighting it and denying it. He did not arrive at it as a result of using his great brain and applying all his learning and knowledge of the law. Nor did any of the others. It is a revelation; it is something that is given by God, something that has been revealed by him supremely in the person of his only begotten Son.

So my argument is as simple as this: as the gospel is purely a matter of revelation given to the apostles by God, we cannot add to it, or subtract from it. So anything that may have happened in the world since the writing of the New Testament makes not the slightest difference. We are dealing here with things about God and eternity, and we know nothing about them. On this subject there has been no additional knowledge during the last two thousand years. None at all.

You see, we are confronted by the fact that the message here is the truth about God and the truth about human beings. God is changeless, he is from everlasting to everlasting, from eternity to eternity. He is 'the father of lights, with whom is no variableness, neither shadow of turning' (Jas 1:17). And he has been pleased to reveal himself in the Old Testament and in the New – he has revealed himself in Christ. You cannot add to that. It is a fundamental misunderstanding of the whole nature of Christian truth to think that our generation should know more than the previous ones. Not at all! Here is the revelation, and it is the only one – the revelation of the changeless God.

And in the same way men and women do not change either. That is where we delude and fool ourselves. We think, because we dress differently and have cars and aeroplanes and bombs, that we are essentially different from everybody who has ever lived before. But we are not! We are exactly what men and women have always been. We are still sinners, we are still failures. However great our learning may be, we are governed by lusts and prejudices and ideas and passions. We remain the same; God is the same. We cannot add to the teaching of the Bible; it is the truth once and for ever given to the saints; there is no change at all.

But my final argument is this: it is in this one person – Jesus Christ – that the light has come, the truth has shone. God's revelation is all incorporated in him – 'In whom are hid all the treasures of wisdom and knowledge' (Col 2:3). 'In him dwelleth all the fulness of the Godhead bodily' (Col 2:9). And as truth is all in him, no increase in human knowledge makes the slightest difference. The thing that matters is to know him and to have an understanding of him. And these men who were with him during the three years; these men who saw him crucified, dead, buried and saw him risen – we read in 1 Corinthians 15:5–8 how he appeared to his chosen company and last of all to Paul on the road to Damascus – these are the men to whom he gave the message. He left the deposit with them. He said, 'Go and preach it – you shall be my witnesses.'

So you see not only the arrogance but the unutterable folly of modern men and women who like to claim that, because they live in the twentieth century, they know more about Christ than the apostle Paul did; that they know more about Christ than did Peter and James and John and all the rest of them. Oh, the arrogant nonsense that we talk! What do we know about Christ and about God over and above what these men knew? The fact is that we know nothing. We are dependent entirely upon what we get from them. So we must face this deposit, this body of doctrine, this theology, this teaching of the church, the creeds, the things so despised today. We have to come back to it, to listen to it and receive it.

'What, then, is this body of doctrine you are referring to?' says someone. I can put it like this. It is simply the facts that we considered in the last chapter plus their interpretation and explanation. What is my doctrine? It is this Jesus of Nazareth, this person; his amazing life; his astounding teaching; the things he did; the way he died; his rising again. It is the facts, not theory nor philosophy, but facts. Yes, and the meaning of the facts. Why he did this. Why the Son of God came. What he did and why he did it. Why he had to do it. That is what I am talking about.

The Apostle sums it up here in his letter to the Colossians when he says: '. . . and knew the *grace of God* in truth' – that is the essential thing about this body of doctrine. It is about the grace of God. It is in the grace of God that we find the explanation for everything that Jesus of Nazareth did and was: the baby in Bethlehem, the young man, the teacher, the miracle worker, the death, the resurrection. So, this body of doctrine does not start with us. It always starts with God – with the grace of God. But our trouble is that we start with ourselves, do we not? We are miserable; we are like that poor man I referred to earlier – in trouble, drinking too much, quarrelling with his wife and his marriage failing. 'Anything that will help me out of my problem!' he cries.

No, my friend, you do not start with your problem. There

is something more important than your problem and mine.
It is you yourself and I myself. Men and women are bigger
and more important even than their problems. That is the
mistake that was made with that poor man. The advice he
was given started and ended with his problem. It should not
have. He should have been made to see that over and above
his problems he was a sinner and he was wrong with God.

This is a message, not about what we have to do, but
about what God has done about us and about our salvation. That is Christianity. What matters supremely to me is
not my happiness, not my moods and states and feelings,
not even my health. Oh, the most important thing to me
and to everybody is our relationship to the everlasting and
eternal God. That is the place to start, whatever my state
and condition may be. If I am happy now, a day may come
when I will be unhappy, and though I may be unhappy
now, I may be very happy later. Yes, but a day is coming
when I will be lying flat on my back, as it were, before God
in the act of death and facing eternity; and happiness and
unhappiness are irrelevant. There are some wealthy people,
there are some poor; it does not matter. I do not care about
your political alignment. I do not care what your temper-
ament is, nor what your gifts are. Nothing matters except
this: you as a being before God and facing eternity in his
holy presence. That is the thing that matters – God.

Do you always start with God in your thinking about
Christianity? Where does he come in if Christianity is just
having a nice feeling and doing good and being brotherly
and friendly? What is my relationship to God? 'Do this,'
says a man, 'follow my technique, go through my steps and
you will find you will be a very happy man.' I have no
doubt you will! Psychology does work, you know, up to a
point. But the question is: What is your relationship to
God? Does this teaching affect that? Does it help that?

That is the fundamental question. Forget everything else, therefore, and look at yourself standing there before God.

And then you come across this term: 'the grace of God'. What is *grace*? It is favour shown to people who are utterly undeserving of it. Grace is kindness to people who deserve nothing but punishment and retribution. Now, says Paul, that is the thing you have got hold of. 'It is come unto you, as it is in all the world; and bringeth forth fruit, as it does also in you, since the day ye heard of it, and knew the grace of God in truth.' You have really understood the message about the grace of God.

But the moment I meet that word 'grace' I am made to ask a question. Am I undeserving? Do I need this favour of God? And the moment I ask that question I am face to face with doctrine – the doctrine of the fall of man, the doctrine of sin, the doctrine of man as condemned by the law of God. You see, you cannot get away from it. It is no use just saying that grace is something marvellous. You need to ask: Why do I need it? Why am I undeserving? And you cannot answer that question or any of the other questions without coming immediately to this body of doctrine which Epaphras taught these people at Colosse.

And what he said to them was this: There is an eternal and holy God who has made us and all the world. You do not know about him. You have been pagans, worshipping your idols. You have not been worshipping and serving the only true and living God. But you have got to stand before him in judgment and he has revealed through the Lord Jesus that he hates sin, that he is going to punish it and that the punishment is death and hell and torment and misery.

That is what Epaphras preached to them. He did not just give them a nice feeling. He did not just say: Come to Jesus and all will be well with you. He said: You are guilty sinners before God; the law of God condemns the entire human race – 'There is none righteous, no, not one' (Rom 3:10). He showed them their need; he instructed them in the sinfulness of man; he gave them the biblical doctrine of the fall and all that it tells us about sin. That is the body of doctrine; that is the message of the Bible.

And then he went on to say: But though you and I and the whole world are thus guilty before God and deserve nothing but damnation and hell everlasting without any intermission, I am here to tell you about the grace of God. I am here to tell you that he so loved the world that, in spite of its enmity and rebellion and sin, he 'gave his only begotten Son, that whosoever believeth in him should not perish, but have everlasting life' (Jn 3:16). And he went on to tell them how God gave his Son not merely to the birth of Bethlehem but to the cross of Calvary, and that he put our sins on him and punished them there that we might be freely forgiven. We do not deserve it but grace is favour to the undeserving, and he has done it – he has done it in his Son.

Believe it, said Epaphras. Believe it is true of you and realize that if you believe it here and now you are saved and you become a child of God, with a hope of heaven. You need not spend time in trying to make yourself fit, you will never do it. He has done it all. You simply believe – 'Believe on the Lord Jesus Christ, and thou shalt be saved' (Acts 16:31), and saved now.

This is the truth and we, too, are called upon to believe and to accept it. And the moment we do we begin to feel it and its power. We want to act on it, and we will find that it gives us the power to act on it and to go after him and follow him all our days here on earth and to spend eternity in his glorious presence.

Chapter 4

The Hope

For the hope which is laid up for you in heaven, whereof ye heard before in the word of truth of the gospel (Col 1:5).

In these words at the beginning of Colossians 1:5 Paul gives a wonderful summary of the Christian gospel and the Christian message. Paul, you remember, is writing to the members of the Colossian church because they had become confused by false teaching.

I am writing to you at Colosse, Paul says in effect, and what I want to do is to confirm what Epaphras has already told you, because he told you the right thing.

So Paul defines the gospel for them, the only true gospel which is for all the world, and we have just been considering it in terms of what Paul calls here a 'word'. The Christian message, we saw, was not just a nice feeling. It is an unchanging body of doctrine; it consists of teaching about the grace of God – God's unmerited favour to undeserving men and women.

That leaves us with a question: What is God's object in doing all this? Why did he ever send his Son out of heaven to be born as a baby in Bethlehem and to do all he did? Why did Christ die on the cross? God always has a purpose; he never does anything just for the sake of doing it; he never does anything haphazardly. God has a great plan according to this message, so what is it? 'The grace of God that bringeth salvation hath appeared . . . ,' says this same writer to Titus (Tit 2:11). But why has it appeared? Why has God's great purpose of grace ever been put into operation?

71

And the answer is here in our passage: 'We give thanks to God and the Father of our Lord Jesus Christ, praying always for you . . . .' What is he giving thanks for? Oh, he says, 'For the hope which is laid up for you in heaven.' That is the object of it all, that is the grand objective of the grace of God – 'the hope which is laid up for you in heaven', for all you who believe.

Now I venture to suggest that this is one of the most surprising and unexpected things that we have ever heard. But here it is, in the summary, in the synopsis at the beginning of Colossians. It is one of the vital, fundamental statements of the Christian gospel; indeed, it is a statement that enables us to see exactly whether we are Christians or not and whether we have ever been right in our thinking as to what Christianity is. Here, you notice, is the only thing that Paul picks out when he talks about the object of salvation, the purpose of grace. This is the one thing he says: 'The hope that is laid up for you in heaven.'

Now it is when you look at a phrase like this that you see that the gospel of Jesus Christ is altogether different from everything the world has ever known or has ever thought. This kind of statement cuts right across all our habitual thinking.

Our idea of Christianity is this. We say that what we want is something practical, something to help us to live in this world. We want something to make this world a better place, because we are conscious of its condition and it is terrible. We see politics failing, the statesmen failing, all the conferences failing. So we come to the Christian church and we say, 'Have you got anything to say? Can you make this world a better place and give us some help to live in it? That is what we want to know from you.'

'And here you are,' says someone. 'You give us nothing but "pie in the sky" – "hope laid up for you in heaven"!

That is just the trouble with your Christianity!'

Is that not the modern man's reaction? Is that not always the reaction of the world to this message?

'I hoped I would have had something to help me here and now,' says the man. 'I am not interested in heaven and hell. I am not interested in some remote possibility. I want something to help me *now*. I am having a difficult time and the world is in flames round and about me. Do you have anything to say to me? Is Christianity a message that will put the world right?'

'Ah!' says the modern man. 'That is why I turned my back on your Christianity long ago. It is too selfish. Fancy thinking of saving your own little soul, your own skin, in a world with these gigantic problems! They are sending rockets up into these vast spaces and you are asking me to think about my soul and its destiny in heaven! It is so disgustingly small,' says the man, 'and, worse than that, it is sheer escapism. That is the trouble with your Christianity. It does not face the facts, it does not stand up to life. You gather together, pull down your blinds, sing your hymns and say, "Isn't it going to be wonderful?" And you are not facing life; you are miserable people looking there into some distant future. Pure escapism!'

Now that is often the way in which the world thinks of its problems and of Christianity, so when it hears a gospel message like this it is annoyed and feels it is all wrong. It is impatient and will have nothing at all to do with it.

Now this is important, and, to be fair, we must grant quite honestly that there have been many people calling themselves Christian who have misrepresented Christianity badly in that way. They have lived a selfish little life and have not been interested or concerned about anything else. I have no doubt at all that the masses of the so-called working people in this country today are outside the church and will not even listen to the gospel because far too many who claimed to be Christians, in the last century and the first fourteen years of this century, were so selfish and self-centred that they gave very little thought to the suffering of others, and there is no excuse for that. That is the failure of Christians to apply what they believe. I would not defend it for a second. That is hopelessly wrong.

But, remember, the so-called social gospel was equally wrong since it taught that Christianity is nothing but some way of introducing the kingdom of God into this world of time by means of legislation; that Christianity is a political, social programme which is going to put everything right. That is equally wrong. They are both wrong. Let us turn from them both, therefore, and look at this message as it is put here before us.

Now it is the apostle Paul who makes this statement; it is not mine. This is what he says to the church at Colosse, and if we want to know what primitive Christianity was, here it is. Now we have already seen this, but I must repeat it again and remind you that you are in one of two positions. You either accept it because it comes with all the authority of an apostle, or else you reject it. It has got to be one or the other. Here is primitive Christianity, and we either admit it and submit ourselves to it, or we reject it and say, 'I do not agree with that. What I want is something that will help me here and now and make the world a better place, and I am not interested in any other message.'

Well, that is your decision. But if you do say that, then you are turning your back on primitive Christianity and believing that something is gospel which is not a gospel. For this is plain New Testament teaching. It is not just an odd phrase at the beginning of the epistle to the Colossians, but is the teaching of the whole of the New Testament. One of the last things our Lord himself said to his followers was, 'Let not your heart be troubled: ye believe in God, believe also in me' (Jn 14:1). Do not be troubled, he says. Why not? Because he is going to make this world a better place? Because he is going to reform it? Not at all! Because, 'In my Father's house are many mansions' (v. 2). That is the comfort, that is the consolation. It is nothing in this world – 'In my Father's house are many mansions: if it were not so, I would have told you. I go to prepare a place for you. And if I go and prepare a place for you, I will come again, and receive you unto myself; that where I am, there ye may be also' (vv. 2–3). 'In the world,' he says, 'ye shall have tribulation: but be of good cheer; I have overcome the world' (Jn 16:33). The whole of his teaching is precisely this, and it is also the teaching of all the apostles.

Look at a man like the apostle Peter writing his first epistle, again to Christian people in great trouble and going through tribulations and trials. What does Peter say to them? What is his comfort to them? Here it is: 'Blessed be the God and Father of our Lord Jesus Christ, which according to his abundant mercy hath begotten us again unto a lively hope by the resurrection of Jesus Christ from the dead, to an inheritance incorruptible, and undefiled, and that fadeth not away, reserved in heaven for you' (1 Pet 1:3–4) – it is reserved in heaven. Then he goes on: 'Wherefore gird up the loins of your mind, be sober, and hope to the end for the grace that is to be brought unto you at the revelation of Jesus Christ' (1 Pet 1:13). It is the same thing and this is also the great burden of Peter's second epistle.

Then listen to James writing to comfort people who were enduring great suffering. This is his comfort: Hold on, he says, 'the coming of the Lord draweth nigh' (Jas 5:8). That is the consolation, and he has nothing else to offer.

It is the same with John. 'Beloved,' he says, 'now are we the sons of God, and it doth not yet appear what we shall be: but we know that, when he shall appear, we shall be like him; for we shall see him as he is' (1 Jn 3:2).

What is the message of the book of Revelation? I know that there are friends who think that Revelation was written for Christians who were yet to appear and that it had no message for Christians of the first century, but that is utterly wrong; it was written to comfort the first Christians. And what is the comfort? It is this great event, this blessed hope. This is its one message from beginning to end, and it is a message of comfort for Christians in all ages and in all generations.

And here we have the apostle Paul: What you have heard, he says, is 'the hope which is laid up for you in heaven'. He keeps on saying this in all his letters. 'Our conversation' – citizenship – 'is in heaven,' he says to the Philippians, 'from whence also we look for the Saviour' (Phil 3:20) – it is in heaven.

Or, again, Paul says:

> Our light affliction, which is but for a moment, worketh for us a far more exceeding and eternal weight of glory; while we look not at the things which are seen, but at the things which are not seen: for the things which are seen are temporal; but the things which are not seen are eternal. For we know that if our earthly house of this tabernacle were dissolved, we have a building of God, an house not made with hands, eternal in the heavens (2 Cor 4:17–5:1).

We could go on, but I have simply quoted Scripture at random in order to establish my contention that this is not just an odd bit of teaching that appears here and there. It is the universal teaching of the whole of the New Testament – of the Lord and all the apostles. So what does it mean? What is this message? Well, let me divide it up.

The first point is that it is a message that emphasizes the

transitory nature of life in this world. That is the great
message of the Bible and it is the exact opposite of what we
all think by nature. We regard this world as the only world.
We say, 'This is the real world – a bird in the hand is worth
two in the bush. This world. I see it; I know I am in it; this
is what I am interested in.' And this, we feel, is the tangible,
the lasting world.

So we talk about 'settling down' in this world and men
and women have always been trying to do that. They try to
perpetuate their life in this world. They look at this world
only. This is everything to them and there is nothing else.
And then the Bible comes and entirely contradicts that
view.

'What is your life?' asks James. What is this life you talk
so much about, this wonderful life, this thrilling, this real
life? What is it? 'It is even a vapour.' 'Go to now,' he says
to the men who talk so glibly and so cleverly about what
they propose to do. Listen, says James, you do not know
what you are talking about. 'Ye that say, To day or to morrow we will go into such a city, and continue there a year,
and buy and sell, and get gain' (Jas 4:13–14).

That is how we speak, is it not, as if we have an endless
lease of life? We think we are in this solid world, not a
world of make-believe, not 'pie in the sky', not this
spiritual unseen that may or may not be there. *This* is the
real world and today and tomorrow and next year and so
on, we plan. But James says, 'Whereas ye know not what
shall be on the morrow. For what is your life? It is even' –
it is only – 'a vapour, that appeareth for a little time, and
then vanisheth away' (v. 11).

Now that is the message of the whole Bible. Life is but a
pilgrimage, says the Bible. We are pilgrims and strangers,
journeymen and travellers. Moses, the author, probably, of
Psalm 90, has put it all in a great phrase: 'So teach us to

number our days, that we may apply our hearts unto wisdom' (Ps 90:12).

This is the message of the patriarchs. Look at those men, those giants, described in Hebrews 11: people like Abel and Noah and Abraham and Moses and David; great men, men who left their impress upon the whole of civilization. What was their secret? Well, 'they confessed that they were strangers and pilgrims on the earth' (Heb 11:13). They had seen the truth that this life is passing, and that they were but moving through it and moving constantly, not able to stay. You cannot settle down in this life, you are always moving. You are always older; every day you are a day older and nearer the end. You come in and you go out. Nothing lives but something dies. 'Change and decay in all around I see'; 'Brief life is here our portion,' say the hymn writers.

The Bible is constantly shouting this at us. Listen, it says, you who want to do everything in this world, and settle and do this and that with your life. It is a transitory existence. You are all moving very rapidly, and you do not know when you will be out of it.

That is what Epaphras preached in Colosse. That is the message of Christianity. He did not preach about the political and social conditions in the Roman Empire; he just said, 'The whole of life is a transient matter.' That is the first note in the message and what fools we are not to recognize it. We see that in the midst of life we are in death and yet we go on living as if we are to be here for ever and that this is the only solid and real world. But we know it is not. Where are our forefathers? They have gone, and we, too, will soon be gone and others will be here.

But having established that, the message moves on to the second point, which is the immortality of the soul. What I mean is this. Having pointed out the transitory nature of life, Epaphras says to the people of Colosse: The thing for you to concentrate on, then, is this. There is that in you which does not, in a sense, belong to this world at all, but belongs to another realm, and that is the soul.

You see, the life lived in this world is a life mainly of the body, the faculties and the powers of the body, even including the mind. That is the kind of life we live. But there is another faculty and this other faculty can penetrate beyond the seen and the visible – this faculty that we all know of if we stop to think for a moment. Men have expressed this in different ways. Wordsworth in his 'Ode on the Intimations of Immortality' writes,

> Our birth is but a sleep and a forgetting:
> The soul that rises with us, our life's star,
> Hath had elsewhere its setting,
> And cometh from afar:

It is that within us that enables us:

> Hence in a season of calm weather
> Though inland far we be,
> Our souls have sight of that immortal sea
> Which brought us hither,
> Can in a moment travel thither,
> And see the children sport upon the shore,
> And hear the mighty waters rolling evermore.

The unseen, the spiritual, the life of the soul and of the spirit, that which is not tangible, that which is not material: we belong to another realm and are here in this tent of clay for just a little while. There is that within us which is bigger than it all: the *soul*. The life lived in the body, says this message, is only temporary. The other life is the only thing that matters because it goes on when the body is finished and we belong to another realm and are here in this tent of clay for just a little while. There is that within us which is bigger than it all: the *soul*. The life lived in the body, says this message, is only temporary. The other life is the only thing that matters because it goes on when the body is finished and left behind, maybe buried in a grave and rotting into nothing. And when all the beauty of the form has vanished, the soul is still there and goes on.

That is what Christianity talks about. 'But I am interested in this world,' says someone. 'I want to get this world better. I want to get some security here.'

But that is where you go wrong. You are putting the wrong thing first. What about your soul? This life has got to end – it will end and the soul will go on.

So Epaphras talked to the Colossians about this – this intangible, immaterial thing, the soul, the human spirit. He said: Listen to me. When you die, you go out of your body; your naked spirit goes on and it stands before God in judgment. And it gives an account of itself, for God gave us this spirit and he meant us to use it to his glory. So he will challenge us and examine us as to what we have done with it; and we will be judged in terms of that. And the result of that judgment is one of two fates. Epaphras said: Believe my message and there is a hope laid up for you which is indescribable in its glory. Reject it and you go to the hopelessness and eternal misery of what the Bible calls hell.

Then, thirdly, the Bible, after laying down this great fundamental principle about the fleeting nature of life and the importance of the soul and its eternal destiny, then gives us a very realistic view of life in this world. And this is what proves to me, if nothing else did, that this is the word of God, because it tells me the truth all along. I read other things, my newspapers and the philosophers and so on, and, with their great idealism, they try to tell me that this world is a wonderful place! The world outside Christ says, 'Isn't life wonderful?' Is it? Have you found it wonderful like that? Is it thrilling? Is it marvellous? Is it just one round of pleasure and happiness? Is that how you have found it? To believe that, to believe that the world has ever been like that or ever will be like that, is to believe a fairy tale.

If you want realism, come to the Bible. It tells you that this world is a place of sin, a place of sorrow, a place of sighing, of bitterness, enmity, fighting, selfishness, greed, malice; that is what the Bible says. And even worse, it tells us that there are times when men and women are so sunk and steeped in sin and iniquity that they become perverts. It is all here. There is nothing you can produce to me in a book or newspaper but that I will show it to you here, described in stark realism. That is life, says the Bible. It is a place of tribulations – 'In the world ye shall have tribulation,' says the Son of God (Jn 16:33). He does not promise anything better. He never promised anybody a life of ease.

A man came running after him one afternoon and said, 'Master, I want to follow you wheresoever you are going.'

Wait a minute, my friend, he said. 'Foxes have holes, and birds of the air have nests; but the Son of Man has not anywhere to lay his head. Are you ready for that?' (see Luke 9:57–58).

No. Our Lord never painted a rosy picture of life. He said that it is a vale of woe. And why? Well, the Bible has its explanation: it is all because of man's sin and disobedience. The world is as it is because it has sinned and rebelled against God and because, in its folly, it is trying to live life apart from him. 'There is no peace, saith my God, to the wicked' (Is 57:21), and there is not. You can become wealthy and learned; you can split the atom; you can organize the Common Market; you can do a thousand and one things, but there will never be peace while you continue to be wicked and live a life apart from God. That is what the Bible says.

I am giving you the message that Epaphras preached in Colosse. He said: That is the sort of world it is and it will never be better. Now, are you finding that all this is sheer pessimism? Do you say, 'This is just depressing'?

But this is truth; this is fact; when you are honest, this is what you know to be true. This is life. Christianity is not a fairy tale; the fairy tale is everything else. The Christian faith is real; it stands up to life and looks at it as it is. It says: That is the sort of world it is; and it is that because of human rebellion and arrogant disobedience of God, and it will never be better until human beings are changed. There is no hope of reforming the world; there is no hope that the world will ever grow naturally into perfection. Believe me, men and women are not gradually evolving into something better; they remain exactly where they have always been because they and the world are under the wrath of God.

Now that does not mean for a moment that we should be unconcerned about our world; that we should not do our best to make it as good as we can. Of course, go and do that for all you are worth, but what I mean is this: Do not tell me that Christianity is out to make the world perfect; it is not. It tells you that the world is under the wrath of God and is doomed. The sentence has already been promulgated and it will be carried out, though I do not know when (it may be sooner than some of us think). And, of course, by now even some modern philosophers are beginning to get troubled about it all. They are beginning to think that the world may end now because of starvation or because of the nuclear problem or the corroding of the land – these dustbowls in parts of the world and other things like that.

'We shall all be starving,' they say, 'if the population goes on multiplying as it does and the food shortage increases.' They are beginning to talk about an end, these men and women who turned their backs on Christianity and used to be so optimistic and say that education will put us right!

There is an end coming because man is sinful and because the world is in rebellion against God: that is what the Bible teaches; that is what Epaphras preached at Colosse. And then he went on to say: Now there is the position. You are moving through this world; you will only do it once and you will never come back again. You have a soul and you decide its eternal destiny while you are here. Do not talk about making the world a better place but make certain that you are somehow delivered from this doom that is coming.

And then, Epaphras said, I can tell you how that can happen. And he began preaching the message of the gospel – Jesus of Nazareth, the Son of God, who came down from heaven to earth and lived and died and rose again. What for? To lift up humanity? To give a fillip to the human march of progress? No! He came in order that 'whosoever believeth' – individuals – might be delivered. He is the one who, when he was thronged by a great crowd of people, felt a poor woman tugging at the hem of his garment and had time to listen to her and to heal and to cure her. He is interested in individuals, thank God! That was the message of Epaphras. He said: You can be delivered out of this. Salvation is a personal salvation. The world is under the judgment and the wrath of God but believe this message of Christ, the Son of God, and you will be delivered out of that doom.

But, he said, your salvation even in Christ in this world is only partial – you do not get it all here. Epaphras did not say: Believe on the Lord Jesus Christ and you will never have another problem. You will go marching down the highway with a new step and a new thrill. You will never meet another temptation; all your problems will be solved.

That is a travesty of the gospel; do not believe it; it is not true. The New Testament has never said that, never! We only receive a little instalment of salvation in this world, but, thank God, it is enough.

What is the instalment? Well, it opens my eyes and enables me to see through this world in which we are living. That is the first thing. We all need this insight – 'This is the victory that overcometh the world, even our faith' (1 Jn 5:4). Are you fascinated by the life in our big cities? If you cannot see through it, you are not a Christian. If you think it is wonderful, if you think that the life depicted on the films and in novels is real life, you have not seen through it. The first thing the gospel does is enable you to see through worldly façades. It makes you see your own need and it makes you see that you are involved in that and its doom.

Then the instalment of salvation that God gives you shows you Christ dying for you and putting you right with God. You become a child of God and begin to live a new life. God begins to smile upon you and you know that he is your Father.

Then you know that as all is well between you and God, you need no longer be afraid of death; you need no longer be afraid of the judgment – you have 'passed from death unto life' (1 Jn 3:14). Christ has put you right with God, he has reconciled you to him. Not only that, he will give you strength and power.

Listen to the apostle Paul praying for these people: 'For this cause we also, since the day we heard it, do not cease to pray for you, and to desire that ye might be filled with the knowledge of his will' (Col 1:9). They had only started! He wants them to 'be filled with the knowledge of his will in all wisdom and spiritual understanding; that ye might walk worthy of the Lord unto all pleasing, being fruitful in every good work, and increasing in the knowledge of God; strengthened with all might, according to his glorious power, unto all patience and longsuffering with joyfulness' (Col 1:9–11).

Paul does not say: We are going to change the world for you and you will walk in a magic circle. No, what he does say is this: You will still be left in this same old evil world. The world will not change, but you will be changed and you will have Christ as your companion. You will have the strength of the Holy Spirit in you.

Paul writing to the Corinthians says that we who are 'in this tabernacle do groan, being burdened', 'earnestly desiring to be clothed upon with our house which is from heaven' (2 Cor 5:4 and 2). He means that in this old, evil, sinful world those who are Christians must be burdened, they must groan. They see sin, vice, evil; they feel its power; it shakes them at times and they groan. They are afraid of themselves, they even wonder whether they can stand, but they are given the strength and the power. They are not made perfect; they are not taken out of the flesh; they are not delivered from all sin in every shape or form. No, they battle and fight. It is the good fight of faith. When they sin, they do not feel full of despair, but say, 'The blood of Jesus Christ still cleanses me from all sin and unrighteousness.' They have only got an instalment of their salvation, that is all they are offered, but that is enough, thank God, to take them through. Yes, but the full salvation is coming – 'For the hope which is laid up for you in heaven.'

If you want a message for this world, here it is. This old world is sinful, it is rotten. All the civilizations throughout the running centuries can do nothing at all with it. Look at the civilizations that have risen in China – gone to nothing.

Look at them in Persia, in Egypt, in Greece, in Spain, and in Great Britain. They cannot touch the problem; they never could, they never will.

But a day is coming when this old world will be put right and that will be when the Son of God comes back into it again. *This* is the hope laid up in heaven; this is my position as a Christian. And what if I should die before he comes again? Then I shall immediately be with the Lord – 'to me to live is Christ, and to die is gain' – 'to be with Christ, which is far better' (Phil 1:21, 23).

But Christ will come again at the end of time and history. He will come back into this world, and what will he come back for? He will come back in order to get rid of sin and evil. Then he will really get rid of it, and not until then. His getting rid of sin and evil and making this world perfect is contingent upon his coming back into it. It will be a crisis, a cataclysm, an apocalypse. The devil and all his agents and his cohorts will be cast to everlasting destruction with all who belong to him, all who have not believed this message concerning the Son of God. And, having purged the universe of sin and evil, Christ will introduce a great renovation. There will be a regeneration of the whole universe and cosmos – 'new heavens and a new earth, wherein dwelleth righteousness' (2 Pet 3:13).

And here is the amazing thing: You know, says Paul, you will be there with me. We will be together in the glory – this is the hope laid up in heaven. You will be in this new universe, this new world, this perfection, where there is no more sorrow, no more sighing, no more sin, no more tears, no more parting – the glory land, Emmanuel's land. All who believe in the Lord Jesus Christ will be living in it, rejoicing in it; glorified themselves, even their bodies, reigning with Christ, judging angels, judging the world. It will be glory unmixed, full, final, free, everlasting. We shall see God and we shall see him, the Son of God, as he is and we shall be like him. 'We are the children of God: and if children, then heirs; heirs of God, and joint-heirs with Christ' (Rom 8:16–17). We will enter into the inheritance with him and we will enjoy it for ever and for ever. That is the object of the grace of God; that is why the Son of God came from heaven and lived and died and rose again. It was in order to make it possible for us to become inheritors of that glory and to enter into it: 'Christ in you, the hope of glory' (v. 27). And Christians are men and women who are concerned about the hope of glory, the hope which is laid up in heaven. If you have never thought about that, I do not care how good you are, how moral; you are not a Christian. You may be a great philanthropist, you may be a great political reformer. I do not care what you are. If your hope is not laid up in heaven; if Christ, the hope of glory, is not in you, you just have not got Christianity. You have never known what it is.

Have you had a glimpse of it? Are you beginning to long for it, that glory that baffles the highest imagination? Oh, make certain of it; realize the truth about life in this world; realize you have a soul, a spirit, that goes on when the body dies and can go to that everlasting and eternal glory.

Chapter 5

The Fruit of the Gospel

And bringeth forth fruit (Col 1:6).

Those who were here last Sunday night[1] will remember my text. We were unaware that there would be any trouble when we met here last Sunday night. But I anticipated the crisis, did I not? My text was this: 'For the hope which is laid up for you in heaven,' beginning in the fifth verse of this first chapter of Colossians. I said that that is the essential part of the gospel message and I interpreted it by saying that the Bible says that this is an evil world, a passing world. It says that the world is not improving and you never know what will happen. It says that this world is under doom and will be destroyed. Thank God the Christian message is that there is 'a hope laid up in heaven'. That is what I said a week ago and the news on Monday verified it.

What if I stood here to say that the world is getting better and better? What if I said that there is a recipe for making this a perfect world, that it can be done, so let's put our back into it? What if I said all that . . . ? You see, I would have been wrong. The world is evil; it is not getting better and better; it is almost the opposite, is it not?

Very well, we have anticipated the very crisis that has

---

[1] This has been left unedited to show how Dr Lloyd-Jones applied his message to the times. The international situation referred to was the Bay of Pigs crisis when the world seemed to be heading towards war. (Ed.)

89

come. I set a hope before you. I said that it does not matter what comes in this world; look beyond it. Make certain that you are going to that eternity which is coming to you in the glory, that hope which is in heaven. Look at that, so that no matter what happens here you will be able to say, 'Here have we no continuing city, but we seek one to come.' You see, I was preparing you for the crisis. *This* is the only practical teaching. This really does deal with the situation; it is prepared for anything at any moment. And those who believe the gospel were ready for it: they were not shaken, they were not dismayed. They knew that hope that is laid up in heaven beyond the present evil time; the glory of God that will be seen in Christ when he comes on earth again to judge and to destroy his enemies and to set up his everlasting kingdom of glory. That is my justification.

In other words, I am going on with my exposition of this summary of the Christian message because nothing else in the world today is ready to meet the problems of the world. No teaching, no philosophy, no religion, nothing but this gospel enables us to meet life as it is. Literally nothing else can equip us for whatever may come. There is nothing that really enables me to be more than conqueror. That is why I am keeping to this message and not allowing myself to be deflected by what is happening round about us in the world.

So if all I am saying is true, the vital question for us is: Do we know this gospel? Does it help us? How do you react to bad news? Do you find that you have something to sustain you? Do you have a solid foundation beneath your feet? Do you feel calm and collected, saying, 'All right, whatever happens, I know where I am and where I stand; I know in whom I have believed'?

The one thing that matters in this uncertain world is, as

we have seen, that we do really know this gospel and that we are sustained and helped by it. Because if we are not, if it is not our mainstay and our solid foundation, then there is something wrong with our whole conception of it.

'On what ground do you say that?' asks someone.

I say it on this ground: When other things have been very doubtful, I have known that this gospel, as our text says, 'bringeth forth fruit'.

Now the word which the Apostle uses, which is translated here 'bringeth forth', carries the notion that it does so by its own inherent power. And the result of this is the idea of a great fullness. It brings forth by its own inherent power a fullness of fruits, of results. That is the fourth fundamental thing which the Apostle tells us about this gospel.

My point is that as this is a gospel that brings forth fruit that really leads to something, then it should be leading to that in us; and if it does not, then we do not have the gospel. I am, therefore, suggesting seriously and solemnly that this is the most urgent problem for us – not the current international or political situation; not whether or not war is coming. Here is the question for us: Is this gospel bringing forth fruit in us by its own inherent power? Nothing else will be left if war does come; nothing else will be left but this gospel, everything else will have gone. Our money, our possessions, our pleasures – they will all vanish; nothing will be left behind. This alone will be left, this alone will be ready to save and sustain us.

So there is nothing more urgent than that every one of us should know whether or not we are truly Christians. Every one of us must be certain that the hope is laid up for us in heaven; we must have no doubt about it. While the world may be in convulsion, and worse may be coming, we must be certain of this before everything else.

How can we be? By examining this fruit which, says

Paul, the gospel always brings forth: 'Which is come unto you, as it is in all the world; and bringeth forth fruit, as it doth also in you, since the day ye heard it.'

So let me be as direct as I can be and put forward a number of propositions. God knows the matter is too serious for anything else. I want to put it in such a way that whatever may come, we shall all be ready, we shall all know where we are.

First, then, the gospel is a *power*. The Bible is always saying this. God says – 'My word . . . shall not return unto me void, but it shall accomplish that which I pleased, and it shall prosper in the thing whereto I sent it' (Is 55:11). That is God's own statement about his own word. It is a power. 'Is not my word . . . like a hammer that breaketh the rock in pieces?' (Jer 23:29).

'I am not ashamed,' says the apostle Paul, writing to the Romans, 'of the gospel of Christ' – why not? – 'for it is the power of God unto salvation to every one that believeth . . . .' (Rom 1:16). Or again, to the Corinthians, 'For the Jews require a sign, and the Greeks seek after wisdom: but we preach Christ crucified, unto the Jews a stumbling-block, and unto the Greeks foolishness; But unto them which are called, both Jews and Greeks, Christ the power of God, and the wisdom of God' (1 Cor 1:22–24). The power of God: it is the way that he brings this thing to pass.

And, of course, we are repeating what our Lord himself said in his parable of the sower. You see, there is power in this seed as it tests the various types of ground. The ground matters, but the power, the life, is in the seed that is sown.

What, then, does this mean? It means that the Christian faith, this Christian message of ours, is not like anything else offering itself to the world, because it is not just a matter of a loosely held opinion. Everything else is opinion:

the statesmen have their varying opinions, hence all wars; one man thinks this, the other that. But the Christian message is not like all these philosophies and views of life. Not only that, it is not a matter of theory, just something to argue about, a good subject for a debating society. How wonderful! Let's have an argument about religion!

But if that is your idea of Christianity and of the Christian message you know nothing about it. This is something that changes you; it is something that brings forth fruit; it has a dynamic power; it has life. It acts with the soil to produce something. We do not sit back and look at it. No, it lays hold upon us.

'It bears fruit among you,' says Paul to the Colossians, and he means that it makes you different from what you were. As I hope to show you, it turned these people who were once terrible sinners into saints. They are now 'saints and faithful brethren in Christ'. There was a time when they were not, when they were living in the gutters of life. What changed them? It was this power that is in the gospel! The gospel is the chief thing in the life of men and women who believe. It controls everything, their whole outlook, their entire vision. They are what they are by the grace of God.

Secondly, it is a power that comes through the Holy Spirit using this word. Now this is absolutely vital. Look at the beginning of the book of Acts. Here were men who had accompanied our Lord for three years during his earthly ministry. They had heard his sermons; they had seen his miracles; they had watched him being crucified; they had seen his dead body taken to a tomb. They knew he had risen from the dead; he had appeared to them. Yet, let us never forget it, he said to these men that they could not witness to him and his resurrection as they were. He said to them, 'Ye shall receive power, after that the Holy

Ghost is come upon you' (Acts 1:8).

And the Holy Spirit came upon them on that Day of Pentecost and they began to preach. And when Peter was preaching three thousand people became believers, not simply because of Peter's sermon, but because of the power of the Spirit in Peter, working on the word of God.

Then look at a man like this Epaphras. He was not an apostle. We know very little about him, but we know that he was a preacher and that he went to Colosse, preached this gospel and delivered this message. Paul reminds them of that when he says, 'As ye also learned of Epaphras our dear fellowservant, who is for you a faithful minister of Christ.' Who was Epaphras? Well, you know, this is the glory of preaching. It does not matter who or what you are. All I know about Epaphras, which is the only thing that matters, is that he was a man who believed this truth, and the power of the Holy Spirit came upon him and used his words, producing fruit in the lives of those Colossians who received it.

It is the Holy Spirit who does it. So we do not merely have a dead-letter; this is not an irrelevant word. You do not take up your Bible as you take up Shakespeare or a book of history or politics. It is not a textbook among textbooks, but God's word. It is a unique word, and, still more important, it is the word that the Holy Spirit of God uses. This is the meaning of 'the Spirit on the word'. The Spirit applies the word. He enlightens the mind, and our minds need to be enlightened because they are darkened by sin. The Apostle says that in great detail later on in Colossians. Our minds need to be quickened, to be given a new power of vision and an ability to see unseen spiritual truth. He alone can do that and he does it through this word.

The Spirit then moves the heart. And our hearts need to be softened, do they not? The world has become hard, selfish and cruel and it needs its heart to be softened. The world knows nothing about love – only about lusts, which it calls love – and it needs to be taught about love and compassion and tenderness and kindness and a forgiving spirit. And these stony hearts of ours must be softened and turned into hearts of flesh before we know anything about love.

And at the same time the Spirit can persuade the will, these stubborn wills of ours, these wills that say, 'I do not care. I am going to have a good time. I am not going to listen to what the preachers say . . . .' That will of ours needs to be taken under control, and the Spirit of God can do it.

This is just a very brief summary of the teaching of the gospel. 'The princes of this world do not know these things,' says Paul to the Corinthians (1 Cor 2:8). They did not recognize Christ when he came; they thought he was just a man. They resisted him; they crucified him; they laughed at him; they ridiculed him. So how does anybody believe? Oh, says Paul, 'God hath revealed them [these things] unto us by his Spirit: for the Spirit searcheth all things, yea, the deep things of God . . . . we have received, not the spirit of the world, but the spirit which is of God; that we might know the things that are freely given to us of God' (1 Cor 2:10, 12). And it is the Holy Spirit in his power who gives men and women the power of understanding, the softened heart, the supple will, and so they become Christians.

Paul makes an amazing statement in Romans 6:17: 'But God be thanked,' he says, 'that ye were the servants of sin, but ye have obeyed from the heart that form of doctrine which was delivered you.' Now that is the Authorized Version, which is not a good translation. This is what he really said: 'But you have obeyed from the heart that form of doctrine into which you were poured,' as melted iron is poured into a mould. So the truth of God is a mould and the Spirit comes and melts us and we are poured into the mould to take the shape and the form of the mould of God's glorious truth and we are new men and women. God be thanked! It is the Spirit who does it through the word.

Then my third point is this: the Holy Spirit employs the gospel to accomplish – what? What does it produce within us? Now this is another important point and here I am going to be intensely practical.

You cannot get figs from thorns or briars! No, a seed always produces the same fruit – it is guaranteed! And the gospel always brings forth the same fruit. There may be differences in detail. I do not want to press that. But unless you know to some extent something of the things I have catalogued to you, then you are not a Christian. If the gospel is not bearing fruit in you, then you are outside Christ and you are not ready to die and face God in the judgment.

So consider this as you value your soul. What is the fruit that it brings forth? Well, here is the first fruit: a consciousness of some constraint and some power upon us. I am putting this very gently. The first thing that occurs, when the Spirit takes the word and applies it to us, is that we become very conscious of the fact that something has happened to us and we begin, for the first time in our lives, to attend to the message of the gospel. Now let me give you an illustration of this which will fix it in your minds.

The first sermon which the apostle Paul ever preached in Europe was at Philippi. He went to a prayer meeting held by some women by the side of the river and there, we are told, he 'sat down, and spake unto the women which resorted thither'. Then: 'And a certain woman named Lydia, a seller of purple, of the city of Thyatira, which worshipped God, heard us' – oh, we can all hear it, can we not? That is not important. But then – '*whose heart the Lord opened*, that she attended unto the things which were spoken of Paul' (Acts 16:13–14).

You see the difference? There is all the difference in the world between sitting in a meeting and hearing words and *attending* to them. Because the Lord opened her heart, she paid attention to Paul's words. We all know something of this, do we not? We know what it is to be in a service, sitting there and apparently listening, but with our minds a thousand miles away. We are thinking of yesterday or of what may happen tomorrow! We are hearing words without *attending*. But the moment the Spirit takes hold and begins to apply the word to us we begin to pay attention. All the motives for not attending are overruled.

Now there is, again, a perfect example in Acts 2. Who was Peter preaching to? What was the congregation? Why were those people listening to Peter? At first they were filled with curiosity. They saw a group of unlearned and unlettered men talking in strange languages and they looked at them and said, 'These men are full of new wine' (Acts 2:13).

'Well, I don't know. I am not so sure about that,' somebody else said. And they began to argue. They started to say, 'What are these men? What is it? What has happened to them?'

Then they said, 'One of them is going to speak. Let us listen.' They congregated together in order to satisfy their curiosity. There is no other reason for it. 'What is this Galilean going to say? He is only a fisherman. Who is he to speak like that? What has he got to say?' Sheer curiosity! But notice that before he had finished the curiosity had been replaced by something else. They were paying attention to Peter's words.

Now let us be very plain about this. There are many reasons for attending a place of worship, are there not? And we have all been guilty of them. A mere attendance at the house of God may be useless. You may attend church out of curiosity, or because you have been brought up to go and have not thought of stopping. You may go to church in order to meet people. I am not condemning you, but what I am saying is that if you continue on that level you are not a Christian, you know nothing about the gospel.

We are all human, we have all done these things. God knows I am not standing in judgment on anybody. There are many reasons why people listen to the word without taking it to heart. Some people may be interested in the technique of preaching. They may enjoy listening to preachers who have some ability to dissect and expound a passage. I have known men using the Scriptures instead of crossword puzzles! But when the Spirit comes upon them, all that goes and they begin to pay attention to the words and the sermon comes alive. They begin to attend, as Lydia did, to the things that are said. They no longer have a general, vague interest but something more definite. They begin to become a part of it.

The second fruit is this: we begin to feel that the message is for us personally. It is no longer a general message; no longer a point of view about the world, or about bombs, or about war, or about industry and peace. No, it is for me myself. I cease being interested in other things, in various people and their messages, and am now interested in myself. The sermon speaks to me personally and individually.

Now no one has ever become a Christian unless that has happened. Christianity is not about having a general Christian outlook on all sorts of subjects. It is intensely personal. Christ always spoke to individuals. He buttonholed people, as it were. He addressed them individually about themselves.

In John 4 we read about a woman of Samaria who wanted to have an argument about worshipping on Mount Gerizim in Samaria or in Jerusalem, about the differences between Samaritans and Jews, and all these wonderful religious questions! And suddenly our Lord looked at her and became personal. He said, 'Woman, go and call thy husband, and come hither.' He spoke directly to her. He said: I am not interested in your opinions on God, nor on worship, nor on Jews, nor on anything else. What about the life you are living? What about immorality and adultery?

The gospel is always personal and if it has not been personal to you, you do not know it and it is not bearing fruit in you.

Thirdly, the gospel always leads to a concern about the soul. We need not stay with this, because I have dealt with it already. There are many people in the world who are tremendously concerned about the death of their bodies. But when the Spirit comes upon the word, they become less and less interested in death and the fate of their bodies and very interested in the fate of their souls and their eternal destiny. They know that they have that within them which is imperishable, so that whether the body is blown into nothing by a bomb or rots in the grave, they go on and will go on for ever and for ever. That is their main concern now. Is it yours?

The fourth thing is conviction of sin. What does that mean? Well, the gospel, you see, makes us think. That is the meaning of the word 'repent' – 'think again'. We do not think, do we? We think we have thought, we think we know all about it, we think we have 'got Christianity taped', as we put it, and we think we can dismiss it. We think we have a philosophy of life that is all right. Suddenly, there is a threat of war! Where are we? We begin to think again. That is repentance – thinking again in the light of this message – and the moment you do that, you begin to become aware of your failure to live to the glory of God.

The first question in the Shorter Catechism of the Westminster Confession is this: 'What is the chief end of man?' And here is the answer: 'The chief end of man is to glorify God and to enjoy him for ever.' And when men and women come under the power of this word they realize that they have not done that. They have lived for themselves; they have not thought of God; they have gone their own way; they have spurned 'the voice divine'. Not only that, but they have quite deliberately broken God's laws; they have thought it was clever to laugh at them and spit upon them. They have deliberately stood against God; they have violated their own conscience. And now they begin to realize all that, though they never did before.

And so they go on to see that their nature is evil and they are vile. Their life is futile, their cleverness, they now know, is monstrous. And so they are filled with a sense of shame and sin. They know they have sinned against God and are unclean. They admit that they preferred evil to good and 'loved darkness rather than light because their deeds were evil' (Jn 3:19).

Our next step is number five: they are now filled with a desire for forgiveness, a desire to be reconciled to God. They now say, 'I want to know that God forgives me, that God is going to receive me, that in my agony I can go to him and know that I will be with him.' This is their real desire. This is a part of the fruit that this gospel always brings forth.

Is it your chief desire to know God and to be blessed of him? Added to that is this: a desire to love God and a desire to please him. These people now see it. They say: 'Create in me a clean heart, O God; and renew a right spirit within me' (Ps 51:10). I not only want forgiveness for my past, I want to live a new life. I want to be clean – 'Wash me, and I shall be whiter than snow' (Ps 51:7). I want to live a God-given life. I want to love the light and hate the darkness. I want to please God, the God I have ignored and neglected and reviled and whose love I have spurned. I want to live the remainder of my life to his glory and to his praise that I may spend my eternity with him. That is their chief desire now.

But then evil thoughts enter into their minds. 'Very well, you had better start to live a new life; you must give up the life you have been living. You had better start to read your Bible; you had better start praying; you had better start doing good. Give up everything and give yourself to the cultivation of this life of God.' But when the work goes on – and the work does go on – they realize that it will not help them. They realize now that their imagination is vile and their will unstable. They hear this message on Sunday, but forget it before they get home and on Monday morning it is not there at all. Why does the blessing of Sunday not carry on for the remainder of the week?

So they say, 'I cannot help it, I am rotten. "In me (that is, in my flesh) dwelleth no good thing"' (Rom 7:18). They try, they fail and go on failing until they come to the conclusion that they are utterly hopeless and helpless and that all their efforts and strivings are futile and valueless. They are beside themselves and they do not know what to do. They cry out saying: 'What shall we do? What can I do? What can I do with myself? I know that nothing else matters but this. All is going from me, the world is receding, it may be blown up at any moment. I am left and God. "What must I do to be saved?"' (Acts 16:30). And they realize that they can do nothing – there is nothing in them that can do anything.

And then the Spirit goes on quietly and gently leading

them to this blessed truth about the Lord Jesus Christ. Listen, 'We give thanks to God and the Father of our Lord Jesus Christ, praying always for you, since we heard of your faith in Christ Jesus . . . .' You see, the Colossians had been listening to Epaphras, and Epaphras had been preaching in the way I have been trying to describe, and they were paying attention and were convicted and condemned. They realized they were guilty and hopeless; they could do nothing and were feeling alarmed and desperate.

Listen, said Epaphras, I have a gospel for you. I have good news. And he told them the good news of Christ Jesus our Lord. He told them the facts. He told them the story of the Lord Jesus Christ. And that, said Epaphras, is God's way of saving men. That is his way of reconciling the world unto himself – 'God was in Christ reconciling the world unto himself, not imputing their trespasses unto them' (2 Cor 5:19). 'The Lord hath laid on him the iniquity of us all' (Is 53:6).

Epaphras said: That is the meaning of the gospel. The Son of God came from heaven, as he said himself, 'to seek and to save that which was lost'. And he did it by taking our sins upon himself; he bore our punishment; he died our death. God smote him that we might be forgiven. That is what Epaphras preached. He said: Though you have sinned so deeply against God, if you believe in the Son of God, you are forgiven and reconciled to God.

Oh, let us be clear about this. This is what the apostle Paul calls 'justification by the faith of Jesus Christ' (Gal 2:16), and 'not by the works of the law'. 'But,' says somebody, 'I am not interested in your theoretical terms.' Aren't you? These are the most important words in the world. They mean not only that you and I can do nothing, but that God does not even ask us to do anything; he has done it in his Son. They mean that I simply believe that

Jesus Christ, the Son of God, came into the world to die for me, for me individually; that the Son of God loved me and gave himself for me.

So I want to test you on this. If you are saying at this point, 'I agree that I have forgotten God and ignored him. I have sinned against him and spurned his voice. I see I have been wrong. I am determined to be a better man or a better woman. I am going to start reading my Bible. I am, I am, I am!' Then do not. If you say that, you are still damned. If you are relying upon anything that you are going to do, you have not got this message – the gospel is not bearing fruit in you. The fruit of the gospel is justification by faith alone, which means this: 'Whosoever believeth in him should not perish, but have everlasting life' (Jn 3:16). It does not postulate our doing anything, but simply believing in him – 'Whosoever shall call on the name of the Lord shall be saved' (Acts 2:21).

And so you thank him; you just fall at his feet and praise him. You do not ask him to forgive you; you thank him now, for what he has done in Christ. You accept it, you receive it, you begin to rejoice in it. And then you get up and say, 'I will give the rest of my life to show my forgiveness.' You do not live a good life in order to get it. You live a good life in order to thank him for giving it.

So, has this blessed gospel of the glorious God borne fruit in you? Do you know that your sins are forgiven? Have you faith, this justifying faith, in the Lord Jesus Christ? Do not delay; close with him while your heart is tender: 'Saviour, while my heart is tender, I will yield that heart to thee.' Tell him now, if you have never told him before, that you see who he is, you recognize his word, you see that he is all sufficient. Then say to him: 'Jesus, you are my all in all, and ever shall be.'

Chapter 6

Saints and Faithful Brethren

We give thanks to God and the Father of our Lord Jesus
Christ, praying always for you, since we heard of your faith in
Christ Jesus, and of the love which ye have to all the saints, for
the hope which is laid up for you in heaven, whereof ye heard
before in the word of truth of the gospel; which is come unto
you, as it is in all the world; and bringeth forth fruit, as it doth
also in you, since the day ye heard of it, and knew the grace of
God in truth: as ye also learned of Epaphras our dear fellowservant, who is for you a faithful minister of Christ; who also
declared unto us your love in the Spirit (Col 1:3–8).

Paul, an apostle of Jesus Christ by the will of God, and
Timotheus our brother, to the saints and faithful brethren in
Christ which are at Colosse (vv. 1–2).

We have been looking in general at the question of how the
gospel brings forth fruit in us and we saw that first the gospel brings conviction of sin. The gospel lays hold on us and
begins to speak to us, making us feel uncomfortable and
condemning us; it convicts us and convinces us of our sinfulness. Then it leads to repentance and it ends in faith in
the Lord Jesus Christ. Paul says here: 'We give thanks to
God and the Father of our Lord Jesus Christ, praying
always for you, since we heard of your faith in Christ
Jesus . . . .'
    So that is the first part of the fruit, the beginning. But it
does not stop at that. That is absolutely vital. It goes on,
and, indeed, it is essential that it should and that we should
go on considering it. Why is this? Well, I suggest to you

that we must go on and examine it further because we cannot even account for our faith and belief in the Lord Jesus Christ without going further. What is it that makes men and women believe in the Lord Jesus Christ? Here is one gospel, the same gospel preached to a number of people. Some believe it, some do not. What makes the difference? Now we must meet that question and fortunately our text does that: again, it is part of this fruit.

But another reason why we must go on with the examination is this: How can I make quite certain that what I think is my faith in the Lord Jesus Christ is a true faith?

'Why do you raise that?' asks somebody.

I ask this question because you will often meet people who say, 'There was time when I thought I was a Christian but I realized afterwards that there was nothing in it!' So what has happened to them? They thought that they had faith in the Lord Jesus Christ. They said everything that was right and yet here they are now denying it all, scoffing at it, laughing at themselves, saying that they made fools of themselves and that they do not want to have anything to do with it! What is the matter with such people?

Now there is such a thing – let us be quite honest about this – as giving intellectual assent to the truth. But that is a kind of intellectual belief; it is not faith. And what Paul is concerned about is 'faith in Christ Jesus'.

We are, of course, familiar with this phenomenon. You can make a child believe almost anything you like – that is why I have always said that people must be very careful with so-called child evangelism and child conversion. There are many who have said in their childhood, 'I believe in the Lord Jesus Christ,' but when they grow up they deny it all. And this is not confined to children. There are people who can say in the emotion of a meeting, in the charged atmosphere of a great gathering: 'I believe.' And they think they believe, but they find out afterwards that there was something wrong with this belief.

You see, I am so concerned about this matter, so concerned that none of us should be deceiving ourselves, so concerned that we should be absolutely certain that we are Christians, that I want to press this point. I want you to understand that we cannot afford to take anything for granted. My responsibility is a very serious one. I shall be held responsible at the Bar of Judgment for the way I have preached this gospel. The apostle Paul says, in his second letter to the Corinthians, 'We must all appear before the judgment seat of Christ; that every one may receive the things done in his body, according to that he hath done, whether it be good or bad.' And then he goes on to say: 'Knowing therefore the terror of the Lord, we persuade men' (2 Cor 5:10–11). And that is what I am trying to do. I must not leave anybody in any uncertainty about this matter. I know that the devil can come as an angel of light and persuade us that we are believers when we are not. We can substitute a kind of intellectual assent, an agreement with a number of propositions, for true and living faith, but it will be of no value to us at all.

So it is important that we should go on with our testing in order that we may determine the reality of what we regard as our conviction, our repentance, and our faith in the Lord Jesus Christ. And the Apostle provided the test for us before we ever saw the need for it; it is here in these verses in Colossians.

Now, I do trust that anyone who is somewhat antagonistic to this Christian message, and regards it as some form of psychological trickery, the attempt of a man to play on people's emotions, and so on, I do trust that such a friend's mind is disabused. Far from trying to trick anybody into saying that they believe, I am doing the exact opposite. I

am asking everyone to examine their belief, to test themselves, in order to make certain that they have a real and not
a spurious faith. I am asking them to make certain that they
really are trusting to the Lord Jesus and not merely giving
an intellectual assent to things they have always been
taught.

Have you been brought up in a Christian home or in a
Christian church? I am asking you to examine yourself to
determine whether you are in the faith or not. We cannot
afford to take risks, the times are too terrible, they are too
uncertain. Sooner than we realize we all of us may find ourselves before the judgment seat of Christ and at the bar of
God's eternal judgment where we shall be stripped naked
and the truth will emerge. I am giving you a preliminary
examination to save you from disappointment at that hour.

Now, I have very high authority for doing this – none
less than the Son of God himself. He tells us at the end of
the Sermon on the Mount that some people will come to
him at the end and say, 'Lord, Lord, have we not
prophesied in thy name? and in thy name have cast out
devils? and in thy name done many wonderful works?'
And he goes on to say, 'Then will I profess unto them, I
never knew you: depart from me, ye that work iniquity'
(Mt 7:22–23). Now that is the terrible possibility. These
people come with confidence and say: Lord, Lord, we have
always believed in you. Have we not done this, that and the
other in your name? We have been great workers in your
kingdom. And yet that will be the answer.

We must, therefore, examine ourselves, and the way to
do this is to continue our study of the fruit that the gospel
brings forth. Thank God it does. We have a test here: I can
find out whether a tree is true and genuine by looking at
the fruit it bears. I am quoting the Lord again. He said, 'Do
men gather grapes of thorns, or figs of thistles?' (Mt 7:16).

The nature of a tree is declared by its fruit. It is exactly the same with the Christian life. 'This gospel,' says Paul, 'bringeth forth fruit in all the world as it doth in you also, since the day you heard of it, and knew the grace of God in truth.'

So what is this further fruit? The answer is this: 'To the saints and faithful brethren in Christ at Colosse.' Now this is a wonderful term; a wonderful name is applied to these people. Here is the Apostle writing, not to great conferences of cardinals and prelates and church leaders, but to a handful of people meeting together in one another's houses: 'the Christian church at Colosse'. And Paul addresses them as 'saints and faithful brethren in Christ'. Here they are, just a little group of people, but, he says, they are *saints*. Officials have not been holding conferences for years to decide whether or not these people are saints! Paul says, 'You are saints'; he canonizes them all. Every Christian is a saint; every church member, he says, is a saint if he or she is a true Christian. This is the term that is used at the beginning of almost all these New Testament epistles. It is universal.

So, then, what does this tell us? Well, it is a very profound and important test and, thank God, a most glorious one. What Paul is saying is that something has happened to these people. They are saints now; they are faithful brethren. There was a time when they were not. Something has happened to them as a result of which Paul can designate them as 'saints' whereas a few years back he could not have done anything of the sort.

Never forget the background. These people, the members of the church at Colosse, had been brought up to a life of paganism in the first century. I need not have added the century. Paganism in the twentieth century, paganism in any city tonight, is exactly the same as it was in the city of

Colosse. Paul's readers had been pagans, yet here Paul addresses them as 'saints'. So what had happened?

Well, you see, we are back again to the point that the gospel is not just a word; it is not just a teaching or a theory; it is not just a pronouncement, but has its own inherent power and this power brings forth fruit. It is like the power in a seed. That is the marvel of a little seed. It is nothing to look at but it has life in it; it has power; it has the energy of the atom. And its power is life-giving. The gospel, says Paul, is like that. And this is the fruit I am referring to now. It is what is known throughout the Bible as *regeneration, new birth*! A great change takes place. When the gospel really comes to men and women and comes in the power of the Holy Spirit, it brings forth this fruit, it changes them. There is nothing more important than this and so many fail at this point.

Now there are many people who have always thought of Christianity like this: 'Oh, yes,' they say, 'I am a Christian; I've been a Christian for years.'

'Why do you say that you are a Christian?' I ask.

'Well,' they reply, 'I believe that Jesus Christ saves me. I believe that Jesus Christ is the Saviour, the Son of God. I believe that somehow or other he puts me right with God.'

And that is all they have to say. Their idea of salvation and of Christianity is that you believe in the Lord Jesus Christ and then, well, you go on and battle with this life as best you can. You stand up to sin and temptation and evil and 'the slings and arrows of outrageous fortune' as best you can and in your own strength. What is a Christian? Well, they say, Christians are people who believe that in spite of all their sin and failure, they are going to heaven in the end because God forgives them in Christ! That is their idea of Christianity!

Others put it like this: 'Yes, I decided for Christ a long

time ago. I was in a meeting and we were asked to come forward if we were ready. So I went forward. I decided for Christ. I decided to go after him and follow him as best I could. I took my stand for Christ!' And that is their notion of Christianity.

But, oh, how that misses the central glory of it all! Do not misunderstand me. As we saw earlier, we start with conviction of sin and repentance and belief in Christ and his shed blood. It is the beginning, but it is not the end, and I can test whether or not my faith is true by this further test. This gospel brings forth fruit – of what? New life!

'What do you mean?' asks someone.

Well, new life is the great thing that is taught right the way through the New Testament, beginning with our Lord himself. Consider the famous incident of our Lord dealing with that man Nicodemus who came to speak to him. You see, Nicodemus' idea of the religious life was that it was a life you lived with your own power. You had certain understandings, you could teach others and you lived a good moral life. So he came to our Lord and said: Now, I thought I knew all about it, but you know more than I do; tell me, what is this extra you have got? I should like to know about it. You must be a teacher sent from God because you have exceptional power. What is this? I want to have it.

Our Lord interrupted him and said, 'Verily, verily, I say unto thee, Except a man be born again, he cannot see the kingdom of God.' And Nicodemus stumbled. He could not understand it. But our Lord went on saying it. 'Marvel not that I said unto thee, Ye must be born again. The wind bloweth where it listeth, and thou hearest the sound thereof, but canst not tell whence it cometh, and whither it goeth: so is every one that is born of the Spirit' (Jn 3:1–8).

This is it, our Lord says. You do not understand it, you

have it all wrong. I am not talking about an ethical system; you do not advance from here to there. It is a new birth. And he told his followers, the apostles, to teach the same thing.

The apostle Paul in his first letter to the Corinthians keeps on talking about the 'natural man and the spiritual man'. He says, 'The natural man receiveth not the things of the Spirit of God: for they are foolishness unto him: neither can he know them, because they are spiritually discerned.' That is the natural man. He does not believe the gospel; he says it is nonsense, folly. It is impossible for him to believe it because he is a natural man. But, says Paul, we believe the gospel. How do we believe it? Well, he says that something has happened to us: 'God hath revealed them unto us by his Spirit: for the Spirit searcheth all things, yea, the deep things of God.' He continues, 'We have received, not the spirit of the world, but the spirit which is of God; that we might know the things that are freely given to us of God' (1 Cor 2:14, 10, 12). We are believers, and not the others, says Paul, because we have received this Spirit that enlightens us.

And that is another way of saying that there is a new creation, that the believer is a new person, someone who has been born again. Listen again to Paul as he puts it in specific terms: 'If any man be in Christ, he is a new creature [a new creation]: old things are passed away; behold, all things are become new' (2 Cor 5:17). Now that is Christianity. That is the fruit – a new creation.

But lest anybody say, 'But that is only the teaching of that man Paul – that legalist who foisted his ideas upon the glorious simple gospel of Christ!' then let us listen to James. People like James because they say that he is a practical man. But this is what James says: 'Of his own will begat he us with the word of truth, that we should be a kind of firstfruits of his creatures' (Jas 1:18). James agreeing with Paul? Of course! They all agreed with one another. It is only so-called clever people who try to produce a disagreement.

Then there is Peter. He says, 'Being born again, not of corruptible seed, but of incorruptible, by the word of God, which liveth and abideth for ever' (1 Pet 1:23). It is a living word, a life-giving word; it leads to a birth. This word has brought forth fruit in us: it has given us a new life.

And John is equally clear about it all. If you read his first epistle you will find that he constantly speaks of the one who is 'born of God'. He says, 'Beloved, now are we the sons of God' (1 Jn 3:2); 'Whosoever is born of God doth not commit sin; (1 Jn 3:9). 'We know,' he says, 'that we have passed from death unto life, because we love the brethren' (1 Jn 3:14). And that is how the New Testament deals with this wonderful fruit.

This is essential Christianity. Thank God for it! Christianity is not just a message that tells you that if you believe in Christ your sins are forgiven, and then leaves you to meet the world and the flesh and the devil just as you are and in your own strength. No, it is regeneration – new birth – a 'new man'.

When you become a Christian, what happens is not so much that you add something to your life as that your life is changed. When men and women become Christians, it is not that they put on new clothes; no, they are changed, inside and out, and the inside is particularly changed, a new creation.

But remember, secondly, that Christianity is not about people deciding to change themselves. They cannot. 'Can the Ethiopian change his skin, or the leopard his spots?' (Jer 13:23). Let them try to do it, then they will find they cannot! People talk about deciding to change themselves.

We have all tried it. It is impossible. But, thank God, there is power in this word which brings forth fruit, and a part of the fruit is that it changes us. We do not decide to change ourselves but we find that we are changed.

That, to me, is the romance of Christianity. A man finds that he is 'a new man' and he is amazed at himself. He cannot believe it is true of him! He says, 'Is it possible that I am the man I once was? I am the same man and yet I am not!' The apostle Paul was always filled with that amazement at himself – 'I live; yet not I, but Christ liveth in me' (Gal 2:20). He had been changed.

And I want to emphasize that it is not a superficial change. It is not merely that we are changed in certain respects; it is an essential change, a profound change. The terms all tell us that. *Birth* – It is not, Nicodemus, that you need to be improved a little here and added to there; a little information at this point and a little taking away! No, no, you have to go back. You need to be born again.

Then – *creation*. There is nothing more profound than that. According to this term, when men and women become Christians, it is an event that can only be compared to that which happened at the beginning when the Spirit of God brooded over the abyss and God said, 'Let there be light: and there was light' (Gen 1:3). Creation was out of nothing – a bringing into being of something that had not been there.

Or take the words I have just quoted from John – 'we know that we have passed *from death to life*'. That is it. Paul has the same notion – 'You hath he quickened, who were dead in trespasses and sins' (Eph 2:1). Is there any bigger change than from death to life? A body dying, corrupt, finished, lifeless, useless, hopeless is suddenly alive; life from the dead!

Those are the terms that are used in the New Testament

to describe this great change we are dealing with. What does it mean? Well, here it is in its essence.

Do you know what makes men and women Christians? It is the mighty action of the almighty God, the Creator. He takes them as they are and smashes them and makes them anew. He, God, is bringing into being something that was not there; a new disposition is put into them, a new principle of life is infused into them. God enters into their lives. The life of God comes into the soul; it is a creative act, so the New Testament says that the Christian is 'a new creature'. The Christians in Colosse were the same people in physical appearance but they were 'saints and faithful brethren in Colosse'. And Paul says that about those who were pagans!

Now there is nothing more wonderful than this. I think this is where the gospel hope comes in. When we have tried and tried and tried again, only to fail, always finding ourselves back at the same point, we stop, and the world stops. Philosophy cannot help us, psychology cannot help us, nothing helps us; but then the Creator says: I will help you. I will make you a new person. I will put a new principle into you. I will infuse a new disposition into you. I will make a new creation.

There is hope there, and it is the only hope. But, thank God, it is the hope that is given in this gospel. And my assertion is that you and I are not Christians unless we have been born again; unless we know that we have received the life of God; unless we become new creatures, new creations.

'But how can I know it?' asks someone.

I will tell you. This is something that shows itself. It shows itself as it did in these people at Colosse. They became saints – 'To the saints and faithful brethren in Christ . . .'. Now the first definition of 'a saint' is this: a saint is one of God's consecrated people. Saints are those who have been set apart by God for himself. The saints are the people of God, so that when they become saints they enter into a new relationship with God. You see, before they become Christians they are not saints nor the people of God. They are in the world, they are not a people. Peter puts it like that – 'Which in time past were not a people, but are now,' he says, 'the people of God.' Formerly just a rabble, but the moment you become a Christian you become a saint, one of God's people. God has set you apart: '. . . who hath called you out of darkness into his marvellous light' (1 Pet 2:10, 9).

Now, here is where the practical test comes in. The gospel brings forth this fruit of new life in us and we know that we have got it because we have become saints. How do I know that I am a saint? In this way: I have a new spirit in me that I did not have before. That shows itself in my attitude towards God. Everyone by nature is a hater of God. 'The carnal [natural] mind is enmity against God,' says Paul to the Romans, 'for it is not subject to the law of God, neither indeed can be' (Rom 8:7). This very epistle will tell us that: 'You, that were sometime alienated and enemies in your mind by wicked works, yet now hath he reconciled in the body of his flesh . . .' (Col 1:21–22).

'Oh, but that is nonsense. I have always believed in God,' you say.

You have not, my friend; you have believed in what you thought was God. You believed in a god that you made for yourself and your god is not the God of the Bible. The God of the Bible is the God of the Ten Commandments; he is a holy God, a righteous God; he is the Judge eternal. Do you like that sort of a God? Of course you do not! You support the man who says he does not believe the Old Testament because it depicts God as a righteous holy Judge. That means you hate God.

We all hate God by nature, do we not? How often have I had people coming to me and saying, 'Why does God allow this to happen to me? What have I done that God should treat me like this? If there is a God, why does he allow war? Why doesn't he stop it all?' They are always criticizing. God, they feel, is against us. They feel that God is some sort of tyrant and monster waiting to crush us and to keep us down!

But, the moment they are born again and become Christians, this whole attitude to God changes. There is a new spirit in them. The hatred is removed, and they no longer feel God is against them. They know now that God has loved them though they have been what they have been; they know that God has loved them in spite of the harsh and cruel thoughts they have harboured against him. They know now that though they have been such vile fools, such ignorant rebels against this almighty God, God so loved the world and so loved them that 'he gave his only begotten Son, that whosoever believeth in him should not perish, but have everlasting life' (Jn 3:16). They know that God has loved them and they in turn love God.

Now they want to know God, and to be blessed of him. Before, they did not want to know about him; they would believe anything in a newspaper that seemed to disprove the being of God. They thought it was clever and marvellous! Now their chief desire is to know him and serve him. They are born again; they have a new spirit in them; they are bearing the fruit. They are saints.

Have you become a saint? You see, what matters is not that we *say* that we believe, but this inward disposition. Is this our attitude towards God?

But let us look at another aspect of the word *saint*. When we normally use the word, we always think of conduct and behaviour and holiness, do we not? The saint is a person who lives a holy life. Quite right! There is an element of truth in that. The real definition of the saint is the one I have given, but this is also true, because when men and women thus come into this new relationship with God, it affects the whole of their being. When people are born again, as the Apostle puts it: 'Old things are passed away; behold, all things are become new' (2 Cor 5:17). And by that, Paul means that a very profound moral change takes place in someone who becomes a saint.

Look at these people at Colosse. Are you interested in romance? Of course you are! Everybody is interested in romance, hence the popularity of romantic films and television plays and so on. But if you want to know anything about romance, here it is in these people, 'saints and faithful brethren in Christ'. Do you know what they once were like? Let me give you a description of them. This passage is from the epistle to the Corinthians but it was true of all pagans.

> Know ye not that the unrighteous shall not inherit the kingdom of God? Be not deceived: neither fornicators, nor idolaters, nor adulterers, nor effeminate, nor abusers of themselves with mankind, nor thieves, nor covetous, nor drunkards, nor revilers, nor extortioners, shall inherit the kingdom of God. And such were some of you (1 Cor 6:9–11).

And that is what they were! That was the sort of life these people were living before Paul went to Corinth, before Epaphras went to Colosse. And that is the life that is being lived in our cities today, not only by the people who live in the gutters, but by the 'smart set', by some of the people who are near the top! 'Abusers of themselves with mankind, idolaters, effeminate, adulterers, wife beaters, live in the gutters, but by the 'smart set', by some of the

people who are near the top! 'Abusers of themselves with
mankind, idolaters, effeminate, adulterers, wife beaters,
drunkards, extortioners.' Yes, said Paul, that is what you
were! And when they were that they were not called
'saints' and 'faithful brethren'. But now they are and it is
because of the profound moral change that has taken place!
'And such were some of you: but ye are washed, but ye are
sanctified, but ye are justified in the name of the Lord
Jesus, and by the Spirit of our God' (1 Cor 6:11).

This is what Christianity is. It came to people who were
living lives like that. The dynamic and the power of God
came into them and made them anew, lifted them out of the
gutters and turned them into saints adorning the church.
That is the power, the fruit I am talking about. This is how
you test your faith. You say, 'I believe in Christ.' Very
well, has this sort of change taken place in you? Are you
washed? Are you sanctified? Are you delivered from your
past sins and put into a new position, justified in the name
of the Lord Jesus?

This means that when we are born again we see sin for
what it is. We see it in our own heart, in our own actions,
in everything we are, and we hate it. We realize that we
have sinned against God; we realize that we have sinned
against ourselves. We sin against mankind, we sin against
human nature, we are beasts and worse, and we hate it.
That is the main effect of this moral change. We want to get
out of it, we want to be rid of it, so we do not continue in
it. We plead for power to enable us to come out of it –
'Whosoever is born of God doth not commit sin,' says
John (1 Jn 3:9), which means that we do not go on living in
it.

No, says John, 'Whosoever is born of God doth not
commit sin; for his seed remaineth in him: and he cannot
sin' – he cannot go on sinning like that, because – 'he is

born of God.' There is a new seed of life in him and it is impossible that he should continue there. It does not mean he is perfect, he may fall into sin, but he does not stay in it. He is not like the sow that was washed returning to the mire, or the dog to his vomit (2 Pet 2:22). No, that is the temporary believer; but this man has got new life in him. The seed remains in him and he cannot be defeated.

And the positive aspect of it is that whereas we used to hate the Ten Commandments and the teaching of the prophets, the Sermon on the Mount and the teaching of the apostles, we now love them. We love the law of God. We are able to say with the psalmist: 'O how I love thy law!' (Ps 119:97). We are able to say with John, 'By this we know that we love the children of God, when we love God, and keep his commandments. For this is the love of God, that we keep his commandments: *and his commandments are not grievous*' (1 Jn 5:2–3).

Tell me, do you love the Ten Commandments, or do you still hate them? Are you still arguing against them? Are you still saying that Christianity is too narrow; you want to live your own life; you want to have your fling; you want really to enjoy life? Is that your attitude? If it is, take it from me you are not a Christian; the gospel is not bearing in you the fruit it always does. When we become Christians we love the law of God, it is no longer grievous to us. We say, 'That is right, that is how I ought to be, that is how I want to be.' That is the meaning of becoming a saint, you see. This moral reformation takes place in addition to the change in our spirit and our attitude towards God, and we become faithful and reliable men and women.

And we must just say something about this word 'brethren' – 'To the saints and faithful brethren in Christ'. It means that the moment this great change takes place in us, the moment we are born again, we become children of

God. So, of course, we become members of the family of God, and, because of that, we are members of a new society. We have been separated from the world and our old associations, because we are new men and women. And we find that there are other new men and women so we join them and align ourselves with them. That is obvious, is it not? – 'Birds of a feather, flock together' – of course! They have that same fundamental constitution. The world mixes with the world but the saint does not. Saints, as we have seen, are, by definition, people who are delivered from this present evil world and put into this new association. We are members of a company, of a number of brethren.

And so, you see, Paul was writing to this little group of people who met together in one another's houses in Colosse. That is the Christian church, not your cathedrals and all that paraphernalia! No; it is hearts blended together; it is people born of the Spirit, wanting fellowship with one another, recognizing one another. They are different from what they were. They are segregated from the world: not that they are Pharisees but that they are children of God. And the moment we are born again, we recognize this in others. And to me this is one of the most wonderful things of all.

So when you become a Christian you will begin to like people whom you have always despised hitherto. You will begin to find that they are the only people worth knowing. They are your brothers and sisters – related to God. You will note them; you will desire to be with them; you will meet with them. 'Faithful brethren': the Christians in Colosse used to meet together. What for? Well, to learn more about these things, to study the Scriptures, to pray together, to ask God to give them power to help others and to bring others out of darkness into the new fellowship.

And notice the point that Paul repeats twice over, that is,

their love to one another – 'Since we heard of your faith in Christ Jesus, *and of the love which ye have to all the saints*', and then he ends in verse 8, 'Who also declared unto us *your love in the Spirit.*' This is a very wonderful test. John, as we have seen, puts it like this: 'We know that we have passed from death unto life, because we love the brethren' (1 Jn 3:14). People who have become Christians, who have received this new life of God into their soul, are those who say, 'I would sooner spend my evening with the simplest, most unknown Christians than with the greatest in the land who are not Christians.' 'I had rather be a doorkeeper in the house of my God,' says the psalmist, 'than to dwell in the tents of wickedness' (Ps 84:10).

We are told that Moses 'refused to be called the son of Pharaoh's daughter'. There was the glittering prize! Life in the court; a prince, perhaps to become the Pharaoh; a great general! Marvellous prospects! The world was at his feet, as it were, waiting for him to go in and possess it. But he 'refused to be called the son of Pharaoh's daughter; choosing rather to suffer affliction with the people of God, than to enjoy the pleasures of sin for a season' (Heb 11:24–25). It is inevitable, is it not? If you have the life of God in your soul you recognize the brethren and you prefer them to anybody else. You no longer judge people by their wealth or poverty, by their intellect or lack of it, by their learning or their ignorance, by their houses or their hovels. You judge them by one thing only; you say, 'Are you a child of God? If you are, you are my brother; you are the one I want; you are the one I can talk to from the depth of my heart. You belong to the family and we are all destined for the same eternal home.'

Are you a Christian? Are you bearing this fruit that I have been holding before you? Have you been born again? Is there a new spirit in you? Do you want to know God?

Is it your chief complaint that your love is weak and faint? Do you love his law? Would you like to keep it and love it? Do you long to know him and to honour him? Do you like his people? Would you put them before the whole world? God give us grace to face these questions honestly. There is no value in a belief unless it leads to this fruit. 'Faith without works' – these works – 'is dead' (see Jas 2:17).

But if you can say 'Yes' to all those questions, you are a Christian, my friend. However weak, however frail, however fallible, however failing, however sinful. You have new life in you and it is God who has put it there. It is this word that has borne forth fruit, even the fruit of a regenerated being, a renewed soul. God has created you anew and he has made you his own child and he is preparing you for the eternity that awaits all his people.

Let us make certain that the fruit of the Spirit is indeed manifest within us. If it is not, ask God in mercy to lay his hands upon you, to breathe his life into you. Ask him that, honestly and truly, and he will not refuse you. He will do it for you and you will be born again. You will become a saint and faithful brother and an heir of the eternal and everlasting glory.

Chapter 7

In Christ at Colosse

To the saints and faithful brethren in Christ which are at Colosse: Grace be unto you, and peace, from God our Father and the Lord Jesus Christ . . . . For this cause we also, since the day we heard it, do not cease to pray for you, and to desire that ye might be filled with the knowledge of his will in all wisdom and spiritual understanding; that ye might walk worthy of the Lord unto all pleasing, being fruitful in every good work, and increasing in the knowledge of God; strengthened with all might, according to his glorious power, unto all patience and longsuffering with joyfulness (Col 1:2, 9–11).

We are, let me remind you, looking at the introduction to this epistle to the Colossians, in order that we may serve two main purposes. The first is that we may be perfectly clear in our minds as to what this gospel is about. And secondly, we also want to make quite sure that we are believers of the gospel, that we are enjoying its benefits, because there is the danger of assuming that we are Christian only to find in times of need that we are not Christians at all and therefore that it does not help us. There are many, many in that position.

Now, the Apostle deals with this and it is this aspect that we are focusing on at this point. So I want to go on considering this wonderful fruit which comes out of the gospel and in particular I want to call your attention now to something which, in many ways, is the ultimate fruit which the gospel produces. It is something that enables us to live triumphantly in this present evil world, and I suggest to you that it is the ultimate test which must be applied to any teaching whatsoever. Many teachings are offering themselves to us at this present time – in the newspapers, on the television and on the radio. People are saying, 'This is what you have to do.' The test is: Does it really help me to live life in this world, to conquer life and to master it?

Now, the gospel meets us and says, 'That is precisely what I enable people to do.' Listen to the Apostle putting it here in verse 11: 'Strengthened with all might, according to his glorious power, unto all patience and longsuffering with joyfulness.'

So here Paul is, writing to this little handful of people who were members of the church at Colosse in a world which was as difficult a place two thousand years ago as it is today. Life has never been easy in this world; biblical and secular history prove that. And here Paul writes to these Colossians who were having a hard, a trying time, many of them enduring grievous persecution. He says: What you need is patience, longsuffering. Life is a stern battle, it is a difficult business. But I know that now, since you have become saints and faithful brethren, you are able not only to go through life with patience and longsuffering, but with joyfulness.

Here, then, is the test, here is the challenge. Does the gospel enable us to face the battle of life as it is today in such a way that we are more than conquerors – not merely conquerors but *more* than conquerors? Does this teaching, which is offering itself to us, enable us not merely to put up with tribulations but to rejoice in them? That is what we find here, 'patience and longsuffering with joyfulness'.

Now the gospel's claim is that it can enable us to face life as it is at this present moment with all the problems in the world and with all that may be coming to meet us. Here is a message which says: Believe this, believe on the Lord Jesus

Christ, and whatever comes you will be able to go through it more than conquerors.

And there is no other teaching under the sun that can make such a claim, not one. The eastern religions are all hopeless, they are all pessimistic. Philosophers? They, too, are all hopeless, they do not understand. There is nothing that offers us this apart from this gospel.

So the question that arises is: How does it do this? Now let me tell you first what it does *not* do. It is not escapism. I have to deal with this because there are many people who still seem to think that Christianity is just a form of escapism. 'Ah,' they say, 'you Christian people, you are working a wonderful trick on yourselves; you just meet together and sing your hymns and work yourselves up into a state of excitement. You are a bunch of emotionalists. You do not face the facts at all; you do not read; you do not think. You have your artificial little life and there, of course, you make yourselves feel very happy and you say, "What a wonderful life this is!" But in reality it is fear and sheer escapism.'

So I want to try to show you that it is not that. Indeed, if you want to talk about escapism, I do not find it at all difficult to show you examples of it. What about the men and women who can only keep going on drugs? What about the people who cannot live without their whisky? That is escapism. What about the people who cannot live without the television or who cannot stay at home any night of the week, but must always be out, having some pleasure or excitement? That is pure escapism! But that is not what we find here, as I shall show you.

Neither is Christianity wishful thinking. You know that attitude of wishful thinking, a kind of false optimism, which refuses to face facts and says, 'Things must surely get better, they cannot go on like this.' There is a great deal of that in the world, but I can show you that that also is not this message.

What about fatalism? Fatalism says: 'What is to be will be! Do what you like about it, you cannot change it. There is something inevitable – kismet! Call it what you like. What is the use of fighting against a thing like that? You might as well give in!' But that is not this message.

And, then, it is not what is called 'stoicism', which is also very prevalent. Stiff upper lip! Bracing back your shoulders! The philosophy of courage, grit and sticking at it! Now that has often been confused with Christianity but it has nothing to do with it at all. That was a pagan philosophy and it still is. Like most pagan philosophies it is very fond of borrowing Christian terminology, but that does not make any of them Christian; that does not turn them into a gospel message. That just means that they are thieves and robbers!

'Well, then, what is this?' asks someone.

Here it is. The Christian life is realism – realism which is based upon an understanding of this message. It is a life which is lived as the result of a series of deductions drawn from the truth that is revealed in the word of this true gospel. Now let me show you this.

What I mean by realism is that the gospel, instead of telling us to stop thinking, urges us to think. That is the great appeal of the Bible from beginning to end – think! 'So teach us to number our days, that we may apply our hearts unto wisdom' (Ps 90:12). 'Come now, and let us reason together, saith the Lord' (Is 1:18). The whole tragedy in the world is that men and women do not think or, if they start thinking, they stop; they do not go right on, they are never thorough. The Bible invites us to think and to face facts exactly as they are. Far from pulling down the blinds and working ourselves up into some emotional excitement when we meet together to consider the message of the gospel, we meet together to face facts.

Now I am never tired of emphasizing this. If I had no other reason for believing the Bible to be the word of God, its realism would be enough for me. Here is the only book in the world that tells me the truth about myself. And what it tells me is that I am a sinner. It tells me 'that in me (that is, in my flesh) dwelleth no good thing' (Rom 7:18). It tells me that I am twisted and perverted, a cad, and a liar; that the human heart 'is deceitful above all things, and desperately wicked: who can know it?' (Jer 17:9). This is the truth, and the Bible is the only book in the world that tells me such truth about myself.

And what does it tell me about life in this world? Does it paint rosy pictures and tell me that this world is a wonderful place? No, it calls it 'this present evil world' (Gal 1:4). You see, it is the most honest book in the world. It has some great men in it, some great heroes, but it gives a true portrait – warts and all, every time! Take a man like David, one of its greatest heroes: the Bible shows us that man as a cad who fell and sinned terribly. It is true of all of them. You have all the facts here with nothing concealed. No more terrible picture of life has ever been presented to the human race than that which you have in this book.

I can sum it up like this. The Bible's whole case, its first postulate, is that this world and its denizens are in such a deplorable and completely hopeless condition that the very Son of God had to leave the courts of heaven and eternity and come into this world in order to save it. Messages were not enough; instruction was not enough; saints raised by God were insufficient. The world is in such an awful condition that nothing less than the incarnation of the Son of God was adequate to deal with it.

So there is nothing that is so pessimistic about life, about the world as it is, than the gospel. And that is what I mean by realism. The people who are guilty of escapism and wishful thinking are the people who persist in saying to us, 'It would be all right if only we all did this and that – if only we made an appeal, if only all the preachers sent messages to the world leaders – then the whole problem would be solved!' Those are the people who lack realism because they are wasting their breath and wasting their time. Realism means facing the facts as they are without manipulating anything at all or without changing anything. Now the gospel does that. This method here in the Bible of enabling me to go through life more than conqueror, starts by telling me, 'Face the facts exactly as they are!'

What next? The Christian faith invites me to believe the gospel because if I do that, it will separate me from this present evil world.

'What do you mean?' asks someone. 'Does it mean you are going to die?'

No, it means that though I still remain *in* the world I shall no longer be *of* it. Did you notice this in the second verse? Never rush through the beginning of any epistle; these preliminary salutations, so-called, are full of doctrine if you have eyes to see them. Paul says, 'To the saints and faithful brethren in Christ *at Colosse*.' He is sending a letter and that is how he addresses it. Do you see the significance? These people who have become Christians are at Colosse.

'What's the significance of that?' you may ask. 'What does he mean by this phrase?'

Oh, these two words conceal one of the most marvellous and glorious facts of that change which is called 'regeneration'. You see, the moment men and women are born again, the moment they become new creatures, they not only become 'saints and faithful brethren', but they immediately have an entirely new relationship to this world.

Now Colosse represents the world and these Christians are 'at Colosse'. We, too, are in this present world, so what does all this mean for us? Well, let me translate it into simple terms.

What were these people like before they became Christians, before this great change took place in them and they were made new men and women? Well, at that time they were not at Colosse but were in Colosse and of Colosse. Colosse was then everything to them. Their whole life was circumscribed by it: Colosse controlled and determined everything. That was true of them, and it is true of all who are not Christians. Their whole life is determined and controlled absolutely by this present world.

Now the apostle Paul has a wonderful way of putting that in his epistle to the Ephesians: 'You hath he quickened, who were dead in trespasses and sins; wherein in time past ye walked according to the course of this world' (Eph 2:1–2). What a perfect description! You walked, he says, you lived; your being and existence were determined by the course of this world. Can you not see it? The translation in the Authorized Version suggests a wonderful picture of a kind of course, a racecourse, if you like, and that is life to those who are not Christians. They are just going round and round in a circle – the course mapped out in this world. It seems to be a wonderfully active life and a moving life! Yes, but you never go outside it, you are always within its confines.

Our Lord put it in still more striking and dramatic terms. This was his description of life: 'When a strong man armed,' he said, 'keepeth his palace, his goods are in peace' (Lk 11:21). This is a picture of life in this world. It is like a great castle, owned by a very powerful chieftain – the devil, the 'strong man armed'. And what are men and women? They are his goods; there they are, you see, inside this castle which has an enormous wall built right round it. Oh, it is very spacious. It has extensive grounds and there are various buildings! You can spend a lot of time walking round and taking up first one interest and then another!

Ah, yes, but, you see, you are never allowed outside the grounds. Try to get outside and you will be clubbed on the head and fall helpless to the ground. Get up and try again and he will club you again. All right, you can be very active within the grounds of the palace but woe betide you if you attempt to get out. If you try to be a Christian, if you try to believe in God, if you try to lead a godly life, you will be struck.

As long as they are in general under him, the strong man armed does not care very much what 'his goods' do. So the devil allows a great deal of culture, he has never objected to that; he has no objection to education and all these things. He knows that men and women may be very cultured and highly educated but still his slaves, and he does not care where they are in the grounds as long as they are there. Colosse limited the whole outlook, all the desires, everything they did. Is that not true of the world today?

The world has never been in greater slavery than it is now. Men and women do not determine how they live; their lives are determined for them, hence advertising! It works; it pays to advertise, of course! Why? Because we are bound by Colosse. Tell the citizens of Colosse, 'Everybody is doing this,' and they will say, 'We must be right if everybody is doing it!' The 'course of this world'. And so, you see, our appearance, the way we speak, the way we dress, everything, is being determined for us. All that happens to us is bound by the world, by what is called here Colosse, the city in which we live.

What is going on? What is holding our attention? Well, we are interested in what we see in the newspapers and on the television. We have no interests outside that at all. We are absolutely confined to these media of communication which put things in front of us and determine our entire outlook. And what matters to us, therefore, is what happens in Colosse. Any change in Colosse affects us; anything happening there must make a difference to us because this is the centre and the circumference of our lives!

And on top of that, of course, such people have their joy entirely determined by their circumstances. If things are all right in Colosse, we are all happy. If things go wrong there, we are all miserable. And is that not the state of mankind outside Christ? 'What's going to happen? My whole life is shaken! What will happen to me, my wife and children? What will happen to all the preparations I have made? It all seems . . . !' I have no basis, you see. It is what happens in the world in which I find myself that determines my joy, my reaction, my everything. I am a part of Colosse; I am of Colosse, I am in it and I cannot extricate myself.

That is how these people were before they became Christians. But that was no longer true; a great change had taken place in them. What Paul says about them is this: 'at Colosse'. What does he mean by this? Well, although they were still living at Colosse, they had been extricated out of it; they had been detached from it. They no longer belonged to it; they were no longer involved in it in the way they were before.

How does such a change come about? The first thing the gospel does is open our eyes to Colosse. It opens our eyes to the vanity of this present world. Before, we said, 'Isn't life wonderful!' Though everything was going wrong, we buoyed ourselves up. Then the gospel comes, it opens my eyes and I see things for what they are. I see the paint and the powder; I see that it is all a vain show! John Bunyan, of course, put this once and for ever, when he called the world 'Vanity Fair'. What has it all led to? It will lead to nothing. So the gospel comes and opens our eyes to things which we once thought were so thrilling and we now see to be utterly empty and vain and evil.

There was a time when the members of the church at Colosse thought it was a wonderful thing to get drunk. They boasted about it and told their fellows how drunk they had become, how marvellous it had been! But they did not think of it like that any longer. They said, 'We were beasts, we made beasts of ourselves.' And that applies to most of the other things they did. Their eyes were opened and so they said, 'What is there in this for my mind, for my morals? What is the value of this? Does it build me up? What does it give me?' And they found that they had got nothing.

When people become Christians their eyes are opened to the life of Colosse which had governed them completely, which had captivated them and which charmed them. They have seen through its vanity! And not only its vanity. Their eyes are also opened to the fact that it is only temporary. You would have thought that when men and women see people die they would stop and think, they would reason and consider. You would have thought that death would open their eyes to the fact that, even at its very best, our existence in Colosse and this world is only temporary. But not so. The facts never open our eyes. We do not like them so we forget them and begin to talk and laugh and joke. You stand over an open grave and say, 'I'll never be the same again.' But you will; you will be the same before you get home. Facts are not enough. It takes the Spirit of God upon this blessed gospel to open our eyes to the fact that this world is only a temporary place. The gospel alone teaches us to see that we are but strangers, but pilgrims, but sojourners in this world.

So when Paul addresses this letter to these people, he addresses it in this extraordinary way. You see the picture? Think of sending on letters to people who are on holiday. The name is already on the envelope, so after crossing out the usual address you write 'At' then the name of the place where they are staying. Mr So-and-so, at Penzance or Aberdeen or wherever it is. He will not settle there permanently, but he is there for the time being. He is *at* . . . .

Very well, 'To the saints and faithful brethren in Christ which are at Colosse.' This is no longer, you see, their permanent address. It used to be before; they were not at Colosse, but of Colosse. They were men and women of Colosse and they were proud of it and would fight for their city and compare its excellencies with others and it was always the best! But this great change has taken place in them. They are still living there but they are only *at* Colosse – it is a temporary residence only. They say, 'We are strangers and pilgrims; we are but travellers and sojourners; we are as our fathers who were before us, here today, gone tomorrow.'

That is how the gospel puts us right; that is how it enables us to live in this world and to be more than conquerors. It immediately separates us from this Colosse in which we are living. It gives us an entirely new outlook upon the world in which we find ourselves so that we realize that we no longer belong to it. Like Christian in *The Pilgrim's Progress*, we pass through Vanity Fair – we no longer make it our permanent residence.

That, then, is the first thing, but let us go to the second, which is positive. 'In Christ,' says Paul. This is a marvellous gospel! It sets us loose from something, but we are never left just free; according to the Bible, we are always joined to something. We are either worshippers of mammon or worshippers of God; we are either the slaves of Satan or the slaves of Jesus Christ; we are either in Colosse or in Christ Jesus. The gospel joins us to Christ.

That is the term and what a term – 'in Christ'! It is the new link, the new address, the entirely new life. It means a new outlook. When men and women believe the gospel, when they become Christians as the result of the operation of the Holy Spirit in the new birth, they see everything in terms of the Lord Jesus Christ and his teaching and their own relationship to him. Let me give you a summary of this.

The moment this gospel begins to operate on you, you begin to be concerned about your soul. Not your clothes nor your appearance any longer; not your food, your drinks, your possessions, your enjoyments, your pleasures; not the prospects of Colosse and the prospects of the world; but your soul! You realize, as we have seen, that there is that in you which is imperishable and eternal, so you begin to be concerned about it and your eternal destiny, and that is the most wonderful thing that can happen to you. The moment you begin to think about your soul you are no longer as dependent as you were upon what happens to Colosse because your soul is bigger than Colosse. A city can be destroyed, but your soul cannot.

Then, having got you to think about the soul, the gospel puts before you a very clear picture of life in this world, this realistic picture which we have just been considering. Our Lord never promised anybody an easy time here. Thank God for that. Here is the only teaching that I know of that prepares me for the worst. Our Lord tells us quite plainly that in the world we are going to have a hard time. He says:

If the world hate you, ye know that it hated me before it hated you. If ye were of the world, the world would love his own: but because ye are not of the world, but I have chosen you out of the world, therefore the world hateth you. Remember the word that I said unto you, The servant is not greater than his lord. If they have persecuted me, they will also persecute you; if they have kept my saying, they will keep yours also. But all these things will they do unto you for my name's sake, because they know not him that sent me (Jn 15:18–21).

That is the sort of world you are in, our Lord says. He prepares us for it all. Then, further on, he says this:

Behold, the hour cometh, yea, is now come, that ye shall be scattered, every man to his own, and shall leave me alone: and yet I am not alone, because the Father is with me. These things I have spoken unto you, that in me ye might have peace. In the world ye shall have tribulation, but be of good cheer; I have overcome the world (Jn 16:32–33).

So, then, our Lord has told us that and he is the only one who does so. This, he tells us, is an evil world and he tells us why: it is because of its sin; because it has rebelled against God; because it is under his wrath. He says God will not bless a world like this. It is doomed and God will punish it and is punishing it. So he prepares us for the very worst that can come to meet us. Thank God for that. I like to be told the truth and here I am told it.

But, then, Christ does not stop at that. He tells me that in spite of all this being true of the world, he is going to put it right. Oh, he will not do that by changing it superficially; he will put it right by coming back into it again. He will not put it right by working in politicians or statesmen or pseudo-politicians, but by coming again, riding the clouds of heaven surrounded by his holy angels. He will come to judgment; he will come to end the world, to end history, to end the universe. It will be the end of time and he will come and judge the whole world in righteousness. He will destroy all his enemies and all who belong to them and will set up his glorious and eternal kingdom – the kingdom of righteousness and peace. 'Peace ... as a river and, ... righteousness as the waves of the sea' (Is 48:18). That is what he tells me.

So he tells me: Think about your soul; think about your final destiny; do not expect anything from this world, expect what you get. While men and women are still sinful and selfish, there shall be wars and rumours of wars, in spite of what these people have said and are still saying. What right has this world to think that anybody will put an end to war when men covet their neighbours' wives and while they still go on cheating and robbing and giving rein to passions and lusts? A nation is nothing but a man writ large and while individuals are like that, the nations will be like that. They always have been, and always will be until Christ comes back to this final judgment. But when he has come, there shall be no more war and then, and only then, there will be the glory everlasting in his wonderful kingdom.

And that is how he helps me; that is how he enables me to go through this world triumphantly and rejoicing. And, indeed, as John says, 'This is the victory that overcometh the world, even our faith' (1 Jn 5:4). It wins the victory by making me see through the world and all its glittering prizes and glamour! I see it for what it is – the tawdriness and the vanity. I see through it, yes, but I am also enabled to see beyond it.

How does this come about? Well, where is he – he who came into this world and who lived in it and endured the contradiction of sinners against himself, who was condemned and crucified on a cross and who died and was buried? And the answer is that he rose again and ascended into heaven. He has conquered the world and the devil and all his forces; he has conquered the flesh; he has conquered death and the grave; he has conquered everything and is seated on the right hand of God in the glory.

Yes, but did you know that if you are in Christ, as Paul says every Christian is, this is what is true of you? 'But God, who is rich in mercy, for his great love wherewith he loved us, even when we were dead in sins, hath quickened us together with Christ, (by grace ye are saved;) and hath raised us up together, and made us sit together in heavenly places in Christ Jesus' (Eph 2:4–6). If I am in Christ I am already seated in the heavenly places in Christ Jesus.

While I know I am still here in London, I am no longer of London. But, you know, there is a sense in which I am not even in London: in spirit I am in Christ. I am in heaven. So if you write to me, write to me like this: at Westminster, London. Temporary address: Westminster; permanent address: heaven in Christ. I am but a stranger here, heaven is my home. 'Our conversation [citizenship] is in heaven,' says Paul to the Philippians, 'from whence also we look for the Saviour' (Phil 3:20). We have already passed through death unto life in spirit; nothing can keep us from him, nothing can separate us.

Now that is how you conquer life in this world. You now see that because you are in Christ nothing in this world can harm you – nothing. Of course, the world can damage your body, it can rob you, and even kill you, but it cannot touch your soul. That is the glory of it. All the bombs in the world can be set off together and it will not make the slightest difference to my soul, because my soul is in Christ and in his keeping and he is in heaven above it all. Even when the end of the world comes it is not the end for me because I know my soul is in him – I belong to him – that is what is eternal.

But, thank God, the gospel goes even further. Did you notice Paul's prayer? 'Grace be unto you, and peace, from God our Father and the Lord Jesus Christ.' Look at it like this: the gospel gives me a right view of Colosse. It takes me out of Colosse and puts me into Christ. It gives me his view and then it enables me to go through the remainder of my time in this present evil world. How? By *grace* – 'grace from God'. That means God's favour; God's blessing; it means that I am assured of his forgiveness; it means that I know that the almighty and eternal God is interested in me personally and that he has a great and a wonderful purpose for me.

Why have I ever become a Christian at all? It is nothing to do with me; it is not because I was born better than anybody else. I was most certainly not. Is it because I have more ability? No. 'By the grace of God I am what I am' (1 Cor 15:10). It is he who has opened my eyes to Colosse and it is he who has detached me from it.

The grace of God! Is there anything comparable to this, anything as comforting in this present evil world, as the fact that the almighty and eternal God who made everything out of nothing is interested in you personally? Listen to his Son telling you that 'the very hairs of your head are all numbered' (Mt 10:30). My Father, he says, knows about you and all that you want. He knows before you ask him in your prayers. 'The grace of God', this undeserved favour of God, is his assurance of forgiveness and pardon, of his interest. He knows our every need and he will give us every needed grace.

The author of the epistle to the Hebrews puts it like this: 'Let us therefore come boldly unto the throne of grace, that we may obtain mercy, and find grace to help *in time of need*' (Heb 4:16). When the foundations are shaking, when we do not know where we are nor what to do, and we feel so weak and frail, then we have 'grace to help in time of need'. We feel the everlasting arms grasping us, taking hold of us and holding us and saying, 'Nothing shall harm you.'

So it is not surprising that the Apostle prayed that these people might 'know the grace of God'. In another letter he tells us about himself, about when he had a 'thorn in the flesh', that illness of his. He felt it was hindering his work, so he prayed to God three times that it might be taken from him, but it was not. The answer he got was this: 'My grace is sufficient for thee' (2 Cor 12:9): I am not going to heal you but I am going to enable you to carry on. I am not suddenly going to give you a dramatic miraculous healing, but I am going to give you sufficient grace to enable you to do everything I ask you to do.

And so Paul says: It is right, his grace is sufficient. 'Most gladly therefore will I rather glory in my infirmities that the power of Christ may rest upon me . . . for when I am weak, then am I strong' (2 Cor 12:9–10). When I am really weak I begin to appreciate his strength. It comes into me and overwhelms me and puts me on my feet, making me more than conqueror. 'Grace be unto you' – all the reserves of the endless, illimitable treasury of God are at our disposal if we are in Christ.

Peace likewise – 'Grace be unto you, *and peace,* from God our Father and the Lord Jesus Christ.' What does Paul mean by this peace? He means peace with God – I do not stay with that, we have already dealt with it. He means also the peace *of* God. Oh, this is a marvellous thing:

Peace, perfect peace in this dark world of sin?

Certainly

The Blood of Jesus whispers peace within.

E. H. Bickersteth

'Be careful for nothing' (Phil 4:6) says Paul, meaning, 'In nothing be anxious' – and 'nothing' means 'nothing'! Have you got that? 'But in everything', again an all-inclusive phrase – 'in everything by prayer and supplication with thanksgiving let your requests be made known unto God.' What will happen? Oh, this is what will happen: 'And the peace of God, which passeth all understanding, shall keep your hearts and minds through Christ Jesus' (Phil 4:7).

You will not understand it all but you will know that though hell is raging round and about you, that though everything has gone wrong and it is sufficient to drive you to despair, you will have a wonderful peace within. You will not know how it has come there but you will begin to realize that it is 'the peace of God, which passeth all understanding'. Paul says: I am praying that you may know this peace. And further on in that passage in Philippians, he goes on to thank these people who had sent him a present, 'I rejoiced in the Lord greatly,' he says, 'that now at the last your care of me hath flourished again; wherein ye were also careful, but ye lacked opportunity. Not that I speak in respect of want: for I have learned, in whatsoever state I am, therewith to be content' (Phil 4:10–11).

Now, can you say that? What if your bank balance were reduced to nothing tomorrow morning? What if you found yourself in prison? What about it? Here is a man who can say: 'I have learned in whatsoever state I am. . . .' and he had been through a great deal. He tells you all about it if you read 2 Corinthians 10 and 11 – imprisonment, shipwrecks, beatings, all sorts of things. 'But,' he says, 'I know both how to be abased, and I know how to abound: every where and in all things I am instructed both to be full and to be hungry, both to abound and to suffer need. I can do all things through Christ which strengtheneth me' (Phil 4:10–13).

'The peace of God.' Listen to our Lord saying it. What a wonderful promise he gave his disciples just at the end of his life – 'Peace I leave with you, my peace I give unto you: not as the world giveth, give I unto you. Let not your heart be troubled, neither let it be afraid' (Jn 14:27). His peace is not like the world's peace. That comes and goes; it can be broken at any moment. But this is a lasting, an everlasting peace. And it will be with you whatever is happening: in life, in death, in illness, sickness, bereavement, sorrow, war, peace – it does not matter. 'My peace I leave with you, my peace I give unto you.'

You have grace from God. You have 'the peace of God which passeth all understanding' and, on top of it all, you will be filled with a might and strength and power that you will never understand but which you will begin to experience. Listen to Paul's words: 'Strengthened with all might, according to his glorious power' (Col 1:11) – the power of his glory. This, remember, is the power that looked at the original chaos and said, 'Let there be light: and there was light;' the power that brings things into being out of nothing.

So, then, 'If God be for us, who can be against us?' (Rom 8:31). If the grace and the peace and the power of God are on my side – and they are if I am a Christian, if I am in Christ at Colosse – then the grace and the peace and the power of God are operating for me and for my soul and its eternal well-being. 'For I am persuaded,' says Paul, 'that neither death, nor life, nor angels, nor principalities, nor powers, nor things present, nor things to come, nor height, nor depth, nor any other creature, shall be able to separate us from the love of God, which is in Christ Jesus our Lord' (Rom 8:38–39).

That is the way the Christian does it: he believes in Christ, so he is in Christ and he knows that nothing can separate him from this life in Christ. Why? Because Christ has already conquered all these things. He has conquered life; he has conquered death; he has conquered the devil; he has conquered hell, the grave, everything! He has triumphed over all. He is risen and I am in him and I shall rise and inherit that glorious mansion in the sky. I shall be in the New Jerusalem that comes down from heaven to earth, in the glory everlasting.

So how am I to address you? I want to send you a message, I want to write you a letter, how do I do it? What do I put on the envelope? Where are you? What is your permanent address? Is it just Colosse, and no more? God forbid that it should be, because all this is going to end. God grant that now you have heard the word of the true gospel, I may with confidence address my message to you thus: 'To So-and-So in Christ at Colosse.'

Chapter 8

What God Has Done

Giving thanks unto the Father, which hath made us meet [fit] to be partakers of the inheritance of the saints in light' (Col 1:12).

We have been considering the first eleven verses of this first chapter of Paul's letter to the Colossians and now we are going on to consider the twelfth verse. But before we come to deal with its message, we must look at its position in the chapter.

In its context verse 12 is a very important verse because here the Apostle moves from one statement to another. In the first verses, Paul has been giving a very general description of the character, nature and content of the Christian gospel. In this verse, which is a kind of connecting link, he goes on to a further statement concerning the gospel but this time in much greater detail.

That is a method Paul often adopted and it is a very good way of teaching. You first of all give an introduction, a very general outline of your theme. Those who are familiar with music and the analysis of a musical composition will know that the great composers often do that in a symphony. There is a general introduction and in that they will give you some hint of their various themes. Then they proceed to take up these themes one by one and work them out, and, at the end, they sum them all up again in a grand climax.

Now that is a very good way of conveying truth, whether it be direct truth, like this, or truth communicated

145

through music or anything else, and that is precisely what the great Apostle is doing here. He has given us a general description of the gospel but that is not enough. He feels he has also got to deal with it in detail. So here, in verse 12, he is beginning to do that, giving us once again a kind of summary of the whole gospel before going on to divide it up into its component parts.

Now my reason for calling your attention to this is precisely the reason which animated the great Apostle himself. I have reminded you how he himself had never actually preached at Colosse – the members of the church there had come into the Christian life through Epaphras who had been sent there, perhaps by the Apostle, in order to do the preaching. And as Paul reminds us, and as we have seen, they had believed the gospel; it had not just been an idle word, but had done something. 'It has brought forth fruit,' Paul says, 'among you, even as it has every where.' And we have seen something of what that fruit is. But now the Apostle feels he must write to them, because, as we have seen, certain false teachers had arisen who were preaching 'another gospel'.

Paul's object is to show his readers the true gospel over against that false message. He is anxious to show the fullness of this gospel, its completeness – to make the Christians at Colosse see that it does not need any addition. He is also anxious to show them the glory of this gospel, and, above everything else, to show them what he calls in verse 18 'the pre-eminence' of the Lord Jesus Christ, for the main trouble with this false teaching was that in various ways it was detracting from Christ's person and from his work. The false teachers made him just one of a series of intermediaries between God and men. They granted that he was the greatest, but, nevertheless, he was only some form of angel, one of the intermediaries. They reduced him from what he really was. And then they reduced his work in the same way. They said that simple belief in Christ was not enough for salvation but that you had to do various things yourself in order to ensure your place in heaven. You had to be circumcised, they said, and also abstain from eating certain meats and follow rigorous ascetic practices. As with so many modern cults, faith alone was not enough.

The Apostle, then, writes in order to counteract all that, to show its falsity, and, above all, to display in all his wonder and glory the Lord Jesus Christ and his perfect, finished, complete salvation. And, in my own feeble way, I am trying to do the same thing, because there is no other gospel but this. This is the only hope for a world in despair, which is coming to the end of all its theories and philosophies. Only this can deliver us and give us comfort and a good hope. Nothing else can meet every eventuality – war, death, anything you like. Nothing else can prepare us for the various things that come to us in the vicissitudes of life. That is why the most important question for us all is this: Do we know what the gospel is? Do we know what the gospel of Jesus Christ really says? People think they know what Christianity is but their whole conception of it bears no relation to what I find in the New Testament. So it is the business of a preacher to tell men and women exactly what it is and that is why we are looking at this verse.

It is our business to see that you understand what it is; that you know the meaning of the facts you believe. It is not some odd feeling; it is not something magical! No, a Christian knows what he believes and can give an account of it.

Furthermore, we must make certain that we are relying upon it. A head knowledge is not enough. We are living in a world of disasters, in a world where death is very near. We cannot afford to take risks. We must know exactly

where we are and what we are trusting to. What if the end
should suddenly come? Are we ready for it? That is the question. So it is vital that we should consider further what the
Apostle has to tell us about this great and glorious gospel.

Here, then, Paul is moving from general introduction to
particular exposition and he starts by putting it all in one
great statement – 'Giving thanks unto the Father, which
hath made us meet to be partakers of the inheritance of the
saints in light.' That is a perfect summary of what Christianity is; but, of course, it at once becomes a test to us, does
it not? Every statement, every definition, of the gospel is of
necessity testing us. We already saw that when we looked
at Paul's great phrase, 'bringeth forth fruit, as it doth also
in you'. We considered the fruit and we asked ourselves,
'Have I borne that fruit?' And now, again, we have the
same sort of test.

Paul's first proposition is that the first great characteristic of the true Christian is always *a sense of thankfulness
and of gratitude* to God. You cannot be a Christian at all
unless you have this, as I can easily prove. Go back to the
gospels, read the accounts of how the gospel came, and
what you will find in every single instance is that it always
had the effect of leading to praise, gratitude and thanksgiving.

Take, for example, the time when the archangel
announced to Mary about the birth of the Son. She went to
visit Elizabeth, the mother of John the Baptist, who greeted
her with the words: 'Blessed art thou among women, and
blessed is the fruit of thy womb.' And Mary's response was
this: 'My soul doth magnify the Lord, and my spirit hath
rejoiced in God my Saviour' (Lk 1:42, 46). Praise and
thanksgiving unto God!

You find the same thing, of course, in the case of
Zacharias, John the Baptist's father. He was made dumb

for a number of months because of his unbelief, but at last
his tongue was loosened again and he was able to speak and
this is how he burst forth: 'Blessed be the Lord God of
Israel; for he hath visited and redeemed his people' (Lk
1:68). He was full of praise and thanksgiving to God.
And, of course, everyone remembers the song of the
heavenly angels when they visited the shepherds who were
watching their flock by night. What did they sing? 'Glory
to God in the highest, and on earth peace, good will toward
men' (Lk 2:14). They started by praising God, by glorifying him.

That is how the gospel is introduced; whatever else
Christianity may or may not be, it is something that inevitably leads to thankfulness to God. It is its great characteristic, and you find it everywhere – 'Thanks be unto God,'
says the apostle Paul, 'for his unspeakable gift' (2 Cor
9:15).

Peter's epistle is no less filled with praise and thanksgiving – 'Blessed,' he says, 'be the God and Father of our Lord
Jesus Christ, which according to his abundant mercy hath
begotten us again unto a lively hope by the resurrection of
Jesus Christ from the dead' (1 Pet 1:3). And when we turn
to the book of Revelation, we find that praise is the occupation of heaven. There they are rejoicing in this great salvation and this is how they put it: 'Blessing, and honour,
and glory, and power, be unto him that sitteth upon the
throne, and unto the Lamb for ever and ever. And the four
beasts said, Amen. And the four and twenty elders fell
down and worshipped him that liveth for ever and ever'
(Rev 5:13–14). Why? Because of what he has done. It is
because of this that they are offering up their praise and
their thanksgiving, their worship and their adoration. Or
take another mighty, glorious passage, again from that
same book:

After this I beheld, and, lo, a great multitude, which no man
could number, of all nations, and kindreds, and people, and
tongues, stood before the throne, and before the Lamb,
clothed with white robes, and palms in their hands; and cried
with a loud voice, saying, Salvation to our God which sitteth
upon the throne, and unto the Lamb. And all the angels stood
round about the throne, and about the elders and the four
beasts, and fell before the throne on their faces, and worshipped God, saying, Amen: Blessing, and glory, and wisdom,
and thanksgiving, and honour, and power, and might, be unto
our God for ever and ever. Amen (Rev 7:9–12).

It is always the same, you see: thanksgiving to God for
what he has done. Every single doxology in the Bible, in
the Old Testament and the New, expresses the same thing.
People think the Bible is a narrow, cramped, miserable
book. But this is a book that is crammed with praise! 'O
magnify the Lord with me, and let us exalt his name
together,' says the psalmist (Ps 34:3). 'Praise ye the Lord';
that is the characteristic note.

And, of course, it is not only the great note of the Bible,
but of the church in every period of revival and reawaken-
ing. At other times the church is preaching ethics and morality and good behaviour; nobody praises! Nobody is
expected to praise and if somebody did praise in certain
places it would be a great shock!

No, religion is respectable: men and women leading
upright lives, the good people who go to church, not like
these other people out on the street! Yet there is no praise
among these good church-goers! Why? They have no salvation; they are not thankful to God. They are like the
Pharisees, thanking God, not for anything that he has
done, but because they are not like other men, because they
are so wonderful. That is something entirely different.

But when the church is in the midst of revival, when it is

really functioning as it should and preaching the gospel and men and women are being converted and built up in the faith, oh, then the church bursts forth into hymns of praise and thanksgiving. You had it in the eighteenth century. Look at those hymns of Charles Wesley, John Newton, Philip Doddridge, and the rest of them – all these men, what are they saying? Well, in a sense they are all saying,

> Praise, my soul, the King of heaven,
> To His feet thy tribute bring;

Why?

> Ransomed, healed, restored, forgiven,
> Who like thee His praise should sing?
> Praise Him, praise Him,
> Praise the everlasting King!
> *H. F. Lyte*

That is the note; it runs right through the hymnbook. All the greatest and the most glorious hymns are full of praise and thanksgiving.

Now, then, this becomes a test of us, does it not? Do we really feel like praising God? Do we enjoy doing so? Is there praise and thankfulness in our hearts to him? Paul says to these Colossians: That is your characteristic note. I have never met you, you have never seen my face, but I know that because you are Christians, and because of what has happened to you, this is a part of the fruit that you have borne as the result of hearing this gospel preached by my friend Epaphras. 'Giving thanks unto the Father.'

This is what tests whether we are Christians or not. Religion does not do that; Christianity alone does it. Religion is hard and cold, there is never this welling up of praise and thanksgiving! That, then, is the first note.

But here is the first question: Why does it do that? Why should we give thanks unto the Father? Why is the New Testament full of this? Why did the angels sing: 'Glory to God in the highest'? Why are they in heaven falling down before him and praising him and vying with one another in ascribing to him all praise and might and majesty and dominion and glory? Why will that be the occupation of the saints through the countless ages of eternity?

Well, it is summarized in this one verse. We should give thanks unto the Father first of all because our salvation is entirely produced and given to us by God. 'Giving thanks unto the Father, *which hath made us meet* to be partakers of the inheritance of the saints in light.' It is he who has done it.

Now here is something, of course, which is primary; here is the first principle about which we must be clear. The gospel of our Lord and Saviour Jesus Christ, in the first instance, does not ask us to do anything, it is primarily an announcement of what God has done for us. I almost apologize for repeating this, but while men and women still think they know what the gospel is and deny that at the very outset, I shall continue to emphasize it. The work of the devil is to twist it, to pervert it, to put blinkers on us, and to prevent our seeing it. The idea is as current today as it has ever been that the message of Christianity is a call to us to do something to put ourselves right, to put the world right, to stop this, to stop that!

But the very first principle of Christianity denies that completely; it is the exact opposite. Christianity is an announcement and a proclamation of what God has done; that is what the angels sang about. They were not calling upon mankind to rise up and do something; they were singing and praising because they knew what God had done – 'Unto you is born this day in the city of David a

Saviour, which is Christ the Lord' (Lk 2:11)! Yet people still persist in thinking that Christianity is a call to them to do something. That is why they do not sing and praise God; that is why their hearts are not on fire and full of rejoicing. It is because they think Christianity is a code of ethics, a way of life and of living. No, says Paul, 'Giving thanks unto the Father, which' – he – 'hath made us meet . . .'; he has done it all.

In other words, we are to give thanks unto the Father because our salvation is altogether of his grace. It is his free gift. So if you think you can pay anything for it, you have not got it. Even the prophet saw that; he said, 'Ho, every one that thirsteth, come ye to the waters, and he that hath no money: come ye, buy . . . without money and without price' (Is 55:1). That is a prophecy concerning the coming of the gospel of the grace of God in our Lord and Saviour Jesus Christ – 'By grace are ye saved through faith; and that not of yourselves: it is the gift of God: not of works, lest any man should boast' (Eph 2:8–9).

Oh, what a tragedy it is that men and women should go wrong thus at the very beginning of the gospel and fail to realize this. How can we be so blind? The Bible is full of this and we would see it at once if we only paid any attention to it and read it as we ought.

> For when we were yet without strength, in due time Christ died for the ungodly. For scarcely for a righteous man will one die: yet peradventure for a good man some would even dare to die. But God commendeth his love toward us, in that, while we were yet sinners, Christ died for us. Much more then, being now justified by his blood, we shall be saved from wrath through him. For if, when we were enemies, we were reconciled to God by the death of his Son, much more, being reconciled, we shall be saved by his life (Rom 5:6–10).

And there are many other passages like that.

But what I am concerned about is this great principle. What is your feeling and understanding about this gospel? What if somebody came to you and said, 'What is the message of this Christianity that they are talking about?' What would you reply? Well, the correct reply is that it is a proclamation to us of what God has made possible for us; a salvation which he has prepared for us and which he gives us as a free gift. It is altogether from him.

This is the message of the Old Testament as well as the New. That is why we still have the Old Testament and that is why it is so important to us. The same God is acting in both the Old and the New. He is preparing in the Old for the New; it is a continuous account and it is God acting from beginning to end. You start with the great act of creation – 'In the beginning God created the heaven and the earth' (Gen 1:1). He made a perfect world and put man and woman into it. Then came the fall, the rebellion. Adam and Eve sinned against God; they thought they could get on without him; they wanted to do what they liked, not what God had told them. And so they found themselves in trouble and in shame. There were the man and the woman in the cool of the evening in the Garden, and when they heard the voice of God they ran and hid themselves behind a tree. They knew they were in the wrong; they knew they had been fools. They knew they had fallen, that they had lost something.

Now that was the beginning of man's dis-ease; there was the beginning of the unhappiness, because not only did Adam and Eve fall, they dragged the world down with them; everything is down and has been down ever since. It has been a place of muddle and shame, of sin, sorrow and war, from that moment. Every one of us knows the sense of guilt, the sense that we have let ourselves down and let

God down. There it all began; we have had it ever since. And there they were, the man and the woman; they did not know what to do, so they ran away and hid; they knew they deserved punishment, but they did not want to be punished, so they tried to escape but they could not. God knows everything. He came to where they were and he called them out.

So the Christian salvation is all there in the very beginning, in the third chapter of the book of Genesis. God came down and spoke to the man and woman in this fallen condition and what did he say? Did he say: Pull yourselves together now. You made a mistake but come on and I will give you another chance to put yourselves right?

He said nothing of the sort! What God said was this: You have dragged yourselves and the world down and you can never put yourselves or the world right; but I am going to put both you and your world right. There will be warfare between the seed of the woman and the seed of the serpent but the seed of the woman shall bruise the serpent's head (see Gen 3:15). That is a prophecy of the coming of the Lord Jesus Christ and it is God who said it; it is God who indicated that he was going to do it. And the whole of the story of the Old Testament is just the story of God preparing for the coming of his Son.

Look, too, at what he did at the time of the flood: he destroyed the whole world apart from eight people – Noah and his family! Why did he keep them? It was to preserve the line of the seed of the woman, the seed of Eve. Then, you remember, he divided up the family of Noah who had three sons – Shem, Ham, and Japheth – and he singled Shem out particularly. Why? Because it was from the line of Shem that this ultimate Deliverer was going to come.

Then follow on the story. With the world in the state it is, I do commend that you read your Bible. Do not get lost in the details. Keep your eye on this big thing that God was doing, this thread that ran right through – follow it on. Come on to Abraham. Here was a man living in paganism in Ur of the Chaldees. Then God called him out. What for? Well, he was a part of this line of Shem. And God said: I want you because I am going to turn you into a nation and I will do that because it is ultimately out of this nation, descended from you, that the Deliverer will come. And in him shall all the nations be blessed.

And so the promise went from Abraham to Isaac and from Isaac to Jacob. Jacob had twelve sons but Judah was singled out in particular; it was from Judah that the 'Shiloh' will come (Gen 49:10). Who is he? He is the great Deliverer promised away back in Eden. And on and on it goes; you can trace the promised line right through the books of the Old Testament until you come to David. He belonged to the tribe of Judah and it was out of him in particular that the Deliverer would come. And so as you go through the Old Testament you read the promises and the prophecies. You hear of prophets saying, 'Comfort ye, comfort ye my people, saith your God' (Is 40:1). Why? Oh, a great deliverer was coming – 'every eye shall see him' (Rev 1:7) – the salvation of God.

But what I am trying to show you is that it was God who was acting from beginning to end. All these men I have mentioned were sinful men and they all failed. If they had had their own way the scheme would have come to nothing. It was not the children of Israel who made a way of salvation; it was not the Jews who produced the Messiah. It was God who produced them, and the Messiah out of them and through them and in spite of them. Look at the sorry figure they cut; look at their recalcitrance, their disobedience, their utter folly. Why were they always running away from God? If it were not for the fact that God had a plan and brought it to fruition, the whole thing would have collapsed.

And then we come to the tremendous statement: 'When the fulness of the time was come, God sent forth his Son, made of a woman, made under the law, to redeem them that were under the law' (Gal 4:4–5). The 'fulness of the times' – whose time? God's time! He had planned it away back before the foundation of the earth; he knew all that was going to happen. He allowed the centuries to pass so that men and women might see that they cannot save themselves; that all their civilization and philosophies come to nothing, so that they might know themselves to be absolutely finished and bankrupt. And when all is done,

> O loving wisdom of our God!
> When all was sin and shame,
> A second Adam to the fight
> And to the rescue came.
> *J. H. Newman*

The human race did not produce the second Adam. God sent him. He made the first Adam; he sent the second Adam. It is always the action and the activity of God.

John 3:16 says, 'God so loved the world, that he gave his only begotten Son, that whosoever believeth in him should not perish, but have everlasting life.' There are people who say that they believe that. Those who think they know what Christianity is say, 'John 3:16 is my gospel,' and yet they do not see it. They do not see that it is the action of God. They still think that our business is to try to imitate Christ and to follow him and to put his teaching into practice. They say that we are going to save ourselves by following him; whereas what we are told is that *God gave* and God gave his only begotten Son.

So the first reason for giving thanks unto the Father is

that he has done everything; salvation is altogether and entirely of him.

Secondly, we give thanks unto the Father because of what he has done to enable us to enjoy this great salvation. We are now coming to the details, which we shall go on to unfold, but first, here is a summary of what the Apostle is telling us.

'Giving thanks unto the Father, which hath made us meet [fit] to be partakers of the inheritance of the saints in light.' First, consider what he has done in his own Son. The next verse describes him – 'Who hath delivered us from the power of darkness, and hath translated us into the kingdom of his dear Son,' says the Authorized Version translation. A better rendering is this: 'And hath translated us into the kingdom of the Son of his love.'

'The Son of his love.' Who is he? He is 'the image of the invisible God, the firstborn of every creature: for by him were all things created, that are in heaven, and that are in earth, visible and invisible, whether they be thrones, or dominions, or principalities, or powers: all things were created by him, and for him: and he is before all things, and by him all things consist' (Col 1:15–17). He is God's eternal Son, God's dear Son, the Son of God's love.

But what do I read about him? Well, what I read here is this: '*In the body of his flesh*' (Col 1:22). And this is the whole story of Christianity: in the incarnation, the Word was made flesh and dwelt among us. How?

> I love to hear the story
> Which angels' voices tell;
> How once the King of glory
> Came down on earth to dwell.
> *Emily Miller*

That is it! 'In the body of his flesh.' He who is, as we are

told here, 'the image of the invisible God' (v. 15); God, the
eternal Son in the bosom of the Father, was sent by God
into this world. He came and was born in a body of flesh;
he was made 'in the likeness of sinful flesh' (Rom 8:3);
born in a stable at Bethlehem and put into the manger.
There he was. God had sent him, and that is why the Father
is to be praised.

But then you notice 'in the body of his flesh *through
death*'. And, too, Paul talks here about 'blood' – 'In whom
we have redemption through his blood, even the forgiveness of sins . . . having made peace through the blood of his
cross' (vv. 14, 20). Oh, it moves my heart, it fills me with
indignation, that men and women should think that
Christianity is something which tells me what I have got to
do: that I make myself a Christian and save myself by
doing this or that. And while they are talking about that
they never say a word about the blood of his cross. They
never tell us that this person came from the brightness of
the glory and though he was God's image, not only was he
born as a babe in Bethlehem but he was nailed to a tree, he
died in helplessness upon a cross, and his body was taken
down and buried in a grave.

That is Christianity. It is the Father who sent him: 'He
that spared not his own Son, but delivered him up for us
all, how shall he not with him also freely give us all things?'
(Rom 8:32). And in the name of Christianity these foolish
people are talking about what we need to do, with not a
word of what God has done, especially there on that cross,
with his body broken and his blood shed to make it possible for us to become partakers of the inheritance of the
saints in light. And then he raised him again to the glory
everlasting and crowned him with glory and honour. Now
there he is, seated at the right hand of God, and he will
come again, sent by God, to wind up the whole universe

and establish his glorious reign. That is something of what God has done in order that you and I might escape hell and might go to the glory; that is why you and I are to thank God. Have you realized that? If you have, you are bound to thank him.

Yes, but there is a second part to this. First there is this great salvation purchased by the Son of God, this great inheritance, this kingdom of God. Yes, but here is the question: How can you and I ever get into it? Have you ever thought of that? Well may we ask the question and it is as you listen to Paul giving the answer to it that you see why salvation must of necessity be entirely of God. Why do we give thanks to the Father? Because it is 'the Father, which hath made us meet [fit for, qualified] to be partakers of the inheritance of the saints in light'.

Now if God had not made me fit, I would never be fit. Not one of us has any hope whatsoever of being partakers of this salvation unless God does it for us. It is the inheritance, remember, of 'the saints in light'. Yes, and what is true of us? We are under the power of darkness – 'who hath delivered us from the power of darkness' (v. 13). That is where we all are by nature; we are in that power. How can we get out of it and become the inheritors in light? Not only that, but we are under the wrath of God. We need to be reconciled to him, to be redeemed. We need to be forgiven – 'In whom we have redemption through his blood, even the forgiveness of sins' (Col 1:14). We are enemies of God. And not only that, but our whole nature and outlook and mind is utterly evil: 'You, that were sometimes [once upon a time] alienated and enemies in your mind by wicked works, yet now hath he reconciled' (Col 1:21). You see, before we can enter into that kingdom we need a new mind.

If you and I went in our old natures into salvation, it

would be hell to us. Do you know what they do in heaven? They spend their time singing hymns of praise and thanksgiving unto God. I venture to suggest to you that by nature that would be the height of boredom, it would be hell! You do not have drinks and jazz and gambling and television in heaven, you know! They spend their time there worshipping God and praising him and falling before him. We need to be fit and meet before we can be inheritors with the saints in light. And, of course, the moment we see what we are and what the inheritance is, we see the utter impossibility of it.

All right, says Paul, that is what God has done for us – he has made us 'meet'. Before we can dwell in that burning light we have got to be absolutely perfect; and we cannot do it. God has got to do it and God has done it; that is why we must thank him.

It is not surprising that the apostle Paul should put it like this, is it? Here he is writing as a great apostle; he is now one of the partakers of the inheritance and he, as it were, says to himself: How did I ever get into this, because look at what I was?

There he was, a proud, self-righteous Pharisee, a blasphemer, a persecutor, and a hater of Christ, doing his best to exterminate the Christian church. How did he ever get in? There is only one answer. It was nothing that he did. He was doing everything he could against Christ and against God. He was going down from Jerusalem to Damascus 'breathing out threatenings and slaughter' (Acts 9:1), trying to ruin Christianity. He was against it with the whole intensity of his great nature and he literally had to be knocked on his back on to the ground! It was entirely the action of God: the Lord Jesus Christ appeared to him. That is how he was made fit and meet to be a partaker of the inheritance of the saints in light.

We are told about Lydia, too, the first convert in Europe, you remember, 'whose heart the Lord opened, that she attended unto the things which were spoken of Paul' (Acts 16:14). And if the Lord had not opened her heart she would never have attended at all. 'The natural man receiveth not the things of the Spirit of God: for they are foolishness unto him: neither can he know them because they are spiritually discerned' (1 Cor 2:14).

How does anyone become a Christian? 'God hath revealed them unto us by his Spirit: for the Spirit searcheth all things, yea, the deep things of God' (1 Cor 2:10). God does it by opening our hearts; by convicting us of sin; by casting us down; by justifying us while we are still ungodly; by giving us a new birth; by sanctifying us and ultimately by glorifying us. It is his work from the very beginning to the very end and therefore we give thanks unto the Father.

Are you thanking him for that reason? Are you thanking him because you know of the work he has done in you? 'Being confident of this very thing,' says Paul to the Philippians, 'that he which hath begun a good work in you will perform it until the day of Jesus Christ' (Phil 1:6). Can you honestly say, 'By the grace of God I am what I am' (1 Cor 15:10)? In all humility and to the praise of God, I say that that is the only reason why I, of all men, am a preacher of the gospel. If I had had my way I would not be doing this.

> I fled him, down the nights and down the days.
> *Francis Thompson*

But he, 'The Hound of Heaven', came after me.

And, lastly, we give thanks unto the Father because of the glorious character of the salvation. It is all of God. We have seen what he does in order to give it to us, but what is it? Here it is: *'the inheritance of the saints in light'*. This is salvation; this is Christianity. It is what we inherit; it is what God gives us; it is what we participate in with all the saints. And notice what he says about it – 'in light'.

Being a Christian is not to have a nice comfortable feeling inside you but to enter into the kingdom of God, the kingdom of Christ. It starts in this world: by believing in Christ you enter into his kingdom – 'Enter ye in,' he says, 'at the strait gate . . . because strait is the gate, and narrow is the way, which leadeth unto life' (Mt 7:13–14). The moment you have passed through that strait gate you have entered into a part of your inheritance. It is the kingdom of God; it is the kingdom of his Son. It means the rule of God; it means to be in his realm and to be blessed of him.

To be a Christian means to be taken out of that horrible darkness, out of a life of sin and shame and evil, to begin to live a new life, to have a new start. It means we now belong to him who says, 'I am the light of the world: he that followeth me shall not walk in darkness, but shall have the light of life' (Jn 8:12). We belong to the one who looks at us and says, 'Ye are the light of the world' (Mt 5:14) – that is what he makes us. He is the light of the world and when we belong to him we in turn become the light of the world. That is Christianity, not just getting this particular blessing and that, which we may think we need! No, it is to belong to God who 'is light, and in him is no darkness at all' (1 Jn 1:5). It is the realm of light and of glory, of holiness and purity and peace everlasting – 'the inheritance of the saints in light'.

Read again some of those wonderful passages in Revelation which show us what it will be like in the final glory.

I heard a great voice out of heaven saying, Behold, the tabernacle of God is with men, and he will dwell with them, and they shall be his people, and God himself shall be with them, and be their God. And God shall wipe away all tears from their eyes; and there shall be no more death, neither sorrow, nor crying, neither shall there be any more pain: for the former things are passed away (Rev 21:3–4).

Then this is an account of the heavenly city:

And I saw no temple therein: for the Lord God Almighty and the Lamb are the temple of it. And the city had no need of the sun, neither of the moon, to shine in it; for the glory of God did lighten it, and the Lamb is the light thereof. And the nations of them which are saved shall walk in the light of it: and the kings of the earth do bring their glory and honour into it. And the gates of it shall not be shut at all by day: for there shall be no night there. And they shall bring the glory and honour of the nations into it (Rev 21:22–26).

This is something of this glory that God is preparing for his people, this is 'the inheritance of the saints in light' – 'And there shall be no night there; and they need no candle, neither light of the sun; for the Lord God giveth them light: and they shall reign for ever and ever' (Rev 22:5).

This is Christianity, this is salvation. And it is possible for you and for me to go to that realm, to that glory everlasting and to spend our eternity there.

So are you giving thanks unto the Father for these reasons? If you are thanking him, you are a Christian. If not, well hurry to him, confess it to him, ask him to have mercy upon you. Say to him, 'Make me fit, I am not. I am unworthy. I see I do not know this. I am not thanking you. Oh, God, make me fit, make me meet, because I want to be a partaker.' Say that to him and you will soon be giving all the thanks and the praise and the glory unto him who has done it all for you.

Chapter 9

Free from the Power of Darkness

Giving thanks unto the Father, which hath made us meet [fit] to be partakers of the inheritance of the saints in light: who hath delivered us from the power of darkness, and hath translated us into the kingdom of his dear Son (Col 1:12–13).

At this point in our consideration of this great chapter, let me start by asking some questions. Why is it that people do not thank God, or why is it that they do not see what God has done in and through his dear Son? Why is it that the whole world is not living in this realm of light and righteousness and truth? Why is the world troubled and confused, doing hidden and dark things, resorting to subterfuges? Why is everything not open and plain and in the light of God? These are the questions that inevitably arise and there is only one answer to them.

Men and women are not thanking God for his great salvation which we have considered in verse 12 because, obviously, they do not realize what he has done, what he has made possible, and why he had to do it. So the whole trouble is due to their ignorance of the real truth about themselves.

Now this is one of the most important things we can grasp. It not only accounts for the failure to understand the gospel and its character, but it accounts for the whole state of this world. The main trouble with men and women, in all their cleverness, is that they are not clear about their own condition and there is no hope for them until they see that.

This is what is put before us so clearly in the Bible and in particular in this verse we are examining now – 'Who hath delivered us from,' or out of, 'the power of darkness, and hath translated us into the kingdom of his dear Son.' That is what happens to a Christian. Let us examine this. Our verse tells us what is wrong with men and women as they are by nature and it tells us what is necessary before they can be put right. And how urgently this message is needed.

What is wrong with the world? Surely that is the first question we should all be asking as we see the world in its trouble, its confusion, and all its terrible possibilities. And the first question, surely, is not a political question – we must go deeper than that. It is not a social, nor a military question. The question we all should be asking is this: What is it that is wrong with men and women that makes them do such folly? What is the matter with them?

Many answers are being given to this. There are some people who still answer the question by saying, 'There is nothing wrong with us. It is just a matter of bad luck; it is just an odd phase through which we are passing!' Or some say our troubles are due to a malign fate, that it is all in our stars, that the elements, as it were, are against us! 'People are essentially good,' they say, 'more sinned against than sinning.' And that is their only way of explaining it, but we shall see how inadequate that is.

Another very popular explanation is the so-called 'evolutionary view'. According to this, what is happening at the present time is just a sort of time-lag in the process of human development. 'We advance,' they say, 'but we have not arrived. Do not be impatient. We have not arrived at perfection yet! We are making tremendous strides,' they maintain, 'history proves that. Look back at primitive man. Look at him living in his caves and scribbling on the walls! Look at how he has developed and look at modern man!'

That is the argument, you see, that the human race is advancing. Of course, it is rather inconvenient for that argument that at the present time the world is in such a terrible mess and seems to be in worse trouble than in the nineteenth century; we are still scribbling on the walls and doing things which are even more ridiculous! But there it is: a time-lag in the evolutionary process.

Then another theory, and this again is quite a common one, is that all the trouble in the world is due to just a handful of bad people; that the world is all right, that men and women are all right and that everything was going well until these people began to arise – Mussolini, Hitler, and so on! Just a handful of evil men were spoiling the whole world! We are all right, there is nothing wrong with us! The ordinary man is a decent, good fellow; it is just these monsters who cause all our troubles.

But let us look at that view a little, because it is so fallacious. Strangely enough, while preparing this very message, I came across a most interesting review of a book that has been written on Goering, one of the Nazi leaders, and one of these evil men to whom everything is being attributed. The authors, Manvell and Fraenkel, have tried to analyze this man and they think that at last they have found the explanation for his behaviour. They could not understand him but then they discovered that he was a morphine addict and that seems to them to be a satisfactory explanation. But not to the reviewer! 'Surely that is wrong,' he says. 'It isn't puzzling at all as to why this man was the monster that he was, unless one seeks refuge in the idea that only monsters are capable of monstrous behaviour! The truth we are reluctant to face is that there is no depravity and no cruelty that is beyond the ingenuity of quite ordinary people who are otherwise amiable and even conventional!'

And how right and how true he is. These men are not monsters. We are all capable of that. You cannot explain the world in terms of the behaviour of a few evil men. The astounding thing, says this reviewer, is that these men, in a sense, were ordinary and, when we are honest and admit it, we find that all of us have got it in us to be what these men actually were!

Strangely enough, another book has been published at the same time giving a pictorial review and history of the Nazi régime in Germany, and the reviewer makes the same comment. A whole series of pictures of different men are given there and he says, 'The amazing thing, as you look at this gallery of pictures, is that you are really looking at quite ordinary people!' In the book there is a photograph of Hitler as a baby. Who would have ever prophesied he would have become the man that he became? He looks like any other baby. And so with all the rest of them.

You cannot explain the state of the world in terms of a few monsters. No; these men happened to have the power and they exercised it. There are other men who are not given such power but who, as far as they have any, are exercising evil power in their families, in their homes, in their trade unions, in their political parties and in the circles in which they turn. Undoubtedly the reviewer is right. That is not the explanation.

But then, let me mention just one other suggestion. This is the view of the psychologists, who are supposed to understand and explain everything – Freud, Jung, and so on. Well, let me say this for them. They, at any rate, have realized that there is a problem. They have done very good work along that line and have shattered the foolish optimism of the late Victorians and the Edwardians. This is how Jung puts it: 'We need more understanding of human nature because the only real danger that exists is man himself. He is the great danger and we are pitifully unaware of it; we know nothing of man, far too little! His psyche should be studied because we are the origin of all coming evil!' Now here is a man who does not believe in God – one of the leaders of this atheistical movement that would explain everything in terms of the psyche, the working of man's own soul, as it were. But there Jung admits it – 'We know nothing of man, far too little!' And yet, he says, we must know more because man is such a terrible danger.

And I want to put one further bit of evidence before you. I apologize, in a way, for doing this, but there are men and women, you see, who say that there is nothing in Christianity; that it has nothing to give. But I am trying to show you that it is the only thing that has something to give and that all these other theories that have caused men and women to turn away from God and from Christ are absolutely bankrupt. There is Jung admitting it.

But also there is a review in the current number of the *British Medical Journal.* The late Dr Charles Berg has written a book and do you know what title he put to it? *Madkind* – not 'Mankind' but *Madkind.* He has coined a new word. *Madkind – The Origin and Development of the Mind* is the title and here is part of the review:

As to the title, the neologism 'Madkind' expresses the notion that we, that is mankind, are all a little mad, victims of a protracted and still uncured psychosis. It cannot be otherwise as superstitious taboo colours our social life and personal conduct to such a degree that human thought is founded upon delusions.

Here is a serious writer. What about the cure? What are we going to do about it? Well, he says:

Practical treatment to alleviate the deplorable human lot

should be commenced in babyhood and continued throughout childhood, yet psychoanalysis of infants and children is
not advised.

So what does he advise? Here it is:

> Those responsible for the very young should have
> psychoanalytical treatment; without it they will assuredly
> contaminate the growing mind with their own disease.

Need I say any more?

There is mankind without Christ and without the gospel.
Here are able, educated men, who say that their great
brains prohibit their believing in God and in Christ and in
the Christian salvation. They understand the problem and
there is their answer – 'Madkind'! And the only hope is
that all parents should begin on their psychoanalytical
treatment as soon as they can before they corrupt their
children any further! And it is a hopeless business, obviously! Indeed, all these men are in despair. At long last they
are having to admit that they do not know the nature of
man. Of course they do not! That is their whole trouble;
that is the trouble with the world and it leaves us with
nothing but despair.

So, then, the only true view of men and women and their
world is that which is found here in this thirteenth verse.
What is it?

The first proposition is that by nature people are in the
grip of the power of darkness – 'hath delivered us from the
power of darkness', which means that we need to be delivered. Christians are men and women who have been delivered, but those who ar not Christians have not. Now
this is not something in the psyche; this is not fate nor anything that can be explained along those lines. Men and
women are not free, and the world is as it is, because it is

under the power of darkness. Or, if you prefer, it is under the power of the devil, the power of the god of this world, of 'the prince of the power of the air, the spirit that now worketh in the children of disobedience' (Eph 2:2). It is in the grip of 'the rulers of the darkness of this world . . . spiritual wickedness in high [heavenly] places' (Eph 6:12). Those are all scriptural quotations saying what is put in our text in a different way. So if the whole world is under the dominion of this power of darkness, how did it ever get there? What does it mean?

Now the whole explanation, as we have seen, is to be found in Genesis 3, and it is the only adequate explanation. The blame does not merely lie in the Hitlers or Goerings, but in every one of us. It is not something that can be psychoanalyzed out of us; it is too deep. And it is not merely us, it is this power that dominates us and governs and controls us. What is it? Well, there is the explanation as far as we are given it by the Bible itself. God made his perfect creation; he created man and put him in it and made a helpmeet for him – the woman. And there they were in Paradise, living a perfect life of communion with God.

Then the devil came in, who is more subtle than anybody else, and he raised this doubt. He said: Has God said? Are you fool enough to listen to God? God knows perfectly well that the moment you eat that particular fruit you will become as gods, you will be enlightened, you will understand as much as he does, so he is keeping you down.

So the devil tempted Adam and Eve and they listened to him and fell and, of course, the result was they put themselves under his power.

'But who is this devil?' you ask.

The Bible's answer is that he is a fallen angel. God created the angels before he created the world and human beings. Angels are spiritual beings whom God made and, again, made perfect. But we are told that one of them raised himself up in rebellion against God. Jealous of God, not content with being blessed by God and serving him, he wanted to be a god. He was the first rebel. He lifted himself against God and thereby fell and was punished and cast down, accompanied by all who followed him.

So he has hated God ever since; he is God's great antagonist. The devil hates God with all the intensity of his nature so that when God created the world, and created Adam and Eve, the devil immediately said: Here is my opportunity. I am going to smash up and ruin his creation.

What better way was there, as it were, of dragging God down than to ruin his handiwork? So Satan entered into the Paradise of God and persuaded Adam and Eve to listen. And it has gone on ever since; ever since that moment, the story of mankind has been trouble and confusion, pain and darkness and war. That is our radical explanation – the power of darkness.

Now I want you to see that this is something that is not only told in the Old Testament book of Genesis, but is revealed everywhere. The Lord Jesus Christ himself taught this as we have seen when he spoke about 'the strong man armed' (Lk 11:21). That is the position, he said. People are like the creatures of a great chieftain, a powerful king, who has a great palace with walls around it and there he keeps his citizens within. It is the same thing – the power of darkness.

The apostle Paul, in answer to the question as to why people do not believe the gospel, says, 'You hath he quickened, who were dead in trespasses and sins; wherein in time past ye walked according to the course of this world, according to the prince of the power of the air, the spirit that now worketh in the children of disobedience' (Eph 2:1–2). And the apostle John has exactly the same teaching when he says, 'Ye are of God, little children, and have overcome them' – the antichrists that are fighting against them. Why? – 'because greater is he that is in you, than he that is in the world' (1 Jn 4:4). There he is, in the world and dominating its life. And John puts it still more plainly in the next chapter. 'We know that we are of God, and the whole world lieth in wickedness,' or 'in the wicked one' (1 Jn 5:19). In other words, he says that the whole world is in the embrace of the devil, lying in the bosom of this wicked, evil one – the whole world!

Now this is a very serious matter. This is why the world is as it is. Notice we are told that we need to be delivered from the power of darkness; it is a *power*. It is very interesting to notice the difference here. Paul says, 'Who hath delivered us from the power of darkness, and hath translated us into the kingdom of his dear Son.' He does not say that there is a kingdom of darkness, it is 'the power of darkness'. The devil is a usurper; he has no right at all; he is a rebel. He is one who has taken authority unto himself. He was never given it; he was never meant to rule over human beings and tyrannize them. We were meant to be governed by God, but the devil has taken it upon himself. He does not have a kingdom; he is a power – only a stolen power!

What else? I am simply expounding all that is contained in this word 'power'. Not only is it not a kingdom, it is not orderly either. It is unruly; it is a confused and troubled power. That is what makes Isaiah say that 'the wicked are like the troubled sea, when it cannot rest, whose waters cast up mire and dirt' (Is 57:20). That is a perfect picture of the power of darkness, the power of the devil. It is like the sea in constant movement. It is a disorderly kingdom.

How unlike God's kingdom! God, we are told, is not the author of confusion but of peace. This is how we read about the creation of the world in Genesis 1: the Spirit brooded over the abyss, over the confusion, over the chaos. 'And God said, Let there be light: and there was light' (Gen 1:3). And then God began to produce order; he began to create: first day, second day, third day, and so on, and he brought order, Paradise, perfection. He looked at it all and saw that it was good. Out of the chaos he had brought order and perfection; but that is not so with the power of darkness, which brings disorder and confusion.

Not only that; it is a capricious, contradictory power. (I am still simply drawing out the meaning of the word 'power'. You can check me: read Bishop Lightfoot, he will tell you all this!) That is always a characteristic, is it not, of somebody who is a usurper? You see, he has no law, no system; all he is interested in is the exercise of power, and all tyrants are capricious. You never know what they will think or do next! They are constantly changing; they have no rule, no understanding, no light; they have no system! All they are interested in is their whim, their desire. They will be this one day, that the next. This is so typical of the power of darkness.

The apostle Paul tells the Corinthians that sometimes the devil turns himself 'into an angel of light' (2 Cor 11:14). He will turn himself into anything to get his own way. The devil can quote Scripture or misquote it. He can interpret Scripture or misinterpret it. He comes as a would-be friend, then the next moment he hits you. Is that not the treatment that sin gives you? It seems so wonderful when it first comes and entices you, then the next moment you are weeping and breaking your heart, in pain and sorrow. It is the same one who does it all. Oh, the capriciousness, the contradictoriness of this usurped power, the tyranny of the devil!

That is the next thing – the tyranny and the slavery. That

is why the Bible so often compares the slavery of the children of Israel in the captivity of Egypt to sin and to what sin does to us. It is such a perfect illustration. There were those children of Israel making bricks; then the tyrant said, 'Give them less straw and make them produce more bricks.' That is it – slash them if they do not and keep them there! A tyranny and a slavery! This is all true of sin, of the power of darkness. How powerful it is!

Our Lord Jesus Christ very deliberately used that image of the strong man armed. He wanted to bring out the impression of force and of power. It is such a terrible power that everyone who has ever lived is as putty in his hands. We are all weak and helpless. The fact of the matter is that we, all of us by nature, are nothing but slaves of this power of darkness. 'God be thanked,' says Paul to the Romans, 'that you who were the slaves of sin but . . .' and are we not all the slaves of sin? Is not the world being governed and ruled in every respect, as Paul tells the Ephesians, by the course of this world, by the thing to do, by what everybody is doing, by what we read in the newspapers and see on the television and hear on the radio? Everybody is – 'the course of this world'.

The world is in unutterable slavery. Oh, the power of this darkness! Why do we keep on doing things that we know are wrong? Why do we do things that we know hurt us? Why do we do these things though we know something of their consequences? Why do we do them? What is it? 'For the good that I would I do not: but the evil which I would not, that I do' (Rom 7:19). Why? It is this power that is gripping us, holding us and manipulating us. It is a terrible power.

Yes, but notice also, it is 'the power of *darkness*'. And that is how the Bible always describes this element, this evil. It always refers to it as 'darkness' because it is the opposite of God. God said, 'Let there be light'; the devil says: Let me bring darkness into this kingdom of light. God says: Order; the devil says: I will bring in confusion. This power of darkness is a dark power. It darkens the mind; in other words, it keeps us in the dark. It creates mists; it creates confusion; it creates muddle; it produces fogs – intellectual and other fogs. I have already given you some examples of them.

But, more seriously, the world is as it is because it is ignorant of God. It is in the dark about God. And it is like that because the devil keeps it there. He comes and says: Do you still believe in God? That is what he said to Eve at the beginning. He said: Do not be such fools; do not listen. God is keeping you down. Religion is against you. Make yourselves free; assert yourselves.

On the other hand, though it wants to be free, the world has to admit that people are monsters and are their own greatest danger. The world cannot understand them. So, you see, it is a mass and jumble of contradictions. It says that men and women are perfect at one moment and do not need God, then the next moment? Well, who knows what they are? And you have these terrible descriptions: they are psychotic; they are ill; they are diseased; they cannot think; their minds are twisted and perverted. It is utter confusion.

Yes, but the real confusion is the ignorance with regard to God. It is because it does not know and recognize God, that the world is as it is; and it is because men and women do not know God that they do not know themselves. They think they are wonderful and find that they are fools. They do not know the truth about themselves; Jung has admitted it.

But still more important, they are ignorant that they are just pilgrims and strangers here. They are ignorant about death and are dabbling with spiritism and the occult, and all these extrasensory phenomena! You see, they know within themselves that there is something else and they are trying to find out something about it but they do not know. What they do not know is that 'it is appointed unto men once to die, but after this the judgment' (Heb 9:27).

We are very interested in death but we rarely speak about judgment. There is a great deal about death in the newspapers, and these authorities, these philosophers and psychologists are doing their best to tell us about it. All right, but why do they not tell us something about the judgment? Have you ever heard of one of them writing a letter about judgment? Of course not! They are ignorant; they are in the dark about it. They are under the power of darkness and blinded. They do not know that when they and every one of us dies, we stand before the almighty God in the judgment.

Likewise, they do not know that our eternal destiny is determined by what we do in this life. They do not know that all who have lived a godless, selfish, foolish life, will go to everlasting misery and perdition. They do not know that, for if they did they would begin to pay attention. But the devil keeps them in the dark. He says: Fancy believing that! Do you believe that? You can't be such a fool!

It is the very thing he said to Eve. He is still saying it and men and women are still listening.

He keeps us in the dark about the real truth concerning God. He says: You will never be turned out of this garden; do not believe that; it is not true.

But out they went and they cannot go back – the flaming sword and the cherubim are there prohibiting a return. And mankind still does not know that and thinks that by civilization or psychoanalysis it can cure itself. Oh the monstrous darkness of it all!

And finally, the devil keeps people ignorant of the gospel. Though God's Son has come into this world to save us and set us free, the devil keeps us in the dark: 'If our gospel be hid, it is hid to them that are lost; in whom the god of this world hath blinded the minds of them which believe not, lest the light of the glorious gospel of Christ, who is the image of God, should shine unto them' (2 Cor 4:3–4).

Had you realized all this? If you are not a Christian there is only one reason for it: the devil will not let you believe. He is blinding you, confusing you with this supposed cleverness, which, the moment you really analyze it is, as I have shown you, nothing but hollowness. That is why people are not Christians – not because they have great minds, but because 'the god of this world hath blinded the minds of them that believe not'.

And then, of course, the devil acts not only on the mind, but on the affections also. What do we like? Lusts, passions, desires, evil things that we should not have; the illicit, the prohibited. These are the things we like and we go after them – that is the darkness.

Where does it lead us? Well, we all know the answer: to disorder, confusion, immorality in politics, in everything! Greed and desire, ambition and envy are in control, resulting in unhappiness, fear, distrust, suffering – innocent suffering. Human nature is never satisfied, it is always looking for something it never finds. And it is full of fear: fear of death, fear of the future, fear of anything. There never has been a generation that is so fearful, living on its tranquillizers and its drugs and its soporifics! Why? Oh, it is the fear resulting from the confusion in the dark. We are in the dark and groping, wondering what is happening. Where are we? We do not know. This is the power of darkness and it is dark in every respect – dark in the mind, dark in the heart, dark in the will, dark in its consequences – and the world is miserable and desperate and does not know what to do nor where to turn. That is the explanation for the state of the world.

Having asked the question: What is wrong with the world?, and having looked at the answer given in verse 13, my second proposition is that God in Christ alone can deliver us from such a position and he does deliver all who believe. There is our condition, every one of us, nobody can deny it. How can we believe? There is only one way and it is the way that is indicated here in verse 13. Nobody else can do anything. The patriarchs could not; Abraham could not; Noah could not; none of them could. The best kings that ever were given to Israel could not deliver us; neither could the prophets or the psalmists; all of them tried and all of them failed. Why? Because the devil was too powerful, the power of darkness was too great. 'There is none righteous, no, not one' (Rom 3:10); not a single one has ever succeeded in conquering the devil; he beats all.

Is there no hope? There is. It is the Lord Jesus Christ – a second Adam, another man. The first man fell and all his progeny has fallen ever since. We need another man, but another man is not enough, because since the devil conquered the first perfect men he will conquer any other man, so God sent his own Son – God/Man, man linked to the Godhead. The Lord Jesus Christ, the Son of God, came into this world. What for? Listen to John: 'He that committeth sin is of the devil; for the devil sinneth from the beginning. For this purpose the Son of God was manifested, that he might destroy' – undo – 'the works of the devil' (1 Jn 3:8). In other words, he came that he might conquer the devil.

And that is why, as you read in the Gospels about the birth of our Lord Jesus Christ, you find that the devil tried to kill him at the very beginning when he was but a baby. The devil put it into the heart of that cruel king Herod to get rid of him. This was because the devil knew that his conqueror had arrived.

Then the devil roused the antagonism of the Pharisees and scribes and doctors of the law. Why? Ah, he recognized that this was one who came as the Son of God. But, you see, he, this second Adam, conquered the devil. Here is the only one who can conquer the power of darkness. He conquered him in his own life – for forty days and forty nights in the wilderness he was tempted of the devil, but he routed him, defeated him by quoting Scripture, and the devil had to leave him alone. He came back, but he conquered him again.

Not only that, look at the record of his casting out devils. They brought to him poor people possessed with the devil – dumb, blind or something else – and in a moment he set them free. Think of the boy at the foot of the Mount of Transfiguration – nobody else could help him (Mk 9:14–29). Look at the man of Gadara. They had done everything; they bound him with fetters and chains and still he was no better. He was violent, desperate. In a moment Christ healed him (Mk 5:1–19)! He could cast out devils; he is the master of devils.

People said:

> He casteth out devils through Beelzebub, the chief of the devils. . . . But he, knowing their thoughts, said unto them, Every kingdom divided against itself is brought to desolation; and a house divided against a house falleth. If Satan also be divided against himself, how shall his kingdom stand? because ye say that I cast out devils through Beelzebub. And if I by Beelzebub cast out devils, by whom do your sons cast them out? therefore they shall be your judges. But if I with the finger of God cast out devils, no doubt the kingdom of God is come upon you. (Lk 11:15, 17–20)

Then he spoke of the strong man armed keeping his goods at peace and finished, 'But when a stronger than he shall come upon him, and overcome him, he taketh from him all his armour wherein he trusted, and divideth his spoils' (Lk 11:22). That is how he put it, that is exactly what he did. Therefore he was able to say at the end of his life, 'The prince of this world cometh, and hath nothing in me' (Jn 14:30).

'But wait a moment,' says somebody. 'Did he not die in weakness upon a cross? Did the devil not get him after all? Did the devil not succeed in his machinations and in his working among the Pharisees and Scribes and Sadducees and doctors of the law? Did he not encompass his death? What is the use of talking about healing the sick and the lame and the blind and the deaf, and even raising the dead, when he cannot save his own life?'

That is what the people said at the foot of the cross: 'Ah,' they said, 'save thyself, and come down from the cross. . . . He saved others; himself he cannot save' (Mk 15:30–31). They said: You are being defeated by the enemy, by your foe.

But wait a minute, my friend! Just before his death our Lord said, 'Now is the judgment of this world: now shall the prince of this world be cast out. And I, if I be lifted up from the earth, will draw all men unto me' (Jn 12:31–32). That was his view of his death.

It is all right, he said. It looks as if my life is being taken from me, but do not misunderstand it; that isn't the explanation – 'Now is the judgment of this world' (Jn 12:31). It is not my judgment; it is the world that is being judged and the prince of this world is about to be cast out.

So the apostle Paul, looking back upon the cross, puts it like this: 'Blotting out the handwriting of ordinances that was against us, which was contrary to us, and took it out of

the way, nailing it to his cross; and having spoiled principalities and powers, he made an open shew of them
openly, triumphing over them in it' (Col 2:14–15). He has
defeated them; he has robbed them of their armour. The
strong man armed is being defeated by the cross and by his
death.

Can I prove it? I can. The resurrection! It is the devil that
has the control of the power of death, says the second
chapter of the epistle to the Hebrews (Heb 2:14), and our
Lord has risen from the dead – he has conquered death and
the grave. He has conquered the devil, therefore, who had
this power. So in the light of the resurrection the Christian
can turn with Paul and say, 'O death, where is thy sting? O
grave, where is thy victory?' (1 Cor 15:55). They are
defeated – 'Thanks be to God, which giveth us the victory
through our Lord Jesus Christ' (1 Cor 15:57).

The devil is already a defeated foe. The Son of God has
defeated him in every respect – personally and generally, in
all his manifestations and power. And more, not only is he
defeated and enchained, but a day is coming when he will
be finally destroyed: 'And the devil that deceived them [the
saints] was cast into the lake of fire and brimstone, where
the beast and the false prophets are, and shall be tormented
day and night for ever and ever' (Rev 20:10). Final destruction!

So here is the one, and the only one, who has ever been
able to conquer the power of darkness and its very prince
– and he has done it. Therefore, here is my message to you:
Believe in him! What will happen to you? You will be
delivered from the power of darkness. He sets us free; he
has conquered the one who has held us in captivity. He is
the Deliverer, and he delivers us with a strong arm, as a
mighty conqueror. It is like Israel being brought out of
Egypt. Though Pharaoh was strong, with his hosts and his

chariots and his army, and the children of Israel had nothing, they were taken out with a strong arm, and Pharaoh and his hosts were destroyed in the Red Sea! That is what happens in Christ.

We are taken 'out of Egypt', yes, but, thank God, we are not left in a wilderness – 'and hath translated us into the kingdom of his dear Son'. We read of these foreign powers, these tyrants, taking whole nations and moving them to another land; taking them out of their homeland and putting them into another. That is the sort of thing we are reading about here in verse 13. We are taken out of the tyranny, the territory, of the devil and are translated, put again, into a new kingdom, into the kingdom of 'his dear Son'. That is the way we are given liberty from the power of darkness. It means we are given light; we are given knowledge; we are given the whole armour of God. We are given order; we are given law; we are given truth; we are given righteousness. We are given understanding about ourselves, about God, about time, death, eternity. All is here before us.

But that is not all – we are given something infinitely bigger! We are joined to the Son of God; we are put in Christ; we are the body, he is the head. We belong to him and all his strength and power becomes ours. 'Of his fulness have all we received,' says John, 'and grace for grace' (Jn 1:16). 'Be strong in the Lord,' says Paul to the Ephesians, 'and in the power of his might' (Eph 6:10).

Not only that, we have his sympathy, his help: 'We have not an high priest which cannot be touched with the feeling of our infirmities, but was in all points tempted like as we are, yet without sin' (Heb 4:15). He knows all about us. Your deliverer and mine has been in this world and met it all at its worst, at its vilest, at its most hellish; but he has triumphed and he is with us. We are in him and he is in us, and his strength, his power, and his understanding are available to us.

What is the result of this? Oh, this is a most glorious thing that John says in his first epistle: 'We know that whosoever is born of God sinneth not' – does not go on sinning – 'but he that is begotten of God keepeth himself, and that wicked one toucheth him not' (1 Jn 5:18). He cannot touch him. When you are translated out of the power of darkness into the kingdom of God's dear Son, you are put into a realm where the devil can never get you back under his power again. You may be fool enough and mad enough to listen to him occasionally, but you will never be back in his power. You are in the power of Christ; you are his slave; you are in his kingdom; and the evil one cannot touch you. You may fall but you will never remain down; you will be raised by Christ and your backsliding will be healed. You are in the power of the Son of God and he will never let you go.

So we can say with the great apostle Paul that 'neither death, nor life, nor angels, nor principalities, nor powers, nor things present, nor things to come, nor height, nor depth, nor any other creature, shall be able to separate us from the love of God, which is in Christ Jesus our Lord' (Rom 8:38–39). And the result of all this is that when the devil comes and tries to get you down, as he tempted the Lord himself in the wilderness, this is what you can say: 'Resist the devil, and he will flee from you' (Jas 4:7). From you! He got everybody down – Abraham, the patriarchs, prophets and kings, but if you are in Christ you can resist him and he will flee from you.

Peter says the same thing: 'Be sober, be vigilant; because your adversary the devil, as a roaring lion, walketh about seeking whom he may devour: whom resist stedfast in the faith, knowing that the same afflictions are accomplished in your brethren that are in the world' (1 Pet 5:8–9). Because we are in the kingdom of God's dear Son, because the strength of Christ is in us, when the devil comes we can resist him and he will have to leave us as he left the Son of God. It is the only way whereby anybody can ever be delivered from the power of darkness.

And we are not only saved by the power of God, but we are kept by his power until we safely arrive at that inheritance which is 'incorruptible, and undefiled, and that fadeth not away' (1 Pet 1:4). It is reserved and kept by God for his people and his children in the safety of heaven and the everlasting glory.

Are you out of the darkness? Are you in the light? If you are still in the dark offer this one prayer – this simple prayer – and you need no other. Ask him to enlighten your darkness and wake your spirit. Ask him for the enlightenment that he alone can give and you will find it in the face of Jesus Christ. Blessed be the name of God!

Chapter 10

A New Nature

And you, that were sometime alienated and enemies in your mind by wicked works, yet now hath he reconciled in the body of his flesh through death, to present you holy and unblameable and unreproveable in his sight (Col 1:21–22).

Slaves of the darkness, slaves of the devil: that is what we were, but we have seen that Christ has delivered us out of that and put us into his new kingdom of light, righteousness and glory. And the moment we believe that, we thank God because God alone could deliver us. That is one reason why we thank him. But it does not stop at that and we must go on now to consider a second reason.

You notice that I am varying the order in which the great Apostle puts these points. I am doing that because I am told that people find it difficult today to understand the Scriptures! So I am trying to help by putting all the verses which deal with the human condition into one group before I bring in the gospel. So I jump from verse 13 to verses 21 and 22.

Now you remember that in dealing with verse 13 we saw that we can only understand human nature and the tragic condition of the world today by looking back to the fall – man and woman listening to the suggestions of the devil and thereby becoming slaves of the devil. But, and this is the point which I now want to emphasize, that is not the only thing that happened. A great change took place in human nature and character and this is the terrible thing to which the Apostle calls our attention in these verses.

189

Look here, says Paul, if you are a real Christian you are thanking God because he has made you fit to be a partaker of the inheritance of the saints in light.

God has delivered you out of the power of darkness, yes, but he has also had to change your nature. And men and women do not thank God, because they do not realize that; they do not realize what their nature is and they do not see the need for changing it.

This, then, is something which is essential to our understanding of Christian doctrine and the way of salvation. Most people who are not saved are in that condition because they have not seen the need. So the business of preaching is to show them that need, but it does not stop at that. This is not only vital to an understanding of God's way of salvation, it is also absolutely essential to our understanding of the world and its condition. Why do people behave as they do? Why is the world in confusion? Why is there so much tragedy, so much bitterness, so much sorrow, so much pain? What is the cause of it all? Here is the answer. We have seen that all the efforts of the philosophers and psychologists to understand this and explain it are ridiculous. Here and here alone is the explanation – we are in the power of the devil.

But, in addition to that, this further thing is true of us and it is very important we should realize it. The position of men and women is not that they are innocent victims who are tyrannized over by the devil, and would really be very good if only the devil gave them a chance! That is not true at all. They are the victims and slaves of the devil but at the same time they themselves have become evil and rotten. So let us get rid of the Peter Pan notion that we are all born innocent and, oh, what wonderful people we would be if only the devil did not hold sway over us! No, even if the devil did nothing, the world would be full of evil because there is evil in us.

So that is the second great consequence of the fall. Human nature changed when Adam and Eve listened to the devil. The Bible says that God made human beings in his own image (Gen 1:26), which means that they were good; they really were innocent – innocent of evil. God made Adam and Eve upright and righteous, and as God made them at the beginning, they delighted in God, their supreme delight was to have communion with him. Adam and Eve lived in the Garden. They enjoyed the fruit of the trees. They were in Paradise and it was a wonderful condition! Yes, but their supreme delight was when God, as it were, came down and talked with them. They lived for God; they enjoyed God and their greatest desire was to please him. That is how they were originally, but from the moment they listened to the suggestion of the devil they not only fell, but a change took place in their nature; a terrible change took place in their character. Before that everything was harmony; everything was happiness and peace. But from that point on it was all different.

Now there is a striking example of that at the very beginning, in the person of a man called Cain. There were two brothers, Cain and Abel, and Cain had murder in his heart towards his brother. He was jealous of Abel. He hated him and determined to get rid of him. So Cain murdered his brother. That is what sin did; that was the consequence of the fall. Man had developed a nature which made him capable of that. It began with selfishness and pride, and ended with murder. Now, you see, this is something in human nature, it is not something that is done by the devil.

And so the Bible goes on describing this. In Genesis 6:5 you find words which speak of the world just before the flood. What do we read? 'God saw that the wickedness of man was great in the earth, and that every imagination of the thoughts of his heart was only evil continually'! Now that would be quite true of our country today, would it not? But it was actually like that before the flood.

The prophet Jeremiah puts it like this: 'The heart is deceitful above all things, and desperately wicked: who can know it?' (Jer 17:9). David in the midst of his sin cried out: 'Create in me a clean heart, O God; and renew a right spirit within me' (Ps 51:10). You see, he was not troubled so much by his actions – though, of course, he was troubled by them – but what really made him feel desperate was the state of his heart. He said: What is this thing in me that makes me capable of doing such a thing? My heart is rotten, my spirit is rotten. It is my centre that is wrong.

That is the teaching that is given to us. It is the same everywhere in the Bible. And it is because the Apostle puts all that particularly plainly here in these two verses that I am calling your attention to them. What is the truth about human nature? Why must God do something to me before I can be fit to be a partaker of the inheritance of the saints in light? What is it that is true about men and women when they are apart from Christ?

Well, the first thing that we are told here is that they are *alienated*, they are estranged from God: 'And you, *that were sometime alienated....*' What a contrast! What a change has taken place! Man and woman who were made in God's image, who were the friends of God, who lived in fellowship with him, have become estranged, alien.

We are constantly reading this word 'estranged' in our newspapers, are we not? An estrangement has taken place between a man and his wife; these two who had become 'one flesh' are estranged. There they were, this couple. They loved each other, they got married, but something came between them, and now – estrangement!

That is the natural condition of men and women in respect to God. There is a barrier between them and God, and, speaking generally, a barrier between the world and God. And, of course, one way in which it shows itself is that in this estrangement, in this alienation, men and women are no longer looking for God, no longer seeking his favour and his presence, no longer yearning for communion with him: a barrier! The wife, who used to look through the window waiting for her husband to come, is no longer doing so; they are estranged!

Am I romancing? Am I just talking theory here? Well, 'Let a man examine himself' (1 Cor 11:28). Are you seeking God? Are you looking for him? Is that your supreme desire? If not, you are estranged. If we only knew who God is and what he is, we would desire him with the whole of our being. But do we? No, we have become alienated. We do not seek God and the result is, of course, that we are no longer experiencing his favour.

That is why the world is as it is: because God is not blessing it. Let nobody think that God is blessing this world in a true and a real sense. He is not! He withholds his blessings because of the alienation of humankind. And we are seeing a world which is resorting to its own devices and ideas! Thank God, he still gives us the seasons and the rain and he fructifies our crops; otherwise the whole thing would collapse. 'For he maketh his sun to rise on the evil and on the good, and sendeth rain on the just and on the unjust' (Mt 5:45). Yes, he does that in a general sense, but the world is not receiving God's favour now as it once was. Of course it is not. He tells us that in his own book! It is because of this alienation and this applies to every individual.

And a further manifestation of this estrangement is that people are living their lives apart from God. They do not stop to think about him; he does not enter into their calculations, and they live as if there were no God. Men and women, because they are alienated from God, are living a kind of independent, autonomous life – at least they think they are! Take the average person, take anybody who is not a Christian – is that not how they live? They do not think about God at all.

They think of other possibilities, of course! The business man says, 'If there is a war, it is going to affect my business.' The farmer complains, 'If there is a terrible storm, it will affect my crops.' They think of all sorts of contingencies that may make a difference to them – 'What if I lose my health?' and so on. But how often do they stop and think about God and their relationship to him? They never do; they have broken the connection and there they are, living this autonomous, self-centred life. They think they are the judge of everything! They do what they want to do, saying with W. Bottomley:

I am the master of my fate
I am the captain of my soul.

They think of nothing outside themselves and people like themselves, and God, as the psalmist says, is not in all their thoughts (Ps 10:4)! Is that not the simple truth?

But let me be personal and ask you: How are you living? Is your life based on God and thoughts of God? What is the basis of your planning? How do you decide what you are going to do and be? Is it all in terms of your relationship to God? If not, it is because you are estranged. You see, you are following the modern philosopher who says, 'I reason it out and what I do not understand, I do not believe; I do not accept!' He is his own god; he believes what he can understand, what he thinks is right! He is his own source of authority; he is his own final sanction and he is everything! Is that you?

And the last manifestation of this estrangement is that in their heart of hearts, of course, people have become afraid of God. That is why they are trying to get rid of the thought of him; that is the real cause of the trouble. It is all described perfectly in that third chapter of Genesis. Here were Adam and Eve – they used to wait for God and look for his coming, and when they heard him, they would rush to meet him. What was more wonderful than to hold converse with the almighty God! But then they listened to the devil and they sinned. Then suddenly they heard the voice of God who was coming to walk in the Garden in the cool of the evening and you remember what happened? They hid behind the trees! They were afraid of God, and they had never been before. Estrangement always leads to that. And so today, men and women are afraid of God. In spite of all their loud protestations they have a feeling that there is a God after all, and that God is all powerful, and so they are afraid of him.

These are the manifestations of the estrangement. That is the first thing, but let us now turn to the second, which is even worse.

'And you, that were sometime alienated and *enemies in your mind.*' That means hostile to God, not merely estranged but actually hostile, hating him, nothing less. Now the Bible is perfectly clear and explicit about this. Let me give you some illustrations to prove what I mean.

'For if,' says the apostle Paul, 'when we were enemies, we were reconciled to God by the death of his Son, much more, being reconciled, we shall be saved by his life' (Rom 5:10). Notice, 'If while *we were enemies . . .*' But listen to him again writing to the Ephesians: 'This I say therefore, and testify in the Lord, that ye henceforth walk not as other Gentiles walk, in the vanity of their mind, having the understanding darkened, being alienated from the life of God through the ignorance that is in them, because of the blindness of their heart' (Eph 4:17–18). There it is and that is but a very brief selection of what I could quote to you in order to establish this point.

So, according to this biblical teaching, every one of us born into this world is by nature an enemy of God, a hater of God.

'But,' says somebody, 'I am not a hater of God. I've always believed in him.'

Wait a minute. Have you? Read what the Bible says about every man or woman who is not a Christian, who does not believe on the Lord Jesus Christ, that is, every 'natural man' with a 'natural mind': 'The carnal [natural] mind is enmity against God: for it is not subject to the law of God, neither indeed can be' (Rom 8:7).

What do I say, therefore, to the man who tells me he has always believed in God though he does not believe in Christ? 'Of course,' he says, 'I worship God. I say my prayers at times! I am not one of your Christians but I have always believed . . . !' But he has not, he cannot have. According to the Bible, he is a hater of God.

So how do we resolve the problem? We do so quite simply, like this: we show that the god such a man believes in is not the God of the Bible; he is not the God of our Lord and Saviour Jesus Christ, but is a god of that man's own creation. That is what is happening today. Instead of taking the authority of the Bible, people say, 'What I think about God is this . . .' and then they make a god for themselves out of their own thoughts. But that is not God! The moment you really meet the God of salvation, the God revealed in the Bible, you will find that he is altogether different and you will find that you hate him. Every natural person hates God and I can prove that to you.

When people truly believe in God they worship him. They bow down before him and humble themselves in his presence. They praise him and magnify him. They seek him. Their chief delight is to know him and to please him in all things. This follows of necessity from knowing who God is and what he is. Really to believe in God means that you absolutely give yourself to him and to his glory. As we have seen, that is what God has asked of us – 'The chief end of man,' says the Shorter Catechism, 'is to glorify God and to enjoy him for ever.' And that is the attitude of men and women who really believe in God. It is their 'chief delight', as Philip Doddridge puts it, 'to hear his dictates and obey'.

But as for those others who say they have always believed in God, the very way in which they say it is almost blasphemy: 'Of course I have always believed in God!' But when you believe in God, you do not speak in that way. Even Job, who had a number of complaints against God, when God revealed himself, Job put his hand upon his mouth and said: I dare not speak. I have said too much. 'I will lay my hand upon my mouth' (Job 40:4–5). And if this was true of a man like Job, how much more of those who have never really known God at all.

The natural person talks about God but does not seek him and does not live for God's glory. I have often been in company with people like this (and God knows there was a time when I was myself). I can remember a group of us young men, all smoking cigarettes or pipes, laughing and joking, being clever and talking about God! If we had known anything about God we would have put our cigarettes out and thrown away our pipes; we would have taken the shoes from off our feet; we would have realized we were on holy ground and we would have got down on our knees. But we were cleverly talking and arguing about

God! We knew nothing about him; had we realized who he is, we would not have dared to speak in the manner that we did – even those of us who were trying to defend the being of God. It was ignorance; we were talking about a god of our own creation.

But that is the position of men and women by nature, is it not? I am proving to you that in their hearts they are haters of God; that the Bible is quite right when it says that the natural mind is enmity against God; that it does not seek him and is always ready to criticize him. Have you not heard people saying this? Perhaps you have said it yourself – when, for example, you are suddenly taken ill and say, 'Why should God treat me like this?' And have you heard people arguing about poor disabled children and others? 'If there is a God why does he allow such things?' they say. All this is hatred of God. They feel that God is against them and they attribute everything evil to him. When anything goes wrong it is God's fault! They have this terrible feeling that God is waiting to crush them.

It has sometimes been my lot to talk to very nice, moral, kind people, who are not Christians, after a sudden death in the family. When I have gone round to see these polite, upright, good-living people, this is what they say to me: 'What have I done to deserve this?' There is bitterness and hatred in their hearts against God; they feel God has been unjust to them. And this means, you see, that they are just doing what Eve did: they are listening to the talk of the devil; they are listening to this suggestion that God is unfair. And they believe it. They believe God is against them. Confront them with God's holy law and they will hate him. They say, 'It is unfair. I believe in living a good life but that is too much and your gospel is too narrow. It is miserable, cramped and confined.' That is hatred towards God.

Furthermore, they not only hate the person of God, they
hate his truth and his teaching. The apostle Paul says, as we
have already seen, that 'the natural man' – that is, mankind
without Christ – 'receiveth not the things of the Spirit of
God: for they are foolishness unto him: neither can he
know them, because they are spiritually discerned' (1 Cor
2:14). In other words, men and women show their innate
hatred of God in their attitude towards the Bible and this
glorious gospel.

Now there is a wonderful proof of all this in the New
Testament, in the Gospels. Has it ever struck you as
extraordinary that when you come to read the four Gospels
– Matthew, Mark, Luke and John – you have to spend so
much time reading about those endless wranglings of the
Pharisees, Scribes, Sadducees and doctors of the law against
our Lord? Have you not felt impatient with them? Why
should we bother about all this? We say we want to hear
his message but he seems to have spent much of his time
arguing with those people! What was the matter with
them?

Let me remind you. These were people who thought
they believed in God; they were the religious teachers. Yet
look at the kind of thing our Lord said to them: 'For the
Father judgeth no man, but hath committed all judgment
unto the Son: that all men should honour the Son, even as
they honour the Father. He that honoureth not the Son
honoureth not the Father which hath sent him' (Jn 5:22–
23).

He brought it right home to them one day when he was
speaking in the Temple. Jesus said:

Ye do the deeds of your father. Then said they to him, We be
not born of fornication; we have one Father, even God.

We have always believed in God and he is our Father. But

> Jesus said unto them, If God were your Father, ye would love
> me: for I proceeded forth and came from God; neither came
> I of myself, but he sent me. Why do ye not understand my
> speech? even because ye cannot hear my word. Ye are of your
> father the devil, and the lusts of your father ye will do. He was
> a murderer from the beginning, and abode not in the truth,
> because there is no truth in him. When he speaketh a lie, he
> speaketh of his own: for he is a liar, and the father of it. And
> because I tell you the truth, ye believe me not (Jn 8:41–45).

What was he saying? What was the matter with those
Pharisees, Scribes and doctors of the law? Here was the
very Son of God standing before them. His Father had sent
him into the world to save the world, that was the only
reason why had come – 'God so loved the world, that he
gave his only begotten Son, that whosoever believeth in
him should not perish, but have everlasting life. For God
sent not his Son into the world to condemn the world; but
that the world through him might be saved' (Jn 3:16–17) –
and yet they took up stones to cast at him! Why did they
argue? Why did they cavil? Why this constant wrangling?
Why did they not believe him? Why did they not accept
him? Why did they not fall at his feet and worship him?

The answer is simple. He brought out the enmity that
was in their hearts against God. He was able to show them
that their belief in God was worthless, a lie. They did not
believe in God at all; they were the children of the devil.
They had a false notion of God; they had twisted God's
holy law. They were listening to the traditions of the
fathers and not to God himself in his Ten Commandments.
They were not really listening to Moses, but were living on
traditions. They were worshipping *their* god not God.
Jesus opened their eyes to this and they hated him for it.

But the terrible thing about their teaching was this. Our Lord said to them once, 'Ye shall know the truth, and the truth shall make you free' (Jn 8:32). And instead of thanking him for that, they were furious. They said, 'We be Abraham's seed, and were never in bondage to any man: how sayest thou, Ye shall be made free?' No thank you! they said. We have never been in need of freedom; we have always been free men! We are quite all right!

And our Lord said: 'Verily, verily, I say unto you, Whosoever committeth sin is the servant of sin' (Jn 8:33–34).

That is what annoyed them. When he said to them: 'The Son of man is come to seek and to save that which was lost' (Lk 19:10), they said: Are you suggesting that *we* are lost? Are you suggesting that God says we need to be saved? Why, we are moral men. We have never done any wrong or harmed anybody. We live to do good and you say that we need to be saved, and to be set free! No, they said, we do not want your freedom!

They hated him for it and they hated God because of it. That is why they did not receive his message. And when our Lord looked at one of them and said, 'Verily, verily, I say unto you, you must be born again' (Jn 3:3), the man replied: What, become a child, start afresh, there is no good in us?

Yes, said our Lord, that is it. You are so rotten that nothing but a new birth will put you right. You cannot be improved, you cannot be trimmed, you cannot be given a new suit. It is your heart that is rotten; you need a new one.

Most of them hated him for that and crucified him. The Saviour of the world was crucified because his preaching condemned them. And hating him, as he showed, they hated his Father.

That is how we prove that Paul is perfectly right when he

says that by nature we are not only alienated, but enemies of God. 'Ah!' says the clever philosopher, the natural man, 'I do not believe in your incarnate God; I do not believe in the blood of Christ.' He laughs at it and pours scorn on it. Why? Because he does not know the truth about himself; he does not know the vileness of his own heart; he has never seen the need of being saved; he does not know God. His enmity against God is the only cause. He believes that his ability to reason can save him and that is why he does not need a Saviour. He does not need the blood of Christ to atone for his sin, he can deal with it himself! He thinks he is self-sufficient and yet he has to admit that he does not understand. Do you ever listen to these people as they display their ignorance, their impotence and their lost estate in their minds as well as in their actions? There you see the bankruptcy of men and women apart from Christ – 'alienated and enemies in your minds'.

And then the third and the last thing Paul mentions is *'wicked works'*. That follows, does it not? – 'As a man thinketh, so he is'; 'Out of the heart proceed evil thoughts, murders, adulteries, fornications', and so on (Mt 5:14). Yes, let me quote it again: 'The natural mind is enmity against God: for it is not subject to the law of God, neither indeed can be.'

Men and women, having rebelled against God and having set themselves up as their own final authority, rebel against the commandments of God, and they constantly let us know that, do they not? They spit upon the Ten Commandments; they advise experimental marriage; they justify unchastity; they contradict the Ten Commandments, every one of them, gloating over their rebellion and thinking it is wonderful. And this is modernity. This is advancement! 'Wicked works.'

It is not surprising that our world is in its present state.

If that is the view of the best minds in our country on morality and decency and the right way of living, then God help us! What right have we to expect moral dealings between nations if we are being encouraged in immoral dealings between individuals! If lust is elevated into chastity, again I say, God help us. If there is no law and no rule, if every man does as he likes, we are back in the jungle. The gratification of lust is called self-expression and the sign of living freely as a human being! That is what we have come to!

'Alienated and enemies in our minds by wicked works:' men and women rebel against God, not only dismissing God's law, but ridiculing it. They have arrived at the position described by our Lord: 'This is the condemnation, that light is come into the world, and men loved darkness rather than light, because their deeds were evil' (Jn 3:19). We have now reached the stage when people love the evil and hate the good. They are trying to prove that evil is the greatest good. 'Evil,' they say, 'be thou my good,' and they glory in it, boast of it and call it enlightenment. Their hearts, in other words, are altogether against God and their works prove it.

So there they are – what can be done for them? How can creatures who are thus described ever hope to be partakers of the inheritance of the saints in light, with God, with holiness, purity, chastity, righteousness and justice? How can they? And the answer is that they can do nothing themselves. 'Can the Ethiopian change his skin, or the leopard his spots?' (Jer 13:23). Of course he cannot! Oh, for a pure heart! Where can I get it? Do what I will, I cannot get it. I cannot obey the law of God. I cannot change my nature.

And this, again, is what God has done for us. God sent his Son into the world in order to do it, because we not only need to be delivered from serfdom and the tyranny of the devil, we need to be changed inside. We need a new heart and a right spirit, and, blessed be the name of God, that is what he gives us. That is the meaning of *regeneration*; that is the meaning of being 'born again'. You start afresh; you are a new creation, a new being. You have a new life. A new principle is put into you – a divine principle – and you become a partaker of the divine nature. Here is hope and it is the only hope.

Then there is the whole process of sanctification. The Holy Spirit is given to you and he works in you 'both to will and to do of his good pleasure' (Phil 2:13). He leads you on by the word and you grow in grace and in the knowledge of the Lord. And what is the result? Here it is: 'You, that were sometime alienated and enemies in your mind by wicked works, yet now hath he reconciled in the body of his flesh through death, to present you holy and unblameable and unreproveable in his sight.' This is the marvel of the gospel! This is what Christ came to do. He came and looked upon people like you and me: enemies, creatures with black hearts, filthy minds and twisted, perverted outlooks. And he took our nature, that he might give us his nature. So he gives us a new beginning, this new birth. He proceeds with the process of sanctification.

And to end, it will be this: he is going to present us *holy*. That means separated to God; free from sin. It means entirely devoted to God. He will bring us to that.

And then, *unblameable*. What does that mean? It means without a single blemish upon us. *Unreproveable*: what is that? It means that we cannot be charged with anything at all. That is what he is going to make of us, and he must. How can I dwell in the presence of a holy God if there are spots on me, if I am unclean? I cannot do it. I would shrivel to nothing. I must be pure. 'Who shall lay anything to the charge of God's elect?' Nobody: 'It is God that justifieth

. . . . It is Christ that died, yea rather, that is risen again, who is even at the right hand of God, who also maketh intercession for us' (Rom 8:33–34). 'Holy, and unblameable and unreproveable in his sight' – God will look at us and will find nothing wrong in us because of the work of his Son in us and upon us. It is indeed his purpose to make us such that we shall not ever have spot or wrinkle or any such thing but shall be holy and without blemish before him.

Do you begin to understand this gospel, my friend? Do you want to spend your eternity in heaven, with God and the angels? Well, do you know the sort of place heaven is? It is holy. God is at the centre, there is no sin, nothing unworthy. You cannot take spots in there; you cannot take evil there; you cannot take lust, you cannot take . . . . Oh, what work needs to be done in us before we shall be fit for that! But that is what he does.

And Christians are men and women who realize that the Son of God left that holiness and that glory and came into this evil world and mixed in its life and endured its contradictions. He even died upon that cross on Calvary's hill, was buried in a grave and there fought the devil and the last powers and rose again and ascended. What for? To make us fit and meet to be able to enjoy God, to enjoy heaven, to enjoy eternity. And the moment they realize that he has done that for them, they begin to thank him.

When this old world has been destroyed and nothing remains of it that is evil, when there is a new heaven and a new earth wherein dwell righteousness, will you be in it? Does it give you a great thrill of joy to think that you will spend your eternity in the presence of God, praising him? No more grumbling, no more immorality, no more vice, no more ambition, no more envy; enjoying God and nothing but God for ever and for ever.

There is only one who can make you fit for that: the one whom God sent into this world, his only begotten Son. He can make you fit if you but believe in him, and once you do, you will spend the rest of your life thanking him and praising the Father who has made you meet to be a partaker of the inheritance of the saints in light.

Chapter 11

By Him

In whom we have redemption through his blood, even the forgiveness of sins. And, having made peace through the blood of his cross, by him to reconcile all things unto himself; by him, I say, whether they be things in earth, or things in heaven (Col 1:14, 20).

I put those two verses together because they both say the same thing. The statement of verse 14 is elaborated and put a little more plainly in verse 20 but they are making precisely the same point. Furthermore, they put before us what is in many ways the most tremendous aspect of the work of the gospel.

So far we have been looking at what needs to be done to us. We are in the grip of the devil; our nature is twisted; we are enemies and aliens; we are God-haters and need a new nature. But all that has been about us; that is what has got to be done to us before we can share this inheritance. But that is as nothing compared to the other aspect of the problem presented to us in these two verses – because there are two sides to it. If we would realize what God has done for us we must look at the problem from God's side as well as from ours.

But this, of course, is what the world forgets. It never thinks of God. Most people think of religion entirely in terms of themselves! God, to most people, is some sort of agency out of which we can get any blessing that we happen to stand in need of! Is that not the common conception of God? Do we not take it for granted that the moment we need anything we just go and apply, and there it is? We may not have thought of God for months or for years, but that does not matter. If we are in trouble, we pray to God and we expect an answer, and we are ready to complain if we do not get it. We are taken ill, so we turn to God and ask him to heal us. Whatever it is, we are always turning to God in our extremity and he becomes just some impersonal agency out of which we can draw blessings as if we were drawing something out of a machine! Is that not the common idea of God? We are all guilty of it because the trouble with all of us is that we do not have an adequate idea of God.

Some years ago I remember reading a book with a most arresting title and the author proved his thesis to the very hilt. The title of the book was *Religion Without God*. And that is true of so much of our religion: it is something nice and comforting. People describe prayer as a sort of spiritual exercise that makes them feel better, or some transference of healing thoughts from themselves to others! That is their view of prayer – God does not come into it at all! We can be busy with religion, active in church work, but again, God does not come into it. We are thinking of ourselves from beginning to end. The whole world is doing this. Indeed, that is why the world is as it is – because it has forgotten God.

Why do the nations and all the rival powers set themselves up? It is because they do not realize that they are as grasshoppers in the sight of God. They think they are great and they boast of their might. Do you know what they are in his sight? Isaiah tells us that they are 'as a drop of a bucket, and are counted as the small dust of the balance' (Is 40:15): your great empires! They forget God. Powerful leaders inflate themselves – leaders like Nebuchadnezzar, Alexander the Great, the mighty Roman emperors, leaders of every other power, our own included! They fail to realize that God is over all and in his presence they are as nothing.

But we assume it is our world and that we are to run it as we think and as we please and that we are ever to enjoy it, going our way. But it cannot be done. Every individual who is in trouble today is ultimately in that position because he or she has forgotten God. We are always forgetting him. How can I get this? How can I improve my lot? How can society be made happier? How can we get world peace? You see, it starts with this life, with this world, and it ends with it. We go on as if the problem is entirely human, and God is never mentioned at all.

And that is the whole trouble, because the truth is that our well-being is entirely dependent upon the blessing of God. The Bible tells us that everything about us ultimately depends upon our relationship to him, so we must start with God. We must consider everything in the light of God.

Now here the Apostle says that Christians are people who give thanks unto God the Father because God has made them meet to be partakers of the inheritance of the saints in light. What is the essence of that inheritance? It is that you are a person who is blessed by God in this life. The blessing, the inheritance, is that you become a companion of God and that he begins to smile upon you and bless you. It begins now, and then, of course, ultimately in eternity and in the glory, you see God and enjoy him for ever.

Isaac Watts put that very well:

> The men of grace have found
> Glory begun below:
> Celestial fruits on earthly ground
> From faith and hope may grow.

Even while we are walking through this world, he says, there are blessings which we can receive and which we can enjoy before 'we reach the heavenly fields or walk the golden streets'. So this inheritance of the saints in light of which Christians become partakers are these blessings of God which we begin to enjoy while we are still in this world and shall enjoy unmixed, and in all their fullness, when we pass through the portals of death and go on into the life and world beyond.

So, then, if we realize that that is the essence of the inheritance, namely, to enjoy God, the question that arises at once is this: How can this come to pass? How can I ever get into that relationship with God in which I enjoy him and enjoy the blessings that he has to give me? Now the Apostle, you see, puts it like this. Here, he says, is a great problem. It is not only that we are, by nature, the slaves of the devil and of the power of darkness. It is not merely that our natures are twisted and perverted and that we are aliens and enemies of God by wicked works. It is that, but it is not only that.

So what else is there? Well, the other aspect of the problem is this: How can I enjoy the blessings of God when God is who he is? Have you ever thought of that? But that is the very question that the Apostle puts before us. So let me summarize what it means.

What God has done for us, and what leads us to thank him, can only really be appreciated – let me emphasize this again – as we look at the whole problem from the standpoint and the aspect of God himself. As we have seen, every one of us depends upon God and his blessing, that is the inheritance. 'So what is the problem?' asks somebody. It is the character of God himself.

Now we are told various things about this in the Scriptures. The first great attribute of God is his *glory*. This is something that cannot be described, it is so great. It is God's essential being, he is a glorious God. Then he is also described as *light*. These are the terms that are used to give us some glimmering understanding of the nature and the being of God.

How often have you considered this when you argue so glibly, 'Why does God allow this?' or 'Why does God not do that?' Do you realize about whom you are speaking? 'God is light and in him is no darkness at all' (1 Jn 1:5); none!

Then God has told us that he is *holy,* and holiness, of course, is the exact opposite of sin. To be holy is to be entirely apart from evil. Holiness is a dazzling whiteness without a speck, without anything wrong. Where holiness is there is nothing unworthy, nothing twisted, nothing unclean. Again, holiness is light, an absolute purity without any suspicion of an admixture of anything else. God is holy; he is eternally removed from sin and evil.

What else? Well, God is a God of *truth*. In other words, in God there is nothing which carries any notion of a lie or anything that is not strictly true. There is no contradiction, there is no modification; there is not even any qualification; he is the everlasting truth.

Then, we are told that God is *just*, that he is *righteous*, that he abominates anything which has a twist in it, anything sham, any pretence or mere appearance or make-believe. God is utterly opposed to that; he is entirely removed from it and everlastingly different from it.

And then another attribute of God that is always emphasized in the Bible is that he is *unchangeable*. It is difficult for us to think of that, is it not? We are so changeable, and everything we know is changeable, but God, we are told, is unchangeable. He is 'the Father of lights, with whom is no variableness, neither shadow of

turning' (Jas 1:17). God is everlastingly the same; he cannot
change because he is absolutely perfect in every respect and
you cannot change that. He always is, so he speaks to the
Jewish nation and says: 'I am that I am' (Ex 3:14). That
includes the notion: 'I become what I become, I am from
eternity to eternity, and I am always and everlastingly the
same.' The unchangeable God!

We must leave it at that, but remember, then, that we are
dealing with such a being. Those are the characteristics and
the attributes of God. So God created human beings; that is
where we come in. He was everlasting and he could live
without us. He did not need us. He is not dependent upon
us but he chose and he decided to create man and to create
the world. Why did he do that?

You see, this is the way to approach the problem. Why
did God ever create the human race? And the answer is
that he created men and women for his own glory; he
created them for his own pleasure; he created them in
order that they might be his representatives here in this
world. He made them the lords of creation, supreme over
all the animals. He gave Adam the privilege of naming the
animals. He was to look after them and they were to serve
him.

Men and women were to be a kind of reflection of God,
God's representatives here in this created universe, and
they are therefore very special beings. They were made in
the image of God. Nothing else was: all the animals were
created, the flowers and the plants and so on, but men and
women were made in the image of God; they are like God.
They have a mind, they have reason; they can think of
themselves objectively; they can look at themselves and
meditate about themselves. That is a part of their image, the
image that they have received from God. God made them
like that and his object was that they might be here, as it

were, running the universe for him, always to see that it was to his glory and to his praise. God did all this out of his own good pleasure and for his own glory and he put men and women here in the central position.

So, having made them in his own image and having endowed them with these special and exceptional faculties, God made certain demands of them. He said: You are my representatives and I want you to live as such. There will be a danger, of course, in this exalted position, that you may think it is your world and your universe and you may try to set yourself up as a god; so, I put you, therefore, into the position that you can do almost anything you like, but . . . .

That was God's way of securing that men and women would always be subject to him and not their own master, as it were; not their own god. So he put them there on probation in that way, and he made those demands of them that always and in all things they should minister to God's glory; that they should always be God's servants; that they should not become rebels and set up a rival kingdom. No, they were to go on as God's representatives among all the creatures of the universe. God made that perfectly plain to them. And in many other places in the Bible and in many other ways God has made it quite plain to men and women what he expects of them.

Take the Ten Commandments, for instance. People joke about them, do they not? They even make films of them. They do everything but keep them! What are the Ten Commandments? Well, you start with God – 'no other gods before me'. Do not make any graven image; do not take his name in vain; do not take his day in vain (Ex 20:1–11). God – you live for him. Why? Because he has made you; because you are his representative; because you have something of him in you.

So you live for him, to glorify him in the world. And you carry it out in detail: you do not kill, nor steal, nor commit adultery, and so on (Ex 20:12–17). These are but the marks of man and woman made in the image of God. That is what I want from you, says God. He puts them in that position and says: Now go and live like that; show my glory; be the lords of creation. What a tremendous position!

Then the next step is this. Man and woman, for whom God had done all that and to whom God had given such a wonderful privilege, did the exact opposite of everything that I have been saying. They listened to the suggestion which said: Look here, this kingdom can be yours; you need not go on being the servants of God. Why not take it yourselves? Why not really become lords of creation? You are only in a secondary position. Why not go to the top? Here's your chance! Take it!

And man and woman agreed. But then, you remember, that meant rebellion; it meant forgetting God's commandments.

But now, this must not be viewed merely from the human standpoint. We have already seen what it has done there. However, though that is bad enough, it is not the main trouble. We all know that life is miserable, all of us experience remorse, and so on. We also know the strains of life; we have brought it all upon ourselves. But our main problem arises when we begin to consider what God thinks of all this.

Now God has told us very plainly what he does think of it. He told Adam and Eve, when he put them there on probation in the Garden of Eden: If you break this rule, this law, you will die; you will be thrust out of Paradise and you will bring misery upon yourself.

And it all happened. Now God was indicating there what he thinks of evil, rebellion and sin, and the transgression of his law. And he went on revealing it as the years and the centuries passed and what he has revealed is this: God hates sin, he is bound to. I say it with reverence, he would not be God if he did not – 'God is light, and in him is no darkness at all' (1 Jn 1:5). How can he like the darkness? How can he like the works of the devil? How can he like the lust and the passion?

God hates it. He is the eternal antithesis to it and he has told us that he hates it with all the intensity of his divine being. He has made this quite clear, as we have seen, in the Ten Commandments and he has done so in many other ways. In the Old Testament, we see what God did to individuals who sinned against him. It did not matter who they were; it did not matter if they were favourites like David! When they sinned, they suffered! God always punishes sin; he said he would and he always has. He said, 'The soul that sinneth, it shall die' (Ezek 18:4) and it does die. So all this is inevitable because of the being and the character and the nature of God.

Here, then, is the position at which we arrive. We have spent some time working out the position of men and women in terms of their slavery to the devil. Then we have considered it in terms of what it has done to their own eternal being and nature. But here is the great and the momentous thing, that because of our rebellion, every one of us is condemned by God's holy law.

You see, it is not a matter of how we feel, nor of what we do nor of what we are – that does not matter here. The point is that we are confronted by God's law which he has given and set out quite plainly. Every one of us comes face to face with this holy law of God. It does not matter who we are – whether moral or immoral, whether a so-called good or bad person, whatever our colour, whatever our continent, it does not matter – 'All have sinned, and come

short of the glory of God' (Rom 3:23). The whole world is
'guilty before God' (Rom 3:19). We are under the condemnation of God – have you ever considered that? You say,
'What I want is guidance,' or, 'I want healing; I want to live
a happy life.' All right! But before you ask for any one of
those things you had better consider this: How do you
stand before God's law?

If you break one of the laws of England that is the only
thing that matters at that point. You go to court and the
charge is read out against you. If you begin to say, 'Yes,
but look here, I hold a very exalted position; I am a most
important person. I do a lot of good and I give a great
deal of money to good causes,' they will say, 'But you
have broken act so and so – regulation number, sub-
section . . . . So there it is and you have got to abide by
the consequences.' The analogy is obvious. Multiply that
by infinity and you see every one of us, standing before
the law of a holy God, guilty and condemned. That is the
problem.

Not only that, we are under the wrath of God. Now
this is not my idea but something that God himself has
revealed. God *is* – God is personal, and not a machine.
God is one whom we address as 'You' and he knows us
individually, and the tragedy of our position is that we
are under his displeasure. When he first made Adam and
Eve, God was well pleased; he smiled upon them and
blessed them. But the moment they sinned, the relationship was upset and God could not look with pleasure
upon them. There are the people he had made in his own
image, sulking and hiding behind the tree – the fools!
Does God rejoice in that? Of course not! God hates it. His
displeasure and his wrath are upon sin.

And, again, I would remind you of how that comes out
in the Scriptures. The Jews, the children of Israel, were

God's own people but because of their persistent rebellion
and disobedience, God himself raised up the enemy, the
Chaldeans, to conquer Jerusalem and the whole country
and to carry them away captive to Babylon. God did that;
he was displeased with his people and he told them so.

You see, I am arguing – and God forgive me if I am
putting it in too familiar a manner – that God cannot help
being like this. He cannot help it, because he is light. He is
just and righteous and unchangeable and altogether holy
and pure, so he hates what we are and his wrath is upon it.
The Bible is full of this. In Romans 1 from verse 18
onwards, Paul says that God sometimes shows his wrath
upon sin by allowing us to get on with it. He abandons us,
he 'gives us over to a reprobate mind' (v. 28).

The Apostle's argument is that when the world did not
believe in God but began glorying in itself and its own wisdom, God abandoned it and the result was that it 'served
the creature more than the Creator' (v. 25). Men began to
have passion towards men; women towards women; they
became unnatural – the horrible perversions came in. Did
you know that that is a part of the wrath of God upon sin?
When God ceases to restrain evil in this world that is what
happens.

I think the modern world is experiencing the wrath of
God. To me this is the only explanation for the two world
wars we have had in this present century. The whole world
said it did not need God.

Very well, said God, if you say you can get on without
me, get on without me!

And the result is these horrible world wars – and worse
things are coming. And all that is nothing but a part of the
manifestation of the wrath of God upon sin; he is showing
his hatred of it. He said: I will let you reap the consequence
of what you do and what you believe.

218   LOVE SO AMAZING

And there we are in the agony and suffering, in the tension and the fear of the modern world. That is the second consequence.

The third is, as we have seen, that there is a state of enmity between man and woman and God. We were meant to be the companions of God – he made us for that reason. I have already referred to the Shorter Catechism which says, 'The chief end of man is to glorify God and to enjoy him for ever.' Jesus said, 'Thou shalt love the Lord thy God with all thy heart, and with all thy soul, and with all thy strength, and with all thy mind; and thy neighbour as thyself' (Lk 10:27). That is how we were meant to be – at peace with God, enjoying his companionship – but sin has done away with it; there is warfare; there is a lack of peace. And God hates all this so that there is enmity between God and the people he has made.

Now here, then, is the problem. How can God remain God – how can he be true to himself and remain the unchangeable God that he is – and have any dealings at all with sinful men and women? Here is the third great problem of salvation – 'made us meet to be partakers of the inheritance of the saints in light'. How can it possibly be the case? To be an inheritor of the saints in light means to have companionship with God, to know God and to enjoy him. But how can God do it? How can he possibly have dealings with us? What of his righteousness? What of his justice? What of his holiness? What of his character? What of his unchangeableness? Have you ever considered the problem from God's side? That is what is put before us here.

'But,' says somebody, 'there is no difficulty at all. You have just been very clever! You stop short with your references to the attributes of God. I did not hear you saying a word about the fact that God is love; you were very careful not to say that. You were equally careful not to mention his mercy and compassion. You are making an artificial problem! All you are saying about men and women is perfectly true, but God is love and because he is love there is no problem! Love means that you do not see things as they are. You just pour out your benevolence on everybody. It does not matter what people are. You just shower your love upon them.'

And my answer is that I agree with you that God is love – I would not be a preacher of the gospel if he were not – but, you see, the way you shout, 'God is love,' shows that you do not know what love is. Your love is a love that contradicts truth, that contradicts righteousness, that contradicts justice and holiness. It is a love that is dark and not light; it is a love that lacks glory.

No, here is the problem. How can God reconcile his love with his holiness? How can he reconcile his truth with his mercy? How can he reconcile his justice with his compassion? Let me put it in the words used by the apostle Paul in Romans 3:25–26. How can God remain just and forgive anybody? Forgiveness is not easy for God because he hates sin, because he has said that 'the soul that sinneth, it shall die' (Ezek 18:4). God is unchangeable and he is just, and everything he has said must be carried out. He cannot modify it; he cannot take it back. He cannot pretend he has not said it; he cannot wink his eye. God is everlastingly right. Righteousness, holiness, justice, purity: all are absolutes.

So is there no way of solving this problem? How can this holy God ever look upon me, leave alone have dealings with me, leave alone make me a partaker of the inheritance of the saints in light? That is the question. Had you considered that before or had you simply thought that this was quite easy? You just say, 'God is love' and think there is no problem. You think God does not see it, or pretends he has not! No, no, that is inconceivable. He would not be God if he did that. He would be denying his own essential attributes. Here is the question of reconciliation with God, and the answer of the gospel is just this; it is the message that is before us. It is the message of the incarnation. God himself has solved the problem and provided the way. Nobody else could. Men and women cannot: they are the slaves of the devil; their nature is perverted and vile; and in any case they cannot change. God, God alone, can do it and God has done it.

Did you notice this – 'Giving thanks unto the Father, which hath made us meet to be partakers of the inheritance of the saints in light: who' – he – 'hath delivered us from the power of darkness, and hath translated us into the kingdom of his dear Son.' And here it is in this verse we are looking at – 'he' – God – 'having made peace through the blood of his cross, by him' – Christ – 'to reconcile all things unto himself; by him, I say, whether they be things in earth, or things in heaven'; all things *by him*.

Here is the message and this is why you should praise God. It is God himself who has solved the problem – 'God so loved the world, that he gave his only begotten Son, that whosoever believeth in him should not perish, but have everlasting life' (Jn 3:16). What Christianity preaches is not that we have to pull ourselves up, live a better life, try to do good – only to find that we cannot because we are hopeless and helpless – but that God has done it. Salvation began in the mind of God. He has put it into practice and he sent his only Son into this world.

I am anxious that we should really see it from the side of God. Do you see the problem there? God's love said: I want to forgive my people.

God's mercy said: I must; I see them in trouble, I see

them unhappy. I must do something.

God's compassion agreed but God's justice said: You made them in your own image; you gave them a perfect chance; you told them exactly what would happen and they broke your law – deliberately. You said you would punish them and you must!

And here it is, a great argument, as it were, between love and justice, between mercy and truth. How can these things be reconciled? There they are – mercy and truth, righteousness and peace – they are opposed and yet they are all in the being and character of God.

And this is the one message of Christmas;[1] this is the glory of Advent; this is the thrill of the New Testament gospel: that God himself has found a way out! How? By sending his only Son from heaven into this world and by making him of a woman and under the law and enabling him to live a perfect life, by putting him on the cross on Calvary and smiting him with his own wrath, that you and I might be forgiven and that God might still be just and able to forgive us. That is how he solved it.

These are the great terms that are used in verse 14: 'In whom we have *redemption* through his blood, even the *forgiveness* of sins' (v. 14). Here is the mystery, that in Christ God has found a way whereby we can be delivered from the curse and the condemnation of the law. This is the way that God forgives us; it is the only way. He says, 'As far as the east is from the west, so far hath he removed our transgressions from us' (Ps 103:12). That is what he has done.

In Romans 5:8 Paul says, 'God commendeth his love toward us, in that, while we were yet sinners, Christ died for us.' While we were without strength, while we were

---

[1] This sermon was preached on 9 December 1962.

sinners, while we were enemies and alienated and utterly in the grip of the devil, Christ died for us and God in him has reconciled us unto himself. As verse 14 says: we have redemption; he has redeemed us.

Then in verses 20 and 21, Paul writes: 'And, having made peace through the blood of his cross, by him to reconcile all things unto himself . . . . And you, that were sometime alienated and enemies in your mind by wicked works, yet now hath he reconciled.' Do you see the process? The Son of God has come into the world and has answered the demands of the law. The curse has been removed; the condemnation has gone; our sins are cast into the sea of God's forgetfulness. And, having done that, he reconciles us unto himself. He is free to do it. His justice, his righteousness, are satisfied, so he now reconciles us unto himself.

How does he do it? 2 Corinthians 5:19 answers the question: 'God was in [and through] Christ' – and what did he do in Christ? – 'reconciling the world unto himself, not imputing their trespasses unto them.' And that means that having placed your sins and mine on Christ, and having punished them there, he can now smile upon us. He puts that perfect life and righteousness of Christ upon us and he looks at us in that and he smiles upon us. He is ready to bless us once more. That is the message; that is the ministry of reconciliation.

This is the good news – 'If any man be in Christ, he is a new creature: old things are passed away; behold, all things are become new' (2 Cor 5:17). But, you see, that cannot happen until I am forgiven. I am first forgiven and then I am given new life. I am 'a new man' and God makes me his child and looks upon me as a Father and smiles upon me – 'God and sinners reconciled'. That is the glory of it all; that is the whole message of Christmas:

Hark! the herald-angels sing,
Glory to the new-born King,
Peace on earth, and mercy mild,
God and sinners reconciled.
                                   Charles Wesley

They have been brought into his favour again. He smiles upon us and so peace is made: 'having made peace by the blood of his cross'.

'Yes,' says Paul again to the Romans, 'being justified by faith, we have peace with God through our Lord Jesus Christ' (Rom 5:1). As an old psalmist had prophesied, in Christ 'Mercy and truth are met together; righteousness and peace have kissed each other' (Ps 85:10). The antagonists are embracing one another. Mercy and peace are satisfied. Mercy and truth and righteousness and peace and all the attributes of God are perfectly harmonized and there is again peace between God and the people he made.

And the result is that we have been made fit, we have been qualified, to be partakers of the inheritance of the saints in light. You see, believing this, I know that I am forgiven, I know that I have been restored to God's favour, not because I am anything but because I am in Christ who has died for me and purchased me and redeemed me and given me his own nature and his own righteousness. I am in God's favour once more. The result is that I now stand in grace; I am not under the condemnation of God's law: 'There is therefore now no condemnation unto them which are in Christ Jesus' (Rom 8:1).

There was once. The law of God thunders it, the justice of God demands it, but, 'Christ is the end of the law for righteousness to every one that believeth' (Rom 10:4), and I believe in him. I am standing in grace and that enables me to go to God with confidence. I can pray to God now without being afraid. I come out of my hiding place and go to God knowing that I am accepted, knowing that I shall find mercy, knowing that I shall have grace to help in time of need (Heb 4:16). I know it because I am restored to his favour; I am not only forgiven, I am made a child of God. I say, 'My Father, Abba Father, look upon me, help me, have mercy,' and he will. He has pledged to do it. He has reconciled me to himself.

So now you see why a Christian gives thanks to the Father! That is what the Almighty God has done in order that you and I might be reconciled to him. Do not sentimentalize Christmas. Do not shed crocodile tears over that baby in the manger. This is tremendous; this is the biggest thing in the whole universe! God did that because nothing else could have reconciled you to him. The love of God alone cannot solve the problem of sin. Love and justice, mercy and righteousness, peace and truth – all of them are involved. All must be absolutely satisfied, and here is the only way.

Never forget what it cost God that you and I might be saved. Stop thinking so much about yourself. Do not say, 'But surely I am not as bad as all that, and I think I ought to have a little love and mercy.' If you say that, you are speaking in ignorance. You do not know the character of God. The moment you realize the truth about him you will see that what you have asked is eternally impossible. He must be just, and in Christ he is. God punished your sin and mine in Christ; he therefore gives us free forgiveness and pardon.

Now, then, you see why, as a Christian, you are bound to give all the praise and thanksgiving unto God. If you bring in even an iota of your own righteousness you are outside. If you want to hold on to anything in yourself to save you, or to your free will, I tell you, you are not a

Christian. Salvation is altogether from God. So are you
thanking the Father? Are you thanking him for having solved the problem and in such a way – through the humilia-
tion, the suffering, the agony of his only Son? Have you
ever thanked him? If you have not, again I say you are not
a Christian. Christians are men and women who know that
they are what they are entirely and only by the grace of
God in our Lord and Saviour Jesus Christ. And they thank
him for it.

Chapter 12

The Heart of the Gospel

In whom we have redemption through his blood, even the forgiveness of sins. . . . And, having made peace through the blood of his cross, by him to reconcile all things unto himself; by him, I say, whether they be things in earth, or things in heaven. And you, that were sometime alienated and enemies in your mind by wicked works, yet now hath he reconciled. In the body of his flesh through death, to present you holy and unblameable and unreproveable in his sight' (Col 1:14, 20–22).

We have been dealing with every one of the problems that must be dealt with before we can be made fit to be 'partakers of the inheritance with the saints in light', and all along we have had to say that God has done it in and through his Son, our Lord and Saviour Jesus Christ. He has not done it by sending a word from heaven, nor by raising up servants on earth and giving them a message. No, he has done it in and through his only begotten Son who 'is the image of the invisible God, the firstborn of every creature: For by him were all things created, that are in heaven, and that are in earth, visible and invisible . . .' (Col 1:15–16).

But that brings us to what is in many ways the heart of the whole matter – the point at which we see most clearly why Christians must of necessity give thanks unto the Father with the whole of their being. For the question confronting us now is: How has God done this for us in and through our Lord and Saviour Jesus Christ? And that is precisely the question that is answered in these verses which we are now considering.

Now the old Authorized Version reads, 'In whom we have redemption through his blood, even the forgiveness of sins.' But in other versions the term 'through his blood' is not there. This is a matter of dispute which does not make any difference to the teaching, because Paul repeats it elsewhere quite clearly. It is simply a question of the manuscripts, some of which omit the expression 'through his blood'. But though the words may not be in verse 14, they are in verse 20: 'And, having made peace through the blood of his cross,' and again in verse 22, where Paul says, 'in the body of his flesh through death'. So if the phrase was an interpolation in verse 14 we are not a bit surprised.

Let me, then, put the Apostle's statement to you in the form of three propositions which will help us, I think, to remember it and perhaps to understand it.

The first, let me emphasize it again, is that it is God the Father who was acting in Christ for our salvation. In all these statements, the emphasis is put there – 'It pleased *the Father* that in him should all fulness dwell; and having made peace . . . by him' – the Son – 'to reconcile all things *unto himself*' – the Father – 'and you . . . hath he reconciled' – that is the Father, remember, it is not the Son, it is the Father who has done it – 'in the body of his flesh' – that is the Son – 'through death, to present you holy and unblameable and unreproveable in his sight' – the sight of the Father.

Now why do I make a point of this? It is because the Bible states it everywhere. The New Testament is full of it. Let us take the favourite verse of all Scripture, John 3:16. What does it tell us? It says, 'God so loved the world' – God the Father – 'that he gave his only begotten Son, that whosoever believeth in him should not perish, but have everlasting life.'

Or take another glorious statement: 'When the fulness of

the time was come, God sent forth his Son, made of a woman, made under the law, to redeem them that were under the law' (Gal 4:4–5). *God* sent his Son.

We could quote many other passages. Take 2 Corinthians 5: 'God . . . hath given to us,' says Paul, 'the ministry of reconciliation; to wit, that God was in Christ, reconciling the world unto himself, not imputing their trespasses unto them. . . . For he' – God – 'hath made him' – the Son – 'to be sin for us, who knew no sin; that we might be made the righteousness of God in him' (2 Cor 5:18–19, 21).

Now it is important that we should grasp this because there are many Christian people who very rarely speak of the Father at all, giving the impression that salvation is brought about entirely by the Son. Some even go so far as to say that the Lord Jesus Christ has to persuade his Father to forgive us; that he has to plead with the Father to do this. They suggest that he urges the merit of his blood and says: Look at me, look at my wounds, listen to me and my pleading. It is as if the Father were opposed to it all and antagonistic and the Son had to plead with him, as it were, to change his mind in order to forgive us and to receive us! And there are many who only pray to the Lord Jesus Christ and never to the Father!

But all that is a terrible error and heresy and that is why I emphasize this point. It is a dreadful thing to say that the Father has to be persuaded by the Son to forgive us. There is not an iota of evidence in the Scripture for that. It is in some of the hymns, but they are not divinely inspired, good as they are. If it were true you would not give thanks to the Father, you would give thanks to the Son, whereas the Apostle here says: 'Giving thanks unto the Father . . . .'

So let us get this clear before we proceed. The way of salvation comes from God the Father. It is his plan, and his

purpose; it is his idea, his thought. The marvellous and
wonderful thing, as the old teachers used to put it, is that
the three members of the blessed holy Trinity had a great
council and conference in eternity. Over what? Over
redemption, the salvation of men and women like ourselves. And there the Father put this great plan and the
Son, as it were, stepped forward and said: Here I am –
send me. I will go and do it. 'A body hast thou prepared
me' (Heb 10:5). He gave himself to be the executive, as
it were; and the Father said: I will send you. Salvation
is the plan of the almighty eternal Father who sent the
Son to do the work – work which is essential if we are
to be partakers of the inheritance of the saints in light.
And the Son having done it, the Holy Spirit comes and
opens our eyes to it and applies it to us and thus we shall
eventually be 'holy and unblameable and unreproveable in
his sight'.

So let us be clear about this. This is the plan of the
Father. It is the almighty Father who sends the almighty
Son, and it is the Father and the Son who send the almighty
Holy Spirit. We praise the Father, the Son and the Holy
Spirit but primarily in this matter of redemption we praise
the Father 'who hath made us meet . . .'. Let us never forget
that the Lord Jesus Christ came into this world and did all
he did not to bring us to himself but to bring us to the
Father.

The apostle Peter says that in 1 Peter 3:18: 'For Christ
also hath once suffered for sins, the just for the unjust, that
he might bring us to God.' That is why he did it; do not
forget that. You must not stop at the Lord Jesus Christ; he
brings you to the Father. It is 'through him we . . . have
access by one Spirit unto the Father', says the apostle Paul
in Ephesians 2:18. This is the teaching of the Scripture
everywhere. Let us not be wrong at this point.

Then the second principle is this: the crucial point of this action of God's in Christ was on the cross on Calvary's hill. Again, this is something that is emphasized everywhere. Did you notice these terms: 'Having made peace through the *blood of his cross*' and '*In the body of his flesh*' – body, flesh, blood, cross! These are the terms that are used in this great statement of the gospel and they should fill us with a sense of wonder and amazement and make us give thanks to the Father. What is their significance? They show us that, in order that we might be made partakers of the inheritance of the saints in light, Jesus Christ, the Son of God, who is spirit eternally, took unto himself a body. He who was 'in the form of God, thought it not robbery to be equal with God' (Phil 2:6), was made in the likeness of men! The Word was made flesh; he was born a baby in Bethlehem.

Is there not something wrong with us that we can listen to things like this without being filled with such praise to God that would take us right out of ourselves? Have we ever understood what God has done about us and about our salvation? 'Body – flesh – blood!' You see, we have not got a philosophy here. This is not just a teaching or a morality. It is not an idealistic theory. No, it is sheer fact! God has made us meet to be partakers of the inheritance of the saints in light by doing certain things. He initiated this big event, the coming of the Son of God into the world in a body, as a man – bone of our bone and flesh of our flesh! Here it is, this astounding and staggering thing!

Yes, but we do not stay with the incarnation now, because we are considering his death: 'Having made peace through the blood of his cross'; 'In the body of his flesh through death'. That is how he has done it; that is how he has reconciled us.

So let us ask this question: Why did the Son of God ever

come into the world? Why did the Father ever send him? Now, of course, one answer that is often given today is that he came in order to teach us. What the world needs is teaching and he is the greatest religious teacher of all, the greatest ethical teacher, the greatest thinker, the greatest philosopher; he is supreme! If only the Sermon on the Mount were put into practice there would never be another war, the world would be perfect and all would be well! We would have no troubles at all. It is the teaching of Jesus we need! That is what many people say Christianity is.

And others put the emphasis not so much on his teaching as on his example. There is, they say, great power in an example. An ounce of example is worth a ton of theory. It is all very well to put emphasis on the teaching, but when you see it incorporated in a body, when you see it exemplified in a person, then you say, 'Now I see what it is and I am going to follow him; I am going to imitate him and I can do it.' And that is another current notion as to what Christianity is: it is the imitation of Christ. He lived like that in this world, they say, so let us rise up and live like him.

And yet the extraordinary thing is that when we come here to this great summary of the Christian gospel, we do not find either the teaching or the example mentioned at all. Now I have shown you why the Apostle gives this summary to the Colossians. He does it in order that they may not be misled by the false teachers and believe a wrong gospel. This is the true gospel, Paul says. You remember how he said that at the very beginning – 'Which is come unto you, as it is in all the world; and bringeth forth fruit, as it doth also in you, since the day ye heard of it, and knew the grace of God in truth.' That is the emphasis that he puts upon it – 'For the hope which is laid up for you in heaven, whereof ye heard before in the word of the truth of the gospel.' He is giving the word of the true gospel over against the false gospels.

Here, then, is a summary of the true gospel and the interesting thing, I repeat, is that there is not a word about our Lord's teaching and not a word about his example. Having described the glory of the person, the Apostle comes straight from the incarnation to the death upon the cross. Now this is the heart of the Christian gospel and this is where there is all this confusion at the present time. God saves us in Christ, by the death of Christ, not by his life and teaching, and there is a very good reason for that. The teaching and the example of the Lord Jesus Christ were never intended to save us. Why? Because they could not.

'Do you mean to say,' asks somebody, 'that the teaching and the example of Christ *cannot* save us?'

My reply is that they not only cannot save us, they damn us more than anything else that has ever come. Let me show you what I mean.

When God gave the children of Israel the Ten Commandments he said to them: If you can keep these they will save you.

But not a single person kept them, not one! 'By the deeds of the law there shall no flesh be justified in his sight: for by the law is the knowledge of sin' (Rom 3:20). Nobody ever kept the law. Now the life of Christ and the teaching of the Sermon on the Mount are infinitely higher than the Ten Commandments. You get God's law there in its most spiritual form and you see it exemplified in Christ's perfect life. So my simple argument is this: What is the use of giving a yet higher teaching to people who cannot keep the Ten Commandments? What is the point of giving an absolutely perfect example to people who have already failed to keep a lower test and a lower standard? The thing is nonsense.

Yet many say that Christianity means the preaching and life of Jesus Christ. They say that we should appeal to the nations to practise the Sermon on the Mount, to turn the other cheek and abolish armaments and then you will get perfect peace! But that is a complete travesty, a denial of the gospel, a complete negation of it. It is impossible.

Well then, why did our Lord teach? Why did he live the life he did?

The answer to that is not at all difficult. The whole point of our Lord's teaching was to show us that it was impossible. Had you ever thought of that? His teaching was just to show us that we could not do it.

'But,' you say, 'that is monstrous!'

Is it? Go back and read the Gospels, keeping your eye on the Pharisees and Scribes, the Sadducees and doctors of the law – why were they so annoyed with our Lord's teaching? There is only one answer: he showed them plainly that they could not keep it, and they hated him for it.

You see, the proud Pharisees felt they could do it. They said, 'Ah, we know the law, we are the experts of the law. We keep it and live it and therefore we are well-pleasing in God's sight!'

Wait a minute, said Christ. Let us examine you for a moment. You say, 'I have never committed murder.' All right, but have you said to your brother in your heart: 'You fool!'? If you have, you have already murdered him. You say, 'I have never committed adultery!' But, says our Lord, you do not understand the law. Have you looked on a woman to lust? If you have, you are guilty of adultery.

Our Lord convicted every one of them. They thought they had kept God's law, but he proved to them that they had not. That is the purpose of Christ's teaching: it is to condemn us all.

Let us say this for the Pharisees and Scribes: they at any rate understood what he was saying, but the modern Pharisees do not! They talk about 'imitating Christ'; they talk about 'putting his teaching into practice'. They do not believe in his death and in a new birth. They say they can rise up and do it as they are! They are even duller than the Pharisees! That is the whole trouble with them. No, there is no mention of the teaching in these verses in Colossians, nor of his example and his life, because they cannot save us. They are simply to show us how hopeless and lost and damned and condemned we are.

But what is emphasized is his death. That is the gospel. And this, I want to show you, is taught universally in the New Testament. So there is no excuse for any mistake about it. Look at John the Baptist. Here is the immediate forerunner of Christ, the herald who goes before, announcing that he is coming. What does John say about him? 'Behold the Lamb of God, which taketh away the sin of the world' (Jn 1:29). There it is already; even before Christ has appeared in his public ministry, John announces him as the Lamb that is to be slain.

We see this again in Matthew 16, after Peter's marvellous confession: 'Thou art the Christ, the Son of the living God.' Immediately after that, our Lord began to tell his disciples that he was going to be arrested and treated badly and that he was going to be put to death. And Peter, who had just made his great confession, said, 'Be it far from thee, Lord: this shall not be unto thee.' The same Peter! Peter did not want him to die; he did not understand that point.

But in reply our Lord said to Peter, 'Get thee behind me, Satan: for thou . . . savourest not the things that be of God, but those that be of men' (Mt 16:22–23). You are thinking in human terms, our Lord said. You think I am just a great

man and you are proud to be with me. You like my teaching and you are going to follow me, you are going to be one
of my disciples, but when I say I am going to die, you do
not like it. You are stumbling, of course, because you do
not understand God's way. You think I am just a new
religious teacher who has a teaching which is a bit better
than anyone who has gone before. You think I am giving a
wonderful example and that this is the way of salvation.
But it is not, and when I tell you that I am going to die, you
are annoyed because you do not know that that is the only
way to be saved.

Then we are told that on the Mount of Transfiguration
'there appeared unto them Moses and Elias' (Mt 17:3); and
what were they doing? They were talking to him about 'his
decease which he should accomplish at Jerusalem' (Lk
9:31); they were talking to him about his death.

There is also our Lord's great statement which is
recorded in Matthew 20:28 and Mark 10:45: 'The Son of
man came not to be ministered unto, but to minister, and to
give his life a ransom for many.' He says: You know, what
I am doing is altogether different from anything in this
world. The great man is one who is served by somebody
else; but in the kingdom of God greatness means serving.

Have you ever noticed the amount of space which is
given in the Gospels to the details of our Lord's death? You
can almost hear the nails being hammered in. Why all these
details? It is because his death is the vital thing. It is
everywhere in the New Testament. In Acts 20:28 we are
told that the church is something that has been purchased
by the blood of Christ. The apostle Paul reminds the
Corinthians, 'I determined not to know anything among
you, save Jesus Christ *and him crucified*' (1 Cor 2:2). 'We
preach,' Paul says, 'Christ crucified, unto the Jews a
stumblingblock, and unto the Greeks foolishness' (1 Cor

1:23). Why? Because he is 'the power of God, and the wisdom of God' (v. 24).

And Paul summarizes his gospel again to those Corinthians in chapter 15: 'I would remind you,' he says, 'of the things that I preached to you at the beginning.' What were they? 'That Christ died for our sins according to the scriptures; and that he was buried, and that he rose again the third day according to the scriptures' (vv. 3–4). This is the theme of his preaching always and everywhere.

Writing to the Galatians Paul reminds them at once that Christ gave himself for us 'that he might deliver us from this present evil world' (Gal 1:4).

To the Ephesians Paul says, 'In whom we have redemption through his blood, the forgiveness of sins' (Eph 1:7). In the next chapter he tells these people that there was a time when they were without Christ, being 'aliens from the commonwealth of Israel, and strangers from the covenants of promise, having no hope, and without God in the world: but now,' he says, 'in Christ Jesus ye who sometimes were far off are made nigh' – How? – 'by the blood of Christ' (Eph 2:12–13).

Then again in Ephesians 5 where he is talking about the church, Paul writes, 'Husbands, love your wives, even as Christ also loved the church, and gave himself for it; that he might sanctify and cleanse it with the washing of water by the word' (Eph 5:25–26).

There it is: we could go on indefinitely; the New Testament is full of this. He 'gave himself for us', says Paul to Titus, 'that he might redeem us from all iniquity, and purify unto himself a peculiar people, zealous of good works' (Tit 2:14). He gave himself for us on the cross on Calvary's hill.

But in many ways the most remarkable statement of this whole matter is in the epistle to the Hebrews: 'We see

Jesus, who was made a little lower than the angels *for the suffering of death*, crowned with glory and honour; that he by the grace of God should taste death for every man' (Heb 2:9). Taste death! He was made a little lower than the angels; he was sent as a man; he was given a body. Why? In order that he might die. He was born to die.

Peter, too, has the same message. He says, 'Forasmuch as ye know that ye were not redeemed with corruptible things, as silver and gold, from your vain conversation received by tradition from your fathers; but with the precious blood of Christ, as of a lamb without blemish and without spot' (1 Pet 1:18–19).

The book of Revelation, the last book in the Bible, makes an extraordinary statement right at the beginning:

> And from Jesus Christ, who is the faithful witness, and the first begotten of the dead, and the prince of the kings of the earth. Unto him that loved us, and washed us from our sins in his own blood, and hath made us kings and priests unto God and his Father; to him be glory and dominion for ever and ever. Amen (Rev 1:5–6).

Now then, have I established my point? It is God who saves us in Christ and the crucial point at which he saves us is in the death on Calvary: by his body, his flesh, his death, his blood.

But now I come to my third principle and ask the most vital question of all: What then was God doing in and through his Son on that cross and in that death? Now I suppose that of everything about him this is the most misunderstood. What is the meaning of Christ dying on the cross? The popular view today is that it is just the supreme example of pacifism. There he is saying: Do what you like to me, I will not hit back. I am not going to defend myself. I have done away with all such thoughts as armaments and self-defence. I am leaving myself. I abandon myself. I stand for truth. You do not agree with me? Very well, I simply stand. I shall not fight.

And so the message of Christianity is that when all the nations and their leaders believe that message and do away with all their armaments, there will be no more fighting or war and the kingdom of God will have come! That is what is taught by men in high positions in the Christian church, and it is sheer pacifism.

There are others who tell us that Christ died on the cross to demonstrate his love and so draw us to himself. As he dies he looks at us and says: Though you have mis-understood me, and though you have even done this to me, it is all right. I will still go on loving you!

You would be surprised to know the number of people who are regarded as evangelicals who say that. That is the position Christians have arrived at. They do not know their own case, their own position, their own truth. They say that when you see him saying that, it will break your heart and you will say, 'I must believe in you,' and so you are saved!

Others say that it is the Father who is saying that. He had already said that he is a God of love and that he does love us all, but we cannot see it, we do not believe it. Well, he says, though you have done that to my only Son, I will still forgive you. Can you not see my love now and give in to him?

Then there are others who would have us believe that our Lord dying on the cross was just offering some great act of repentance and penitence on our behalf. We have not understood the nature of sin, but he has, and there he is making a final confession of the utter sinfulness of human nature with which he has aligned himself.

But I must not keep you with these false theories. Why

are they wrong, every one of them? For this reason: that every one of them regards what happened on the cross as a tragedy. They do not talk about the 'wondrous cross'; they talk about 'the shameful cross'.

Secondly, they think that the cross was entirely the result of human actions, and they put all their emphasis on that. Cruel men did not understand him and crucified him in their jealousy and rivalry, and so on. He was a human being among human beings. And these theories in turn leave everything to us. *I* must understand his teaching and *I* must cease to defend myself. *I* must let people hit me, knock me about and do anything they like; it does not matter as long as I do that. I am imitating Christ and so I am saved. In this way I am forgiven and become a child of God!

But the true teaching says that whatever else was happening on that cross it was *God* who was doing something there. As we have seen, the whole emphasis in these verses is upon what God the Father has done. It is always the Father acting, so that anything that tells us that it is human action is already wrong.

Not only that, this wonderful teaching tells us that not only was God doing something there, but that God has done something there once and for all. And that it was by doing what he did there that God redeems me and makes me meet to be a partaker of the inheritance of the saints in light. Furthermore, let us remember Paul's terms – 'And, having made peace through [or by] the blood of his cross, by him to reconcile all things to himself . . . yet now hath he reconciled in [or by] the body of his flesh through death . . .' It is always put like that. It is the Father who does it through this medium, by this means.

And finally, the mistake people make is to read the New Testament only; they do not know their Old Testament.

The New Testament is the fulfilment of the Old. The Old
Testament is a book of prophecy pointing forward to the
New, telling us what is going to happen. If only people
knew that and looked at the Old Testament in this light,
what would they find? They would find that there in that
Old Testament God gave his servant Moses instructions to
build a tabernacle. God told Moses that certain animals
were to be taken and that the high priest was to put his
hand on the head of the animal as a sign that the sins of the
nation were being transferred to this animal. Then that animal was to be killed, its blood was to be collected and taken
into the presence of God, into 'the holiest of all'. It is in the
book of Leviticus in great detail; and all this is a prophecy.

Then you have the explicit statements in the prophetic
books, in passages such as Isaiah 53. There you get the key
to the meaning of the cross. We have it in a word here:
redemption – 'In whom we have redemption' – a word
which means 'to set at liberty by the payment of a price'.
It was something that was very common in the ancient
world. People who were captives could be bought, could
be set at liberty, if somebody paid a given price. It was a
ransom price which was paid and the captive was set free.
That is the very term that the Apostle uses and it is the
term that is used everywhere in the Bible. We need to be
set free; we have already seen from what. But how can I
be redeemed? What is the price? The price is death. God
was there executing and taking the price of my redemption, through the death and blood-shedding of his only
begotten Son.

Now in Romans 3:25 the apostle Paul uses a great word:
'Whom God,' he says, 'hath set forth to be a *propitiation*
through faith in his blood.' And, as we saw earlier, that
means that the holy, eternal, just and righteous God cannot
play with sin. What he says, he must do; and sin must be

punished because 'the wages of sin is death' (Rom 6:23) and 'the soul that sinneth it shall die' (Ezek 18:4). There it is, and only one price is enough; it is death. But who can pay it? Where is the man who is innocent, pure and sinless, who can pay the price and not die himself eternally? There is no one – 'All have sinned . . .' (Rom 3:23). Every one of us has to die for our own sins and, therefore, no one can redeem another. Is there no redeemer? No, there is not, and that is why God sent his own Son, 'made of a woman, made under the law' (Gal 4:4). He can redeem us because he is God as well as man; he can be put to death but not eternally; he rises in the power of his Godhead; he can finish dying and go on living because he is God as well as man. That is why he is the Redeemer and that is why he is 'a propitiation through faith in his blood'.

Read Isaiah 53 for yourselves and notice these tremendous phrases – 'He was wounded for our transgressions, he was bruised for our iniquities: the chastisement of our peace was upon him' (v. 5). 'We did esteem him stricken, smitten of God, and afflicted' (v. 4). 'The Lord hath laid on him the iniquity of us all' (v. 6). It is God, remember, who is acting right through. 'It pleased the Lord to bruise him; he hath put him to grief' (v. 10).

And the apostle Paul puts it in his own words in 2 Corinthians 5:21: 'He hath made him to be sin for us, who knew no sin; that we might be made the righteousness of God in him.' That means that God has taken our sins, and the guilt attached to them, and has put them on his own dear sinless Son. God smote him in order that we might be forgiven. It was the only way: sin must be punished and it has been punished. That is why he came into the world. He had to be a man; he had to have a body that he might be smitten. A word from heaven cannot do it, a man must die for a man and a man has come, the man

Christ Jesus, who is also the Son of God.

As Paul says: 'For what the law could not do, in that it was weak through the flesh, God sending his own Son in the likeness of sinful flesh, and for sin, condemned sin in the flesh: that the righteousness of the law might be fulfilled in us, who walk not after the flesh, but after the Spirit' (Rom 8:3–4).

And the New Testament is full of this; this is what they all preached. Listen to Paul again: 'If when we were enemies, we were reconciled to God by the death of his Son . . .' (Rom 5:10). And: 'He that spared not his own Son, but delivered him up for us all' – by his death on the cross – 'how shall he not with him also freely give us all things?' (Rom 8:32). That is why Christ came into the world; that is why God the Father sent him. It was that he might pay the ransom price, that he might redeem us. It was God who was acting on Calvary, not the Jews or the Romans, not even the Son; he was passive, he was the Lamb of God. The Father was doing things to the Son. The Son said: Here I am; put them on me.

On the cross we see the Son's passive obedience. The activity was entirely the activity of God the Father who laid our sins upon his Son and made his soul an offering for sin. He so dealt with him that that Son turned to his Father and said, 'My God, my God, why hast thou forsaken me?' (Mk 15:34). The Father, seeing my sins on his Son, turned his face away. He smote him, and bruised him. The Father did that to his only begotten, dearly beloved Son in order that he might forgive me; in order that he might reconcile me unto himself.

That is why a Christian praises and gives thanks to the Father. Can you say, quite honestly,

> Love so amazing, so divine,
> Demands my soul, my life, my all?
>   *Isaac Watts*

If you see the meaning of the cross, you will thank him for the remainder of your life and throughout eternity in the glory. Have you seen it?

Chapter 13

The Pre-eminence

... that in all things he might have the preeminence (Col 1:18).

In her hymn 'In the bleak midwinter', Christina Rossetti begins the last verse by asking, 'What shall I give him?' And the words of our text provide the answer: Give him the pre-eminence, because, as I am hoping to show you, it is his and his by right; and it is his and his alone.

We have been working our way through this great statement of the gospel in Colossians, and we have seen that Paul tells us that the ultimate test of whether we are Christians or not is that we give thanks unto the Father. To what extent are we thanking God for what he has done for us and our salvation? Men and women who really believe inevitably give thanks to God. So we have been working through the reasons which the Apostle here adduces as to why we should thank him, and we have seen, of course, that they are almost endless in number. But there is one thing which we have kept on saying and that is that in every instance it comes to this person, the Lord Jesus Christ. So the Apostle keeps on repeating his name, but here in the phrase we are looking at now he emphasizes it. What he has been implying, what he has been saying implicitly, he now says explicitly – 'that in all things he might have the preeminence'.

Now it is very interesting to notice the way in which the Apostle came to say this. The pedants, the mere literary critics, the people who are more interested in form than in

245

substance, are very fond of criticizing Paul for his bad style. What they mean by that, of course, is that he constantly interrupts what he is saying to go off at a tangent, as it were, and then he comes back again. And we have a perfect illustration of that in this whole passage that is before us. Paul starts off in verse 12 by saying:

> Giving thanks unto the Father, which hath made us meet to be partakers of the inheritance of the saints in light: who hath delivered us from the power of darkness, and hath translated us into the kingdom of his dear Son: in whom we have redemption through his blood, even the forgiveness of sins.

Then Paul obviously intended to go on with that particular matter but instead he turns aside:

> In whom we have redemption through his blood, even the forgiveness of sins.

And he begins to tell us something about this blessed Lord:

> Who is the image of the invisible God, the firstborn of every creature: for by him were all things created, that are in heaven, and that are in earth, visible and invisible, whether they be thrones, or dominions, or principalities, or powers: all things were created by him, and for him: and he is before all things, and by him all things consist. And he is the head of the body, the church: who is the beginning, the firstborn from the dead; that in all things he might have the preeminence. For it pleased the Father that in him should all fulness dwell.

And there was no more to be said. That is everything – all the fullness of the Godhead in him – so back Paul comes in verse 20 to where he broke off: 'And, having made peace through the blood of his cross' – that is what he was saying

in verse 14 before he digressed – 'In whom we have
redemption through his blood, even the forgiveness of
sins.' Now he comes back to it and, as we saw in the last
chapter, he works it out again and says what he originally
intended to say.

But in verses 15 to 19, the verses we are looking at
now, and especially in this great phrase which sums it all
up at the end of verse 18, the Apostle turns aside in order
to remind the Colossian Christians of the person of the
Lord Jesus Christ. He feels it incumbent upon him to go
into a certain amount of detail and to remind his readers
of who Christ is. And Paul does so, you remember,
because false teachers have appeared and are creating conditions which make it more or less imperative for him to
do so.

Now the main reason why the Apostle was troubled
about these false teachings was that they were detracting
and derogating from the pre-eminence and the glory and
the majesty and the wonder of the Son of God, our
blessed Lord and Saviour Jesus Christ. And that was
something the Apostle would not tolerate. He said some
very plain and mighty things about it, not only because
of his love for the Saviour, but because he saw that these
other theories were robbing men and women of their salvation. These teachings were the invention of the devil
and were to be unmasked for the counterfeit and sham
that they really were.

The false teachers were saying, you remember, that there
were a large number of angelic intermediaries between God
and man. They were created beings, all of them. You
started with an angel who was just a little bit higher than a
human being; then came another higher than he, and on
and on through a great hierarchy of angelic beings, until
you eventually arrived at God. And the heretics were say-

ing that Jesus of Nazareth was but one of these. They admitted that he was created before time; they said he was greater than man and that he existed before man, but he was still only an angelic being.

So they were denying his deity, his co-equality and co-eternity with the Father. And by doing that they were taking from the glory of the Lord Jesus Christ. That is why Paul wrote his epistle. He said: You are being confused by what is mere human philosophy; it is a muddle of philosophy, asceticism and moralism and it is of the devil. It is made up of the rudiments of the world. Do not listen! Do not go back to that, but realize who this blessed person is in whom you have believed; realize the full truth about him. Realize that 'in all things he must have the preeminence'.

And, of course, such a teaching is as necessary for us today as it was in the first century. There are people who go about thinking that they honour God and serve him by denying these great truths about the Son of God. They stand for Jehovah, they say! And they do so at the expense of the Son. There is nothing new about it, though its particular form is new, of course, and it comes with all the trickery and the sleek business acumen which is associated with most of these cults. It is as old as this heresy which was troubling the church at Colosse. But it sounds very clever, does it not? Its proponents sound as if they are defending God against some attack; but they are insulting him, for whoever insults the Son insults the Father.

The Lord Jesus Christ himself said that. He said, 'He that honoureth not the Son honoureth not the Father which hath sent him' (Jn 5:23); so anybody who tries to take anything from the Son is of the devil. We Christians are not merely believers in God. 'Ye believe in God,' said our Lord, 'believe also in me' (Jn 14:1). We are trinitarians;

we believe in 'God in three persons, blessed Trinity': God the Father, God the Son, God the Holy Spirit. Yes, this is the essential truth; there is no gospel apart from it.

But we must be clear about this and that is why I am calling attention to it. I also have a subsidiary and practical object and that is that we may look again into the mystery of the first Christmas[1] to understand what has taken place in and through our Lord and Saviour Jesus Christ. That is the trouble with all of us who are Christians: we do not realize these things as we ought. The thing is so stupendous, so majestic, so immense, that we cannot rise to it – our minds boggle, our imaginations are utterly defeated – but we must try. And thank God that the Apostle has put it in this form. So let us follow him.

Paul says: 'That in all things he might have the pre-eminence.' He means this. God's way of saving us, as we have been considering, and the reason why we should give thanks unto the Father, is that he has done it all in and through his only begotten Son. So as we give the Son pre-eminence we are obviously giving the glory to the Father at the same time. We praise, we adore, the three blessed persons – Father, Son and Holy Spirit.

But why should he have the pre-eminence in all things? The Apostle gives us three main answers. The first is *because he is who and what he is*: his own person demands it. 'Who is,' says Paul, 'the image of the invisible God.' What a statement! That is what Christmas is about. God is spirit. No one has seen him at any time; no one can see him, he dwells in a light which is unapproachable, but this baby is the image of the invisible God!

This is tremendous, is it not? You see, we are already in a realm entirely removed from what the world calls 'the

---

[1] This was preached on 23 December 1962. (Ed.)

Christmas spirit'. But you must understand who that baby
is. What does *image* mean? Now it does not just mean a
mere likeness, a mere resemblance; you can often get that
quite accidentally, as the authorities have pointed out. You
may have a great collection of eggs and suddenly notice
that two appear to be identical; but that is not what Paul
means by image, that it is nothing but an accidental similar-
ity, a very superficial likeness.

No, here are the best illustrations of what this word
'image' means. Look at a postage stamp and there you see
the head of the Queen. That is an image; it is not something
accidental, but has been produced deliberately. Or take out
a coin and there you see that head again. Now that comes
nearer to defining what we mean by an image. An impression has been made in the metal; it is an exact likeness. But
we can go further, there is something even stronger. Do we
not often say about a child, 'He is the image of his father –
the image of his mother'? That brings us nearer still. That
is what the word really means: there is something here of
that father or mother which is being reproduced exactly in
this child. You look at the child and you see the father or
mother – the image.

So what we are told here is that the Son of God, the Lord
Jesus Christ, is the exact likeness, the express image, the
very embodiment of the Father and is a complete revelation
of him and of his nature. This is a term that is used constantly
in the Scriptures. Paul, in writing to the Corinthians, says
that if people do not believe in the gospel it is because they
are lost: 'The god of this world hath blinded the minds of
them which believe not, lest the light of the glorious gospel
of Christ, *who is the image of God*, should shine unto
them' (2 Cor 4:4). In verse 6 of the same chapter he says,
'God, who commanded the light to shine out of darkness,
hath shined in our hearts, to give the light of the knowledge

of the glory of God in the face of Jesus Christ.' You look
into his face and you see the Father. He said it himself: 'He
that hath seen me hath seen the Father' (Jn 14:9).

Or take that exposition of this truth in Hebrews 1:3:
'Who being the brightness of his glory' – of God's glory –
'and the express image of his person . . .'. Now you cannot
get beyond that. Language finishes at that point! But what
it does say is that this baby born in Bethlehem in that stable
is the very image of the invisible God! Here is the greatest
thing that has ever happened in this world. We all get so
excited about the marvellous and wonderful things we are
doing these days – advances in science, exploring outer
space and so on. All right, I do not want to detract from
them, but put them by the side of this and they are a mere
nothing – nothing at all! Look at it! Here it is. Look into
that manger, look at that baby: he is the exact likeness of
the eternal and everlasting Father!

But Paul goes on! You can take no risks in these matters.
These false teachers who sound so clever and so plausible –
you have only to examine what they say, bring them to the
Scriptures, and you will soon be able to explode their
sophistries. 'Who is the image of the invisible God' and
then *the firstborn of every creature.* Now here, the
Authorized Version is not quite as good as it could be;
indeed, it is almost misleading and people have often mis-
understood it. 'The firstborn of every creature,' they say,
just means that he is the first creature to be born; he is the
first of a succession of creatures. But this phrase actually
means the exact opposite.

Let me say this for the New English Bible: it puts this
phrase very well. It says, 'His is the primacy over all
created things.' And in the margin: 'He is born before all
created things.' That is much better.

Or take other translations: 'He is the one who has priority

of and over all creation.' Or another: 'He is the firstborn before every creature.'

These are vital statements, of course, and we must be quite clear about them. The word translated here 'firstborn' implies priority; it conveys the notion of priority and sovereignty at the same time. He is before and he is over all, the firstborn who has the primacy over all creation.

Now this statement is vital because it tells us that Christ existed before all created things. So if he is before everything that is created, it is obvious that he himself is not created, which means that he is therefore eternal. That at once puts him in a category on his own and gives the lie to all who argue that he is the highest and the greatest of all created beings.

But, then, put that statement with verse 19. We are looking at this person and we read, 'For it pleased the Father that in him should all fulness dwell.' (The word 'Father' is supplied here by the translators.) All the fullness of what? And the answer is 'all the fulness of the Godhead', and the Apostle says that quite explicitly in verse 9 of the next chapter, where he says, 'For in him dwelleth all the fulness of the Godhead bodily.'

This is the way to approach Christmas. There is that baby in a manger, yes, but, remember, all the fullness of the Godhead is in that little body. He is the sum total of all the divine attributes and powers. That is what the Apostle claims for him, that is what he says is the truth about him: that he has primacy over everything that is created. Why? Because he is God – God the Son. The translators of the Authorized Version are perfectly right to supply the word 'Father'; everybody agrees about that. The idea conveyed by the Apostle is that it pleased God the Father that in him should all this fullness dwell. He sends his own Son and the Son has all the fullness of the Godhead in him.

In other words, Paul's claim is that he is to have the pre-eminence because he is not a creature like all the rest, not merely the first in time and rank of a succession that is to follow. That was the Arian heresy of the early centuries. It troubled the leaders of the early church who denounced it as heresy and put an end to it, but it comes back in different forms and, as I have reminded you, it is coming back today. No, he is the eternal Son of God, co-equal, co-eternal with the Father. He is not just the brightest and the greatest of the angels, but is before every angel.

Now there is an extended exposition of this in Hebrews 1. The writer takes it up and says, 'Unto which of the angels said he [God] at any time, Thou art my Son, this day have I begotten thee?' (v. 5). Never! The angelic hosts have all been created: there was a time when they were not. They have been brought into being in order to be God's servants; they are ministering spirits. But he is not one of them – 'Thy throne, O God, is for ever and ever' (v. 8). There is no beginning to him. He is before the skies, the heavens; they will all be rolled up as a cloth, but he abides. Why? Because he always was, without beginning or end of days. He is God's only begotten beloved Son; he is God's only Son eternally generated by the Father.

'I do not understand that,' says somebody.

Of course not. Who does? How can we? This is a great mystery. We are simply confined to what has been revealed to us and what has been revealed is that this Son is God as the Father is God, as the Spirit is God – three persons but one Godhead eternally.

There, then, is the first reason: he must be given the pre-eminence because he is the eternal Son of God, begotten not created. Let us worship him; let us adore him; let us say that he is alone, that he is unique, that there is nobody like him. Give him the pre-eminence because he is who and what he is.

But secondly, he is also to have the pre-eminence, says the Apostle, *because of his relationship to the universe.* 'For by him,' Paul says, 'were all things created, that are in heaven, and that are in earth, visible and invisible, whether they be thrones, or dominions, or principalities, or powers: all things were created by him, and for him: and he is before all things, and by him all things consist.' Again, what a statement! All I can do is to give you some headings about it and then plead with you to think about it and meditate upon it.

What, then, does it say? Well, look at it like this. 'By him,' Paul says, 'were all things created,' and that really means in him and through him. Now there is a familiar statement about this at the beginning of the Gospel of John: 'In the beginning was the Word, and the Word was with God, and the Word was God. The same was in the beginning with God' (Jn 1:1–2) – that is what we have seen. Then – 'All things were made by him; and without him was not anything made that was made. In him was life; and the life was the light of men' (vv. 2–4).

Turning again to Hebrews 1, we read in verse 2: God 'hath in these last days spoken unto us by his Son, whom he hath appointed heir of all things, by whom also he made the worlds'. And this, also, is something that substantiates our exposition of 'the firstborn of every creature'. He cannot be the two opposing things: a creature and the one who made creatures. Not only is he not a created creature, it is in him and through him that every creature has been created. Do not ask me to explain it. All I know is that when the Father came to create, he did it through his Son. He was somehow the agency of creation, and that means, you see, that he was before creation. When there was nothing and when the Father decided to create, he said to the Son, 'I am going to do all this through you.'

And then Paul gives us this extraordinary classification: Everything, he says, that is in heaven, everything that is on earth, everything that is visible, everything that is invisible. Now you cannot add to that, can you? That includes heaven, earth, things visible, things invisible, material things, immaterial things, substantial things, spiritual things, things belonging to time and things belonging to eternity. God created in him and through him the vast universe which we see and which we explore. All the flowers, the mountains, the rivers, the animals, man, everything; all were made by him.

But there is an invisible realm of the angels, spirits, angelic beings; they also were created in him and through him. And in order that we might be quite clear about this and not imagine that he is but one of these angels or great powers, Paul puts it like this: 'By him were all things created . . . visible and invisible.'

'But what do you mean by "invisible"?' asks somebody.

I will tell you, says Paul: 'whether they be thrones, or dominions, or principalities, or powers'. And that is an exhaustive and all-inclusive term that takes to itself all the angelic hosts and powers; they were all made in him and through him.

And then, knowing our propensity to listen to an error and to think that lies are better than the truth, Paul comes back at the end of verse 16 and says, 'All things were created by him, and for him.' He starts by saying it; he ends by saying it.

But what does that mean?

I confess that I do not know exactly. I have read everybody I can read on it and they do not know either.

People often ask this question. They say, 'If you believe in God and if you say that God is the Creator, why did he ever create the world?'

I think that the answer is this: he created it for his Son. Human fathers often do the same kind of thing. A father likes to make something that will please his son, something for the son to have as his own, something for the son to play with and enjoy, something for himself.

And I believe that the Apostle is telling us here that God the Father created the whole universe for his Son and gave it to him as a gift. It is in that sense that everything is made through him and everything is made for him. Everything is made with that intent, that it may minister to his glory. It is in order that the Son might be manifested in his glory that God made the universe. This is the topmost point of spiritual speculation, but in the case of the Apostle it was not speculation – he was writing under divine inspiration. God made the cosmos for his Son and you can see that it is through this cosmos that we have come to know what we do know about this Son and this is the reason why we should give him the pre-eminence always and in all things.

But let us go a step further. The Apostle again sums it all up in verse 17 when he says, 'He is before all things' – all created things have come after him. He was before them because he is uncreated, because he exists eternally in the bosom of the Father. Then – 'and by him all things *consist*'. So when you think about the baby in Bethlehem, you must realize that that baby means nothing to you if you do not know something about this. It is that baby in Bethlehem, in the manger, who keeps the whole universe together!

Now the exact meaning of the word 'consist' is 'to cohere', 'to hold together'. Christ is the reason for the unity and solidarity of the whole universe, the cosmos. Scientists seeking to understand the origin and continuation of the universe should look to Jesus. There is no conflict between science and the birth of that baby; on the contrary, his birth is the key to a true cosmology. What is the great character of this universe in which we find ourselves? Is it not this cohesion? This universe in which we find ourselves is not a chaos; it is a cosmos and a cosmos means that everything is held together. That is what makes scientific investigation possible: there are rules, there are laws. Look at the tremendous activity within the atom and it is all held together so that until recently scientists said that an atom was indivisible. There is a tremendous power, this force, the ion, the electron; they are all playing a part and yet they are all held together.

What, then, is it that holds them? The answer Paul gives is 'Christ'. The whole universe is held together, everything depends upon everything else. There is this marvellous order, this system, this arrangement, this design, this repetition. That is why we must reject as the most idiotic sophistry the theory of those who tell us that all this has come into being by accident. An atom alone is enough to disprove that. There is only one explanation: Christ is holding it together, he assists it all. He is the explanation of the perfect order and the interdependence that we find everywhere in nature; without him, it would all collapse. So let us give him the pre-eminence. There he is, eternal Son of God. Yes, and this is his relationship to the whole of creation, the entire cosmos.

But then, having said that Christ is the eternal Son of God, that he is supreme and sovereign in the whole universe, Paul goes on to suggest the third reason for giving him the pre-eminence: '*And he is the head of the body, the church:* who is the beginning, the firstborn from the dead.' Now this is something different. He always was the Son of God; it was through him that creation took place away back at the beginning, whenever it was. But here is something new, something additional. We are looking now at something that does not belong to eternity but to time.

There was a time when there was no church. 'And he is the head of the body, [which is] the church: who is the beginning. . . .' The beginning of what? The beginning of the church. He has brought it into being; he is the real and only explanation of its existence. So here is a reason for giving him the further pre-eminence. He is the head of the church, the life of the church, the power of the church and the substance of the church.

What Paul means is that the church has come out of Christ. He came from heaven and from the glory into this world in order to form it. You cannot be a Christian without belonging to the church. I did not say a particular local church, but 'the church', which is his body. He saves the church, he saves his people and he is the beginning, the source, the origin, the fount of the church and her life; and he assists it. He is everything to the church.

So how has the church come into being? Here is a wonderful thing; here is a new humanity that will people the new earth and the new heavens. This is how God redeems humanity. Old humanity had gone wrong in Adam, and we have seen that it is hopeless. God was starting a new humanity, so he sent a new man. Adam was the first; here was the second, the last Adam. There had never been one like him before. He is the first in a new succession; that is why he must have the pre-eminence in this respect.

But you see what it involved: it involved his being born as a baby; it involved the fact that the eternal Creator should become a helpless child and be made flesh. It not only involved his incarnation, it involved his passion, his death upon the cross and it also involved his resurrection.

So let us summarize it like this. Christ is the originator of this new humanity, this new succession of people. Here is the first man to have kept God's law perfectly and honoured it in its every detail. Here is the only one who could bear the load of the guilt of the world's sin and really bear it in the sense that he could carry it away and still go on himself. The only one, and as the Apostle reminds us, he 'is the beginning, the firstborn from the dead'. Here is the first to have passed through death and come out the other side. Many people had died before him, but nobody had risen from the dead before. Only he could conquer death and the grave and rise triumphant so that it cannot touch him any more. He ascended into heaven and took his seat at the right hand of God: the first new man, the first to give God's law a perfect obedience, the one and only person who could make atonement. He and he alone has done that and he has done it for the church. And, therefore, he and he alone is the head of the church and for that he should be given the pre-eminence, says Paul.

But there is one further reason. We must also give him the pre-eminence *because of his all-sufficiency*. Paul says: Do not put anybody near him. Do not add anybody to him. He has done it all.

That had to be said in those early days to the Colossians, and it has to be said today. He did everything that needs to be done for our salvation and he did it alone. Born alone; misunderstood, 'a man of sorrows, and acquainted with grief' (Is 53:3); in his life a lonely man. He died, he trod the winepress alone. Nobody was with him, he did it all himself. He arose alone, he ascended to heaven alone and then he took his seat at the right hand of the Father in the glory.

He did it alone; he needed no help, he needed no supplement. I say it in his name and to his glory. Mary his mother cannot add to what he has done. She is no co-redeemer, he needs no co-redeemer; he and he alone is the Redeemer. You need not pray to Mary; go to him, he is all and all in himself. By going to Mary you are taking from his pre-eminence. Do not add the saints to him; do not pray to them; pray to him. He is everything; he is all-sufficient. He is the beginning, he is the end – the Alpha, the Omega – the all and in all.

Shame upon you Christian people, if you dabble with the modern cults and think they can help you or add to your salvation. He is enough; his all-sufficiency is the ultimate reason why we should give him the pre-eminence in all things – 'There is none other name under heaven given among men, whereby we must be saved' (Acts 4:12). It is the only name, there is no other.

So are you giving him the pre-eminence? 'What can I give him?' says Christina Rossetti. What have I got to offer? All he wants is that you and I give him the pre-eminence in all things; that we look at him and say, 'My Lord and my God'; that we say, 'Yes, you are the eternal Son of God, the image of the invisible God and you were born miraculously of a virgin – "the Word was made flesh".'

So go to him, fall at his feet and say, 'I do not regard you as a man only, as only a great teacher or great exemplar. You are God who left the courts of heaven and came on earth, into this sinful, evil world for me.' Give him the pre-eminence in his Godhead; give him the pre-eminence by saying that you are a hopeless sinner and that you believe that he came into the world in order to save you. Say to him, 'I cannot save myself. I thought I could, but now I see that it is impossible. I thought my good works would do it, but they cannot.

> Nothing in my hand I bring;
> Simply to Thy cross I cling.'
> *A. M. Toplady*

So give him the pre-eminence, live for him, praise him, tell others about him. And as you do you will give him great joy. You will be giving him the pre-eminence that is his by right. It is his and he will have it, and the whole world will be compelled to give it to him. But give it to him willingly and say with the psalmist, 'Bless the Lord, O my soul: and let all that is within me, bless his holy name' (Ps 103:1).

Chapter 14

All Things

And, having made peace through the blood of his cross, by
him to reconcile all things unto himself; by him, I say,
whether they be things in earth, or things in heaven.
   To whom God would make known what is the riches of the
glory of this mystery among the Gentiles; which is Christ in
you, the hope of glory (Col 1:20, 27).

We come now to take a last view of this great statement of
the gospel which the Apostle gives us here in Colossians, in
order that we may see the ultimate of the message which
the gospel brings to us. We have considered how in all
things the Lord Jesus Christ must have the pre-eminence
because he is who he is; because of his relationship to
everything that is created; and because he is the head of the
church, the originator of the church and of this salvation
which we enjoy. He is the first, 'the author and finisher',
the file leader of our faith, as the author of the epistle to the
Hebrews calls him (Heb 12:2). And we saw also that he has
done it all alone; he is all-sufficient.
   But there is one further reason why we must give him
this pre-eminence. So far we have been looking at the work
of Christ mainly in terms of ourselves as human beings, our
condition in this world of sin and of shame, and our need
of personal salvation. We have been thinking of our personal deliverance from the power of darkness, from the
threatenings of the condemnation of the law, from the evil
nature that we have in us as the result of the fall. We need
to be delivered from all that and, thank God, we have seen
how he has provided it for us, in and through his only

begotten Son. But there is something further. Did you notice it? 'And, having made peace through the blood of his cross, by him to reconcile all things unto himself' – not only human beings but *all* things – 'by him, I say, whether they be things in earth or things in heaven.'

Now we have hinted at this before, because the Apostle has been throwing out suggestions with respect to it. We had it in verse 5, for instance. Here Paul has been thanking God for these people, and tells them he has been praying for them, 'Since we heard of your faith in Christ Jesus, and of the love which ye have to all the saints, for the hope which is laid up for you in heaven, whereof ye heard before in the word of the truth of the gospel' (vv. 4–5).

And in verse 12 the phrase 'inheritance of the saints in light' also conveys something of the same notion to us, so we emphasized the fact that we are now a people, we are Christians, we are 'in Christ at Colosse'.

But now we must look at this more directly and explicitly. In verse 20 Paul lifts us up and gives us a view of God's ultimate end and object, the completion of his great plan and purpose of salvation and redemption.

Now there are two very special reasons why we should look at this. One is a charge that is very frequently brought against the Christian message and the Christian faith, and especially the evangelical presentation of it. The charge is that we are always concerned about personal salvation only. It is said that we are selfish, self-centred, narrow little people and that we are not a bit interested in the world in which we find ourselves. And they say that because we do not spend all our time preaching about bombs and war and telling the Government what to do and writing letters to world leaders and so on! So we must meet this charge and face it.

But there is also a second reason why it is important that

we should look at this particular subject, and it is this. There are many honest, sincere people who are in a genuine difficulty about this matter. They say, 'Now you Christians, you believe in God and you say that God has made the world, that he sustains it and that he is righteous and holy and just and loving. Now,' they continue, 'our difficulty is this. If that is so, why does God allow the world to be as it is? He seems to have failed. Your God,' they say, 'has been defeated. If you make all these claims for him, then what have you got to say about the state of the world at this present time?'

That is a very common difficulty and it is important that it should be answered – because it can be answered. And what we are considering now deals with both these objections which people raise against the evangelical presentation of the Christian faith.

Let us look, then, at this first one, this idea that Christianity is only concerned about the individual and about personal salvation. Now we have already touched on this and have seen that there is only one answer to give, which is that it is a false charge. Now there may be some Christians who give that impression and I shall not defend them because they are very wrong if they do. If we give the impression that salvation has reference only to the individual, then we are not being true to the Scriptures; we are not taking account of this very text that we are examining together. I want to show you that the Christian faith has a message with respect to the world, the whole cosmos, in addition to what it has to say about the individual.

Then take that second view which does not understand why things are as they are in the world. We have everything to say to that also because we shall be able to unfold what God's plan and purpose are and how he really is still concerned about the world and will be until it has been restored and reconciled to its original condition.

In other words, we not only claim that the Christian message has something to say about the state of the whole universe but we go further and add that it is the gospel alone that really has anything to say about that. Now that may astonish you, but it is true and I can prove it. All the other views are doubly wrong because they say that if Christianity is not improving this present world, then it has failed. That is what they think Christianity should do; that is what they expect it to do. They think that this is a teaching that is to be applied to the world as it is and as a result of which the world will be improved! And then they go on to say that if that is not done, then there is nothing for us but disaster!

But such people fail to understand the biblical message in two respects, which we will go on to consider. I repeat that it is a very different message, and is the only true message with respect to this world. Here is a definite plan, which is being carried out and which will be brought to its final and ultimate completion.

So, then, let us look at it. The Christian message *is* first and foremost a message to the individual. We must be clear about that; that is where it starts. But my point is that it does not stop there. The tragedy is that people will persist in regarding it as some sort of general message. They say, 'If only we can apply this message, we will lift this world and make it a better place!' But that is all wrong; that is a denial of the Christian message; that is not its function. The Christian message primarily is one which says that we need to be delivered as individuals out of 'this present evil world'. And, thank God, we have seen that we can be delivered: 'Giving thanks unto the Father . . . who hath delivered us from the power of darkness, and hath translated us into the kingdom of his dear Son.' So we are in the world but we are not of it.

That, then, is the first message of Christianity. It starts with this individual, this personal emphasis, and it says to every one of us, 'Do not be worried about the world; instead of spending all your time thinking about what the nations are doing, be worried about your soul. Stop, and ask yourself, "What am I doing?" You will be dead long before the world will ever be put right. What, therefore, will happen to you?'

You will not find any political programmes in the Gospels. People came one day and tried to take our Lord by force, to bring him up to Jerusalem and make him a king. But he escaped from them and went up into a mountain by himself. He had not come to do things like that; he had come 'to seek and to save that which was lost' (Lk 19:10). His message, blessed be his name, was to 'whosoever believeth', to the individual. And from the beginning to the end you always find him dealing with individuals. Even when he was dying on the cross he dealt with an individual thief; there in that mighty transaction he remembered this individual and he dealt with him.

That is Christ's message; it always starts with individuals and tells us: Do not pin your faith to world improvement or to any advance of civilization. You must be delivered out of that; you must be delivered from the world, the flesh and the devil. And in Christ Jesus and what he has done you can know and experience that deliverance. You can become a partaker of 'the inheritance of the saints in light' here and now. You can become a child of God and, if a child, therefore an heir of God and joint-heir with Christ (Rom 8:17) while you are still in this present evil world. The heir has not received it yet; he is waiting for it but he knows that he will get it.

But the message does not stop at that. And we must make this equally clear because that is how we refute the

charge that we are only interested in ourselves. Of course
we are primarily interested in ourselves; if we are not, we
are fools! If your house is on fire and a fire-escape is put up
at the window of the room you are in, surely your business
is to take advantage of it and get out of the house instead of
standing there to have a discussion about the architecture,
and about whether something cannot be done to save
other portions, and so on! First of all make sure that you
are in a place of safety, then consider the house as a
whole.

That is how Christianity does it and the tragedy is that
men and women are unaware of this individual personal
emphasis and, indeed, dislike it in their supposed concern
about world conditions. So they go on talking about these
conditions and as they do so the world gets worse and
worse. No, we start with the individual but we do not stop
there. We go on to this larger, ultimate message, which we
find in these verses and which is emphasized everywhere in
the Bible.

I want, therefore, to show you how these two aspects are
related and how God does in both realms very much the
same thing and in the same way. Now the Bible puts this in
a number of propositions. Here is the first: the world needs
to be put right – 'And, having made peace through the
blood of his cross, by him to reconcile *all things* unto himself.' 'All things': obviously they need to be reconciled;
something has gone wrong and it needs to be put right. So
the Bible starts by making that statement and I find it very
comforting. The people who depress me are those who try
to persuade me that everything is all right in this world –
the foolish people who say, 'Isn't life wonderful!' Is it? I
prefer the Bible which says that everything has gone
wrong. The times are out of joint, everything is out of
joint. They need to be reconciled; they need to be united

again. Things must be put back into their right places, into
their respective positions and with a right sense of propor-
tion. The Bible says that the world needs this.

But why does it need it? Why is it a part of God's purpose to reconcile all things unto himself by Christ? And
here I can show you that it is the Bible alone that really
gives us any hope or any comfort, or that has any message
at all for us at this present time, because the Bible alone tells
us why the world is as it is.

Now, when I say 'the world' I am not thinking of men
and women, but of everything in the whole cosmos. Why
are things as they are? The biblical answer is perfectly
plain. There is a relationship between the individual and the
cosmos in general, so the world is as it is because of the fall.
We have seen that men and women fell because the devil
came and tempted them. And why? Because the devil hates
God and is jealous of him. The devil's great ambition, of
course, is to bring God's universe into disorder. God made
the whole universe and it was perfect; it was paradise; there
was nothing wrong in it in any respect. Nothing wrong
with vegetation, nothing wrong with animals, nothing
wrong with the man and woman. And the devil's one idea
was to bring disorder and chaos into this perfection. So he
tempted Adam and Eve and he did that because he knew
that God had made them the lords of creation. God had not
only made them in his own image, he had put them over
everything; there was this relationship between them and
the universe, and the result is that when they fell, the creation fell with them.

This is what people do not understand. You find the full
statement of it away back in the book of Genesis:

And unto Adam he [God] said, Because thou hast hearkened
unto the voice of thy wife, and hast eaten of the tree, of which

I commanded thee, saying, Thou shalt not eat of it; *cursed is the ground* for thy sake; in sorrow shalt thou eat of it all the days of thy life; thorns also and thistles shall it bring forth to thee; and thou shalt eat the herb of the field; in the sweat of thy face shalt thou eat bread, till thou return unto the ground; for out of it wast thou taken: for dust thou art, and unto dust shalt thou return (Gen 3:17–19).

Now the point is that there were no thorns and thistles in nature before the fall; there was nothing like that. There was nothing, as it were, that was cutting across the order and the perfection. It is as the result of the fall that the ground was cursed. Thorns, thistles, pestilences, diseases, earthquakes, cataclysms – all these things have come because of the fall. And, notice, what we are told is that God himself said that the ground should be cursed. So, you see, we are let into part of the explanation of why the world is as it is. The universe – I mean the cosmos – is as it is as a part of the punishment of sin. When the lord of creation fell, creation fell; it was a part of the punishment. In Genesis 3:17–19 we see that Adam had these problems; these things were now working against him. The sweat of his brow was involved; he did not have to sweat before, he was never meant to, but now he had to sweat because of his fall and because of his sin.

There are many great statements of this in the Bible. For example, the apostle Paul puts it like this:

For I reckon that the sufferings of this present time are not worthy to be compared with the glory which shall be revealed in us. For the earnest expectation of the creature [of the creation] waiteth for the manifestation of the sons of God. For the creature was made subject to vanity, not willingly, but by reason of him who hath subjected the same in hope, because the creature itself [the creation itself] also shall be delivered from the bondage of corruption into the glorious liberty of the children of God (Rom 8:18–21).

Now let me show you what that means.

This is a description of the world. It is in a state of *vanity*, that is why it needs to be reconciled to God. 'Vanity' means not fulfilling its function, not measuring up to that which was originally intended for it. Vanity means a tendency to dissolution, a tendency to deterioration which ultimately leads to a void. That is how the Bible describes the world as the result of the fall.

But then there is this other term – 'bondage of corruption'. That means purely physical corruption, the tendency to decay, to putrefaction, to death and destruction and this is true of nature, is it not? Beautiful flowers soon begin to fade, they wither and they die: 'Change and decay in all around I see.' It is everywhere. Look where you will, nothing is stable, everything is changing, everything is in movement. It is bound to, it cannot help it; it cannot escape. So Paul says that 'the whole creation groaneth and travaileth in pain' (Rom 8:22); it is trying to get out of it.

Creation tries to escape every spring, does it not? It makes a great effort, as it were, to lift itself out of death and destruction, but it never succeeds! There is always an autumn and always a winter! It knows something about this 'groaning', you see. The creation is making its protest against human sin and folly. The Apostle is using a great picture here in Romans 8. He is personifying nature and he says: Nature itself is complaining. It knows that it was never meant to be like this and it is trying to get rid of it but it cannot. The creation 'waiteth for the manifestations of the sons of God' (Rom 8:19). Nature, Paul says, has an idea, a feeling within itself, that not only was it meant for something better but that this something better is coming.

says: Nature itself is complaining. It knows that it was never meant to be like this and it is trying to get rid of it but it cannot. The creation 'waiteth for the manifestations of the sons of God' (Rom 8:19). Nature, Paul says, has an idea, a feeling within itself, that not only was it meant for something better but that this something better is coming. So the whole of creation is waiting for this manifestation of the sons of God. It is looking forward to it, stretching its neck out, as it were. That is Paul's picture.

What a description of creation! What a description of the world! That is the biblical view. So, to sum it all up, we can put it like this. As you look out upon the whole of the world of nature what you see is a great confusion: depravity, animals killing one another, ferocity, living on one another, cruelty! Do you not see it everywhere? Watch the insects, beetles, spiders and others, watch this tremendous activity. Here it is, 'Nature red in tooth and claw'! Do you think that this is how God made our world? Of course not! That is what it has become; that is why it needs to be reconciled. It is not man and woman alone who went wrong; but because they have gone wrong, everything else has too. This is the result of the fall as you see it in brute creation. You see it everywhere, animate and inanimate, right through the whole cosmos. The fall has led to this further collapse and this terrible calamity.

So that is the first statement of the gospel. All things need to be reconciled to God because they are out of joint; they are out of position; they are not what they were meant to be.

My second principle is this: that no natural effort, no human effort, can ever deal with this condition. Now here we are making a challenge. People say to us, 'What have you got to say about the world?' And our answer is that men and women do not understand the condition of the world and because they do not understand it they think they can improve it. But not only can they not improve it, nothing else can improve it either.

Of course, they like to believe that there is a process, a power in it. You know the evolutionary idea, particularly that form of it which emphasizes what it calls this 'élan vital'. That is not Darwin, it is another! But it does not matter – it is one of the popular theories that there is this life principle, this something, which is pushing the whole cosmos up until eventually it will have evolved to perfection. It is just rubbish! The whole history of the universe proves that in and of itself.

Man cannot do it either. Man is greater than any conceivable élan vital, but even he cannot. Now my justification for saying that is history. The history of the world is just the story of civilization, or still better, it is the story of civilizations. A great civilization rises and is going to lead the whole world and conquer it all and make it perfect. Then down it goes! Another comes up, down it goes! And so on. That is the whole history of the world: it all comes to nothing! It goes in circles.

'But there are wonderful periods,' people say. 'Two hundred years ago, there was the Enlightenment!' That is what the rationalists of that period called it. 'At last,' people said, 'learning is coming in. It is going to flood everything with light and the world will be made perfect.' There was a hangover from this in the Victorian period. The Victorians sang about it and thought this perfect world was coming! But by now we do not believe much in enlightenment, do we? No; the world has known that sort of thing many and many a time before.

Think of the ancient civilization in China. It was wonderful! But it has gone! The Chinese, you know, discovered penicillin two thousand years ago; they did not call it penicillin, of course, but they discovered the very thing. That is how they used to treat distemper in dogs. They would search for old stones with that blue kind of mould which they would scrape off. When they gave it to their dogs they found it cured distemper. They had all that knowledge, but it disappeared.

At one time, a friend of mine, doing some research on smallpox, thought he had made a grand discovery when he found that one of the best ways of protecting rabbits against this disease was to put it into their nostrils. And he prophesied very optimistically that a day would come when we would no longer be scratching the vaccine into children's arms; they would just have a little kind of snuff and put it in their nostrils and the children would be protected. He had made a brand new discovery! But he went to read in the libraries before he wrote his report and there he found in a footnote that whenever anyone had smallpox in ancient Egypt, it was the custom to go out into the country and cut a bit of wood into the shape of a cone to fit a nostril. Then they would rub the cone in the bed clothes of someone suffering from smallpox and put it into the nostrils of the people who had never had smallpox, and they found that somehow it protected them! I will repeat his words to you. He came to my room and said, 'I am going to chuck up this research work; we are simply rediscovering what has already been known!'

It is perfectly true; it goes round and round in cycles, there is no advance. Look at our age; look at the whole condition at the present time; not only that, look at it in another way. We are very proud, and rightly so, of the diseases that can now be cured that used to be incurable. But have you not noticed that as they cure one a new one seems to come?

No, there is no élan vital; there is no process innate in

nature that will lift up the cosmos. Nor can men and women do it, for all their research, invention and power. There is no hope.

Now, I am old enough to remember a day when people pinned their faith in politicians. But I do not think many people do that today. That is not to say that I justify this habit of trying to ridicule everybody; it is thoroughly bad and needs to be condemned. But there is a lot of truth in it. It is wrong to ridicule politicians, but it is still more wrong to pin your faith in them. No, there is no message of hope whatsoever with regard to the world and the universe apart from the message of the Christian gospel which is God's programme in Christ – 'Having made peace through the blood of his cross, by him to reconcile all things unto himself.'

God, therefore, has a programme for the universe as well as for his own people. I will go further – I say with reverence – God must have a programme for the universe because if he has not the devil is ultimately the victor. It is inconceivable that God could leave this universe as it is. We have seen that he never created thorns and thistles; they came in as a part of the curse, the punishment. God cannot leave this world with such things and with nature 'red in tooth and claw'. If he did the devil would have triumphed and would go on triumphing throughout eternity and taunting God with his failure. So, I say, God not only has a plan, he must have a plan, and here we are told exactly what it is.

God's plan is to reconcile all things unto himself: 'by him, I say, whether they be things in earth, or things in heaven'. What is this? Well, our Lord himself referred to it in a very striking statement – I think we do not attach the significance to it that we should.

Peter answered and said unto him, Behold, we have forsaken all, and followed thee; what shall we have therefore? And Jesus said unto them, Verily I say unto you, That ye which have followed me, *in the regeneration* when the Son of man shall sit in the throne of his glory, ye also shall sit upon twelve thrones, judging the twelve tribes of Israel (Mt 19:27–28).

Do you notice it: the regeneration, the remaking? A great remaking is coming. How are you and I saved as individuals? By regeneration. How is the universe to be put right? By regeneration. It is the same method.

How, then, is this to happen? Will it be by a process of gradual improvement? No, nothing happens that way. We do not become Christians like that. We may not know it, but our new birth is a definite act of God, in a moment. And the regeneration of the universe will happen in much the same way – not by a gradual improvement. According to our Lord's own prophecy, it will be almost the exact opposite: 'When the Son of man cometh, shall he find faith on the earth?' (Lk 18:8); 'And ye shall hear of wars and rumours of wars' (Mt 24:6). That is what he says but, thank God, he says also that, in spite of that, there will be a great regeneration. God will put everything right; he will reconcile it all again in and through his dearly beloved Son.

How does he do it? Well, this is the process. What is happening at the present time is that God is preparing a people for himself to live in that restored cosmos. That, you see, is the ultimate purpose – all things in earth and heaven reconciled, brought back to where he wants them. But now he needs a people to live in that, and that is what is happening to you and me. We are saved as individuals out of this present evil world and are being prepared for that land, that cosmos, which is coming. God in Christ is calling out a people for himself. He rescues us, takes us out

of the power of darkness and puts us into the kingdom of
his dear Son. He is preparing us for the inheritance of the
saints in light.

And at the same time he is doing something else: he is
keeping evil in this world within bounds. God is definitely
doing that – the whole of the Old Testament teaches it. It
is God, remember, who ordained 'the powers that be'
(Rom 13:1). It was not that somebody suddenly thought it
would be a good idea and fine thing to have magistrates! It
is God who brought that about. It is God who appointed
kings; it is he who fixed the boundaries of the nations; it is
he who introduced culture: you will see all this in the book
of Genesis. He did all this in order to limit the power of
evil. And that has happened. The world is being kept
within bounds, and though sometimes God abandons it in
order that he may punish it, he never lets evil go too far.
Read your Old Testament; there you will see people rising
up and threatening the whole universe. God tolerates them
for a while and then he strikes them down. There is always
a restriction upon the power of evil. God has his hand even
upon the devil and he is under God's control.

But we can go further. Since our Lord came into this
world and did what he did, he has been reigning. Just
before his death our Lord said, 'Now shall the prince of
this world be cast out' (Jn 12:31), and he was. When our
Lord died upon the cross, the prince of this world was cast
out and the Lord Jesus Christ began his reign. He himself,
when he had risen, spoke to his disciples and said, 'All
power is given unto me in heaven and in earth. Go ye
therefore, and teach' – make disciples of – 'all nations . . .
and, lo, I am with you alway, even unto the end of the
world' (Mt 28:18–20). Never forget this! He is reigning
already; he has already conquered the devil but not yet in
a visible form. Everything is under the hand of this Lord.

He is seated at the right hand of God waiting 'till his enemies be made his footstool' (Heb 10:13). That is the teaching; that is the position at the present time.

But, thank God, we look forward to something – 'By him, I say, whether they be things in earth, or things in heaven.' He is going to reconcile all things unto himself. When? Well, ultimately, when our Lord comes back again. That is the second coming of Christ; that is what the Apostle is talking about here – 'the hope of glory'.

Now, you see, it is always in Christ. I said at the beginning that in all things he must have the pre-eminence, yes, and he must have it here also. He is pre-eminent in creation, pre-eminent in redemption, pre-eminent in the new regeneration in the world to come. He will come back into this world. He said so himself. All the apostles teach this message. This is, you see, the thing which is not believed by the people who tell us that Christianity is just a teaching to improve the world; they do not believe in the second coming! They think that when a man dies that is the end. They do not believe that the Lord Jesus Christ is coming back into this world visibly in the body, riding the clouds of heaven, surrounded by the holy angels. They do not believe it, so they say that if we cannot persuade the nations to practise Christianity it is the end! But it is not; he is coming back again! That is the teaching of Paul, as it is the teaching of all the apostles.

And what does he come back for? He comes back for judgment. He is coming back to judge the world in righteousness and all his enemies and all God's enemies shall be put under his feet.

Take those tremendous words in 2 Thessalonians:

To you who are troubled rest with us, when the Lord Jesus shall be revealed from heaven with his mighty angels, in flam-

ing fire taking vengeance on them that know not God, and
that obey not the gospel of our Lord Jesus Christ: who shall
be punished with everlasting destruction from the presence of
the Lord, and from the glory of his power; when he shall
come to be glorified in his saints, and to be admired in all them
that believe . . . in that day (2 Thess 1:7–10).

And Paul repeats it again in 2 Thessalonians 2:8:

Then shall that Wicked be revealed, whom the Lord shall consume with the spirit of his mouth, and shall destroy with the
brightness of his coming.

Here is the only hope for the cosmos. It needs to be delivered from bondage, corruption and vanity, and the power
of the devil, and it will be: Christ will do it. When he comes
back he will defeat all his enemies, the devil included. They
will vanish when they come into his presence; by the word
of his mouth he will destroy them. And so we read in the
book of Revelation:

And the devil that deceived them was cast into the lake of fire
and brimstone, where the beast and the false prophet are, and
shall be tormented day and night for ever and ever. . . . And
death and hell were cast into the lake of fire. This is the second
death. And whosoever was not found written in the book of
life was cast into the lake of fire (Rev 20:10, 14–15).

That is what Christ will do and then he will purge the
whole cosmos of every vestige of evil.

That is the particular message that was revealed to the
apostle Peter. He tells us that 'The day of the Lord will
come as a thief in the night; in the which the heavens shall
pass away with a great noise, and the elements shall melt
with fervent heat, the earth also and the works that are

therein shall be burned up' (2 Pet 3:10). It is coming; evil is
going to be burned out of the whole cosmos, and there
shall be a 'new heavens and a new earth, wherein dwelleth
righteousness' (2 Pet 3:13).

Now that is it. Everything that leads to 'nature red in
tooth and claw' will be destroyed; everything that produces thorns and thistles will be destroyed. All that is evil
and against God will be purged, burned out of existence –
new heavens and a new earth wherein dwelleth righteousness.

What will it be like? Well, Isaiah has had a glimpse of it
and this is how he puts it:

> The wolf also shall dwell with the lamb, and the leopard shall
> lie down with the kid; and the calf and the young lion and the
> fatling together; and a little child shall lead them. And the cow
> and the bear shall feed; their young ones shall lie down
> together: and the lion shall eat straw like the ox. And the
> sucking child shall play on the hole of the asp, and the weaned
> child shall put his hand on the cockatrice' den. They shall not
> hurt nor destroy in all my holy mountain: for the earth shall
> be full of the knowledge of the Lord, as the waters cover the
> sea (Is 11:6–9).

The regeneration! God will have reconciled all things in
the whole universe unto himself and that is what it will be
like. No more war and bloodshed, no more thorns and
thistles, everything perfect, Paradise regained, restored,
reintroduced. And you and I, if we belong to Christ, will
be in it! We shall reign with him. That is what we are being
prepared for; that is why he redeems us; that is why he
does what he does to us; that is why he has made Christ
unto us 'wisdom, and righteousness, and sanctification, and
redemption' (1 Cor 1:30). He is preparing us for this glorious cosmos in which we shall dwell with him and reign

with him as children of God in the glory everlasting.

But the most wonderful thing of all is the place that will be given to Christ himself in all this. He must have the pre-eminence and he will have it. Paul puts it like this when he writes to the Philippians about the work of Christ: 'And being found in fashion as a man, he humbled himself, and became obedient unto death, even the death of the cross.' Then, 'Wherefore God also hath highly exalted him, and given him a name which is above every name: that at the name of Jesus every knee should bow, of things in heaven, and things in earth, and things under the earth; and that every tongue should confess that Jesus Christ is Lord, to the glory of God the Father' (Phil 2:9–11).

He will be supreme over all because God will have done it all in and through him and every knee will bow to him and will ascribe unto him all the glory and all the praise. And then, at the very end, he will hand back this perfected cosmos, this perfected kingdom, to God the Father, 'that God may be all in all' (1 Cor 15:28).

That is God's programme for the universe – the only programme. It is a certain programme because it depends upon the power of Almighty God, and nothing can frustrate it.

So, my dear friend, you are interested in the world, you say? That is what is going to happen, and therefore I ask you a personal question: Have you got this hope of glory in you? That is what this gospel is about, says Paul to the Colossians. Did you not notice it in verse 27? 'To whom God would make known what is the riches of the glory of this mystery among the Gentiles; which is Christ in you, the hope of glory.'

So do not be too concerned about this world; you cannot do anything about it and nobody else can. Do not attack this personal gospel, it is your only hope. Do not say, 'I wish you would deal with world conditions. I wish you would express yourself politically.' It is because I value your soul and your eternal destiny that I do not do that. I cannot influence such things. But what I can do is this: I can repeat to you this message that can make you fit to have a place and a part in that glory which is coming – 'Christ in you, the hope of glory.'

Are you ready for that world? Do you believe in it? Do you know anything about it? Are your affections fixed upon that? That is what makes a man or a woman a Christian. This old world of ours is dying and I feel like adding, 'Let it die!' If we were truly Christians we would all be saying, 'Even so, come, Lord Jesus' (Rev 22:20). Hasten the day, bring in your great salvation.

He will bring it in and the urgent question for every one of us is this: Are we looking forward to this glory? Do we realize we are being prepared for it? Do we realize we have got to be delivered from the powers of darkness, from the condemnation of the law? Do we realize that the Son of God came into this world in order that we might dwell in that glory and enjoy it for ever and for ever? Do we believe that this is the urgent matter?

Years come and years go and it will soon be the end of your life in this world, but it will not be the end, you know. You either go on to everlasting destruction or into this glory. All who have not obeyed the gospel, says Paul, go with the devil and the beast and the false prophet to the lake of destruction and terror and alarm and suffering, and go for ever and for ever. But all who have obeyed the gospel, who have believed in the Son of God and in what he has done, who have given themselves to him, and whose desire is to please him and follow him, they will all certainly go to the glory that is being prepared for them.

This glorious regeneration, this perfected universe, that is going to come is 'Christ in you the hope of glory'. Are you concerned about this? I beseech you, realize you have got to face it, you cannot evade it, it is either the one or the other – the everlasting misery or the eternal glory. Believe on the Lord Jesus Christ as the one who came from heaven to earth and died and rose again in order that through him, and through what God did to him there on that cross, you might be reconciled to God first, and ultimately take your place in the reconciled cosmos and share in that eternal and indescribable glory. Amen.